CULTURAL PRACTICES OF LITERACY

Case Studies of Language, Literacy,
Social Practice, and Power

CULTURAL PRACTICES OF LITERACY

Case Studies of Language, Literacy, Social Practice, and Power

Edited by

Victoria Purcell-Gates
University of British Columbia

LAWRENCE ERLBAUM ASSOCIATES, PUBLISHERS
2007   Mahwah, New Jersey   London

Lawrence Erlbaum Associates, Inc., Publishers
10 Industrial Avenue
Mahwah, New Jersey 07430
www.erlbaum.com

Cover design by Kathryn Houghtaling Lacey

Library of Congress Cataloging-in-Publication Data

Cultural practices of literacy : case studies of language, literacy, social practice, and power / edited by Victoria Purcell-Gates.
    p. cm.
Includes bibliographical references and index.
ISBN 978-0-8058-5491-6 — 0-8058-5491-6 (cloth)
ISBN 978-0-8058-5492-3 — 0-8058-5492-4 (pbk.)
ISBN 978-1-4106-1791-0 — 1-4106-1791-2 (e book)
1. Literacy—Social aspects—Cross-cultural studies. 2. Sociolinguistics—Cross-cultural studies.   I. Purcell-Gates, Victoria.
LC149.C796   2006
302.2'244—dc22   2006018291
                                                  CIP

Printed in the United States of America
10 9 8 7 6 5 4 3 2 1

Contents

Preface   vii

1   Complicating the Complex   1
Victoria Purcell-Gates

Language, Literacy, and Hegemony   23
Victoria Purcell-Gates

2   Appropriation and Resistance in the (English) Literacy   25
Practices of Puerto Rican Farmers
Catherine Mazak

3   Language and Literacy Issues in Botswana   41
Annah Molosiwa

The Immigrant Experience: Language, Literacies,   55
and Identities
Victoria Purcell-Gates

4   Sharing Stories, Linking Lives: Literacy Practices   57
Among Sudanese Refugees
Kristen H. Perry

5   Multiple Border Crossings: Literacy Practices of Chinese   85
American Bilingual Families
Gaoming Zhang

6   Literacy Practices in a Foreign Language: Two Cuban   99
        Immigrants
        Kamila Rosolová

Literacies in and out of School and on the Borders   115
    Victoria Purcell-Gates

7   Breadth and Depth, Imports and Exports: Transactions   119
        Between the In- and Out-of-School Literacy Practices of
        an "At Risk" Youth
        Stephanie Collins

8   Literacy and Choice: Urban Elementary Students'   133
        Perceptions of Links Between Home, School, and
        Community Literacy Practices
        Jodene Kersten

9   "You Have to be Bad or Dumb to Get in Here":   155
        Reconsidering the In-School and Out-of-School Literacy
        Practices of At-Risk Adolescents
        J. David Gallagher

10 School and Home: Contexts for Conflict and Agency   169
        Chad O'Neil

New Pedagogies for New Literacies   179
    Victoria Purcell-Gates

11 Digital Literac(ies), Digital Discourses, and   181
        Communities of Practice: Literacy Practices in Virtual
        Environments
        Douglas Eyman

12 Comprehending Complexity   197
        Victoria Purcell-Gates

Appendix A: Cultural Practices of Literacy Study: 217
Semistructured Literacy Practices Interview

Appendix B: Demographic Information   225

Author Index   229

Subject Index   233

Preface

This book is the result of an advanced doctoral seminar that I designed and directed during my final year at Michigan State University, 2003–2004. I designed this seminar in a pique of selfishness: My research interests had increasingly centered on my desire to more fully explore the ways in which different people actually use the literacy that they, for the most part, acquired in the context of some sort of formal instruction. I had just concluded a large and very complex experimental study during which my co-investigator, Nell K. Duke, and I studied the effect of explicit teaching of genre features in the context of authentic reading and writing. This study was longitudinal, and for 2 years we directed a team of 12 research assistants, collecting classroom data, and designing and conducting assessments that would enable complex statistical analysis. I was exhausted and I missed the up-close contact with real people in out-of-school, real-life situations. I was ready to return to ethnographic case study.

My timing, however, was totally off. The climate for research funding in the United States had taken a forced, but nonetheless real, turn away from qualitative research. Although I had benefitted from this for my previous study, I was up the proverbial creek when it came to interesting federal funders in any study that looked at literacy outside of instructional contexts and in a decidedly qualitative manner. What to do?

In a fit of perhaps not brilliance but hubris, I decided to forge ahead as if I had funding. I created the Cultural Practices of Literacy Study (CPLS) out of thin air and whole cloth. I found a brilliant and dedicated assistant in Kristen Perry, a doctoral student at MSU who agreed to work with me to invent a study design and analytic procedures—for free! Another graduate student joined our group—Gaoming Zhang, who at the time was a literacy masters student who had been bugging me for a research job. Well, this was not a paid job, but she willingly threw her coat in the ring and we had a research "team."

The three of us met for slightly more that a semester, talking theory, reading books and articles, and designing and conducting pilot studies. The notion that I was eager to play with was one of multiple case studies of literacy practice. Because we were working within the theoretical frame of literacy as cultural or social practice, these case studies would be bounded by sociocultural categories, or dimensions. My view of culture is one of fluidity, multiple and nested. People always act, think, create, believe within describable sociocultural contexts that are reflections of gender, race, socioeconomic status, religion, age, education, geographical location, and power relations. Literacy practice reflects, mediates, and, in many ways, coconstructs these sociocultural contexts.

Significant and seminal work had already been done in this area by Brian Street and others, notably David Barton and Mary Hamilton. The construct of *multiple literacies* and *literacy as social practice* was increasingly well-known and accepted. I did not feel, however, that we knew all there was to know about literacy as multiple and social. I believed that there was a need to examine many more case studies of literacy in practice within specified social contexts.

I also wanted to explore the possibilities of cross-case analysis of such studies of literacy practice. Is it possible, for example, to look across many case studies of literacy practice for greater insights into how technological literacies actually play out in the lives of people both across and within sociocultural contexts? Or can we trace, in a more generalizable way, the movement taken by immigrants in taking up new literacies in new contexts and languages?

Finally, because I am, at core, a teacher of reading and writing, I wanted to come to a better understanding of the forces and factors that prevent children from socially and economically marginalized communities from acquiring an empowering literacy in school. This goal speaks to the, apparently, essential achievement gap between the Haves and the Have Nots in developed and developing countries around the world. My approach to this is to study and theorize from the ways in which literacy practices in communities either do, or do not, align with literacy as it is practiced, taught, assessed, and rewarded in formal instructional contexts.

All of these goals called for multiple case studies of literacy in actual use. I began this process with the seminar, mentioned in the first paragraph of this preface. I put out a call across the university for students who wished to study literacy as social practice and to examine the multiple ways that social and cultural contexts, within relationships of power, played out in the practice of literacy. The authors of the 10 chapters contained in this volume con-

stituted the first research team for the CPLS. Kristen Perry and Gaoming
Zhang also joined the seminar, continuing with their case studies. Each researcher identified the case he or she wished to explore. We read as many
works on literacy as social practice as we could, all the while building theory
and data collection techniques. Each case reflects the unique focus and
background of the researcher, but each case contributes equally to the
growing database on literacy as cultural practice. Several of them also contribute more directly than others to the goal of understanding the align-
ments and misalignments of literacy as practiced in school and as practiced
in homes and communities. The work of the CPLS continues, now located
in Canada at the University of British Columbia. Several of the case studies
in this volume are being followed by new studies centered within the same
sociocultural communities as their authors (Perry & Mazak) continue with
their work.

The case studies reported in this book contribute toward the real need to
fill in the picture of literacy as multiple and social. They do this by adding
new information to the picture of heretofore unexamined sociocultural
groups and their literacies. They also do this by adding further detail to the
ways in which language and literacy practices transact with issues of global
economics, politics, and power. Finally, they add much needed *range* to our
understandings of literacy as cultural practice, with studies situated in countries around the world, developed and developing.

This book will be informative for a range of audiences. Scholars working
in the field of literacy studies and literacy practice will welcome the additional data and insights that come from the case studies, both individually
and taken as a whole. The book is a natural selection for graduate seminars
and courses on literacy. Those who study and/or implement policy related
to education and, in particular, language and literacy education will also
find much needed information, and food for thought, in these portraits of
real people using real literacy for their own purposes. Too often, policymakers operate out of hypothesized networks of assumptions about the outcomes of education and the effects on the lives of people once they "attain
literacy." Greater knowledge and insight into the reality of the actual practices of literacies can only benefit future policy and its implementation.

Following my introduction (chapter 1), in which I provide the theoretical
frame for the volume as well as a description of the CPLS methodology, we
begin with the case studies by Cathy Mazak and Annah Molosiwa. Together,
these studies delve into issues of linguistic hegemony and the contexts of
historical and continuing imperialism. In chapter 2, Mazak describes the
ways in which Puerto Ricans exercise linguistic agency in resisting the hegemony of English and the United States, while taking from their schooling in
English to meet their personal, economic, and political needs and desires.
Molosiwa, in chapter 3, provides an insider's perspective and knowledge on

the ways that native languages and English are taken up, mediated, and transformed in the African country of Botswana.

The next three chapters address issues of immigration and examine the ways that literacy practice plays out within the lives of three different groups of immigrants to the United States. In chapter 4, Kristen Perry focuses on the group of Sudanese immigrants, known widely in the United States as the "Lost Boys," a label coined by the press. She provides a compelling description of literacy as shaped and parceled out in the Sudan by different religious groups as well as the ways the Sudanese took up English literacy in the United States to suit their personal, cultural, and political purposes. Gaoming Zhang, in chapter 5, looks at the bi- and multiliteracies of two children of Chinese immigrants in the Midwest of the United States and describes the complexity of cultural retention, familial educational expectations, and developmental stage as factors that shape their literacies. Kamila Rosolová (chap. 6) delves into the multiple social and political factors that shape the English and Spanish literacies of two refugees from Cuba who won lotteries to come to the United States. These portraits of language and literacy practice add detail and texture to the complexity of language practice by demonstrating the diversity of immigrant experience.

The next four chapters take us into the school room. Stephanie Collins, Jodene Kersten, and David Gallagher (chaps. 7, 8, and 9, respectively) provide us with fascinating descriptions of children from inner-city neighborhoods who, in various and different ways, struggle to find a fit between their out-of-school lives and that of their schools. Chad O'Neil (chap. 10), on the other hand, using primarily retrospective data from his informants, gives us an inside look into the literacy lives of two middle-class, mainstream college students. We need many more studies of mainstream groups to provide perspective and fullness to our portrait of literacy as social practice.

In chapter 11, Douglas Eyman selects a college class focused on learning a particular technology to explore one aspect of the "new literacies." His exploration of this class as an instantiation of situated pedagogy provides a much needed portrait of what can be as we move into the new and multiliteracies' era. In addition, Eyman gives us a welcome definition of the construct of *digital literacy*, something that will be most useful for future researchers.

I conclude the book with chapter 12, wherein I answer some of the questions I raised in chapter 1, and raise further ones. I also provide some examples of the possibilities of cross-case analyses of literacy practice case studies, using the studies included in this volume.

ACKNOWLEDGMENTS

I would like to take this opportunity to thank and acknowledge all those who helped make this project possible. Kristen Perry was invaluable in the beginning stages of the CPLS project, particularly with the construction of the metamatrix of literacy practices across studies. Kedrick James, the CPLS project manager at the University of British Columbia, takes credit for coming up with the term *sociotextual domain* to replace *social domain* in a way that better reflects my particular interest in texts and textual practice within social contexts. Naomi Silverman, as always, is editor extraordinaire, and her calm, but persistent, manner in the face of exhaustion and rebellion is unmatched anywhere. Barbara Wieghaus, Lawrence Erlbaum Senior Book Production Editor, handled the challenge of moving the project along while I was somewhat out of touch in Costa Rica (conducting another CPLS project). I also wish to thank copyeditors for their careful work that makes us authors look better than we are. Finally, I thank the reviewers of this volume, for their interest in the work and their insistence that I make it better. I appreciate it.

—*Victoria Purcell-Gates*

Chapter 1

Complicating the Complex

Victoria Purcell-Gates
University of British Columbia

A revolutionary paradigm shift has taken place over the last 10 or so years in literacy studies and literacy educational theory, and this shift has complicated and challenged notions of what literacy *is*. The ongoing pedagogical and theoretical debate regarding *how* people develop literacy is affected by this theoretical shift in new and interesting ways. Previously, albeit from differing disciplinary bases, the prevailing beliefs about the nature of literacy converged around the notion that literacy is reading and writing, that is, people who can read or write are literate, and those who cannot are not literate, or illiterate. Relatedly, people became literate by learning to read and write in school, or within some type of intentionally instructive context. People who did not have access to schooling, thus, were not literate in the generally agreed-upon sense.

In retrospect, this was a simple world. It is true that there was disjunction, if not disagreement, on what was meant by literacy level, or degree of reading or writing ability that was needed to qualify someone as literate—able to read and write. However, this issue was of import, for the most part, only to those compiling statistics for national and international policy and political purposes.

Although this rather straightforward and simplistic (or at least, simplified) view is still prevalent, I believe, among the majority of educators, political leaders, and the general public, another, more complex one has emerged. As for all complex theories and paradigms, this one reflects the convergence and cross-fertilization of experience, theorizing, and research from a number of disciplines and takes unique form within each. Within the literacy studies and education discipline(s), we have experienced this "new" perspective on literacy as falling under such labels as *multiple literacies, literacy as social practice (or social literacies)*, and *new literacies*. The basic, most obvious distinction, and one to be recognized immediately on the surface lexical/morphemic level, is the recognition that *literacy* is now pluralized to *literacies*. Many books and articles have been, and are presently being, written, theorizing, explaining, describing, and arguing this multiple and social literacy paradigm. I limit my discussion here first to a brief gloss of the basic principles of this theoretical perspective on literacy and, second, to raising some issues that result from this new view that appear to complicate and add complexity to how we think about the relationships between schooling, literacy, and literacy development.

THEORETICAL MOVES TOWARD THE COMPLEX

The move toward considering literacy as multiple must first be viewed within the larger theoretical shifts over the last half century. We have moved with philosophers along an epistemological path from Enlightenment theories, through Marxism, structuralism, and modernism to postmodernism and poststructuralism. From a belief in the autonomy of the individual mind and its ability to understand an objective reality, the structuralist and modernist perspectives led us to view individuals as shaped by dominant systems such as the economy or religion. These so-called "grand narrative" frames positioned individuals as subject to powerful forces that crossed contexts and did not recognize in the lens such factors as individual agency.

The ideological (Althusser, 1969, 1971) and social reproduction models (Bourdieu, 2001; Bourdieu & Passeron, 1977) were heavily influenced by structuralism (Canagarajah, 1999). Although Marxism gave control over the individual to the material dimension, structuralism moved us to view the individual as constructed more by the social symbol system.[1] Within these models, schools were seen as agents of social and cultural reproduction, ensuring the continued grasp on social and political power, status, and privilege by those who held it, at the cost of ongoing marginalization of the underclasses of the world.

According to an analysis by Canagarajah (1999), structuralism cut loose the Marxist tie of the institutions to the economy with its focus on linguistic mediation. This led to increased awareness and focus on the fluidity and relative independence of institutions from larger, basic forces. It still held, however, that linguistic and discourse codes were socially constructed and beyond the control of the individual. Thus, looking back, we can see the

---

[1]Of course, language and discourse never exist outside of an economic system, and this differentiation of structuralism from Marxism is seen as a specification as it related to issues of discourse, rather than a repudiation of Marxist theory.

path we have traveled epistemologically from the assumption of complete autonomy of the individual and individual thought of the Enlightenment frame, to the view of thought and development as constructed through socially constructed codes and discourses.

The deterministic and generalistic aspects of structuralism have given way in more recent decades of postmodernism and poststructuralism to theories of specificity, localism, and indeterminateness. This is the result of powerful critiques of structuralist perspectives by subjects representing positions of marginality who argue that structuralist analyses continue to privilege dominant discourses and ideologies and leave little room for other realities that are often hybrid, flexible, and fluid (Foucault, 1980; hooks, 1989). In the postmodernist world, grand theories no longer hold, and local contexts are seen as wholes, providing ground for "little theories" that reflect local cultural contexts. As I will discuss further in the last chapter, this theoretical move has opened the door to greater exploration of individual agency and resistance as regard linguistic and discourse domination.

Literacy as Multiple and Social

It was within the epistemological landscape just described—somewhere between structuralist and poststructuralist theorizing—that the notion that literacy, itself, could be viewed as more than just a unidimensional construct, free of contextual constraint. Street's (1984) book, *Literacy in Theory and Practice*, was among the first of the scholarly works to be taken up by educational theorists that challenged the dominant view of literacy as singular and autonomous. Street, a British anthropologist, challenged the assertions of language theorists (Hildyard & Olson, 1978; Olson, 1977) and social anthropologists (Goody, 1968, 1977) that literacy itself was responsible for such cognitive development as the development of rationality and the ability to think in decontextualized ways. Drawing on his work with non-western cultures, Street argued that literacy itself does not possess isolable qualities nor confer isolable, decontextualized abilities. Rather, literacy is always embedded within social institutions and, as such, is only knowable as it is defined and practiced by social and cultural groups. As such, literacy is best considered an ideological construct as opposed to an autonomous skill, separable from contexts of use. Its ideological nature, according to this view, reflects the fact that literacy is always constructed and enacted within social and political contexts and subject to the implications of differing power relationships. It is best, Street suggested, to think of literacies rather than literacy. Being ideologically bound, different literacies are recognized by the established institutions of time and place as more and less legitimate. Some literacies provide access to power and material well-being, others are marked as substandard and deficient.

Within this frame, there are many literacies—discursive literacy practices with their texts and purposes for reading and writing those texts[2]—and each of these is shaped by and interpreted within the sociocultural/sociolinguistic contexts within which they occur (Barton & Hamilton, 1998; Street, 1984, 1995). This highlights the fact that different texts are written and read for varied purposes within specific sociocultural/sociolinguistic contexts by literate people. Meaning in written language, as for oral, is never autonomous, and free of contextual constraints (Bakhtin, 1981). From this perspective, literacy development is not seen as linear, building in skill and fluency toward one type of literacy, nor as hierarchical (e.g., low, functional literacy to high, educated literacy). Rather, it is seen as multiple, occurring across the complex plane of life itself.

Within this frame of literacy as multiple, and socially and culturally bound, school literacy, or academic literacy, is but one of many literacies. The forms and functions of academic literacy are shaped by the social and cultural suppositions and beliefs of the academic community. The academic community is intricately linked to state dictates, composed by the powerful and enfranchised, who decide which literacy is to be valued, taught, and assessed. By nature of the social and political power wielded by this community, the manners and modes for how literacy is to be defined and assessed throughout sanctioned society is decided within the frame of literacy as autonomous and academic, rendering this practice of literacy (academic, schooled literacy) perhaps the clearest example of the ideological nature of all literacies.

Research Spawned by the Construct of Multiple Literacies as Social Practice

With this new lens through which to view literacy, a number of research studies were launched to elaborate on the theory and to explore its ramifications. The everyday practices of literacy were now interesting, and several to-become-foundational studies were conducted, documenting what came to be known as *local literacies* (Barton & Hamilton, 1998), *literacy practices*, and their embedded *literacy events* (Barton, Hamilton, & Ivanič, 2000; Purcell-Gates, 1996; Purcell-Gates, Degener, Jacobson, & Soler, 2002). Researchers documented people reading store signs while purchasing food and clothing for their families, reading print on food containers as part of nurturing their children, reading notices of meetings while participating in

[2]Here I focus on reading and writing, or print literacy. However, this view is embedded in a larger frame for literacy that includes other semiotic systems, including oral language mode. This is not to privilege print literacy over other literacies like visual literacy, digital literacy, or oral literacy. It merely reflects a bounded area for purposes of research related to practice (teaching of reading and writing) that is of personal interest to me.

local governance of their communities, reading news articles as part of their developing a political stance in preparation for upcoming elections, reading essays in church materials while participating in their religious lives, reading bus schedules for transportation to work sites as part of providing for their economic well-being, reading personal letters from friends and relatives while maintaining personal relationships across time and space, and seeking relaxation at day's end by reading novels, magazines, poetry, and short stories.

Similarly, research documented people regulating their lives by writing memos, reaching out to friends with written messages on greeting cards, contributing to community interests by writing reports for organizations, participating in public life and writing notes on a public lecture, developing personal beliefs and writing private reflections in a journal, and so on. These literacy practices are patterned by—and pattern—the personal, social, spiritual, and work lives of literate people.

In their ethnography of the uses of reading and writing in one community in England, for example, Barton and Hamilton (1998) documented the local literacies, or vernacular literacies, throughout the community. They describe people using reading and writing to get things done in their lives: to manage households (e.g., writing lists, notes, paying bills); to shop (e.g., reading food ingredients, reading laundry requirements, writing grocery lists); to communicate with others (e.g., writing notes and letters to loved ones, writing formal letters to school personnel, sending and receiving greeting cards); to learn (e.g., reading books, writing essays, reading and following directions); to relax (e.g., reading novels and poetry, doing crossword puzzles); to reflect (e.g., writing in diaries).

Other researchers looked at the ways in which literacy is historically situated. In *Literacy in American Lives*, for example, Brandt (2001) examined the changing economic, social, and political conditions for the literacy learning of 80 people between the years 1895 and 1985. With Brandt's study, we are able to see literacy learning within the context of large economic systems such as increasing industrialization and the fading of farming as a prevalent way of life. Brandt's analysis makes clear the ways in which literacy is both enacted and made possible by historically situated movements and institutions.

Vernacular Literacies and School

With the spotlight on *vernacular literacies*, or out-of-school literacies, some researchers sought to examine ways to bring children's vernacular literacies into the schools to enhance their academic literacy learning. This approach reflects the turn from considering the nonacademic literacies of primarily nonmainstream learners as deficient to viewing them, rather, as different from the literacy privileged in schools, if not as strengths heretofore unrecognized by schools. The work of Dyson (2003), for example, highlights the ways in which young, urban African American children call upon their symbolic resources pulled from popular culture to move into traditional literacy, as taught in school. In *School's Out!*, Hull and Schultz (2002) presented a series of separately authored chapters in which authors detail and celebrate the out-of-school literacies of children from different sociocultural groups while, at the same time, they highlight the failures of schools to recognize and capitalize on them. Lee (1993) researched and then created instructional recommendations based on the out-of-school language and literacy abilities of African American youth. Morrell and Duncan-Andrade (2002), Mahiri (1998), Cushman (1998), Moll (1990), Moll and Gonzalez (2003), and Gregory and Williams (2000), in England, are among this group of researchers who have focused on recognizing and documenting community-based knowledge and discourses with implications for teaching.

Cultural and Social Reproduction

The subtext of much of this work is the clear implication that the ideology of privileging academic literacy is used by those in power to continue the persistent academic underachievement of students marginalized by language, gender, ethnicity, and race. In this way, power is maintained, and threats to that power by "underclass" groups can be fended off under the guise of academic failure. Many of the literacy researchers just cited explicitly work to resist this hegemony and to find ways to "legitimate" the literacies of marginalized groups within academic settings.

Theories of social and cultural reproduction, epitomized by the writings of Bourdieu (2001), frame much of the theorizing and research by literacy researchers working from a multiple and/or social literacies perspective. As briefly noted previously, Bourdieu holds that dominant discourses are perpetuated and reproduced through official institutions of schooling, which control access to cultural and social capital. Schools commit "symbolic violence" by disallowing marginalized discourses as capital and convincing even those marginalized that dominant discourses of the privileged, to which they will have no real access, are legitimate. This position, in the eyes of many, represents a frustratingly closed discourse/power loop.

Now What? So What?

From this brief overview of the theoretical and research turn to multiple literacies and literacy as social practice, I now consider where all of this leaves us. Increasingly, teachers and academics alike have critiqued this body of research with the challenging "Now what?" It has been interesting, many say, to document the ways in which literacy events are embedded in literacy practices and to examine the multiple variations of these practices as they are patterned by such sociocultural factors as class, race, gender, education, language, and geopolitical positioning. Clearly visible through this lens, and research, is the aligning of academic underachievement with these sociocultural dimensions. Although this visibility has always been there, the research of the multiplicity of literacies has, among other things, brought the nonacademic literacies of the underachieving into sharper focus and to greater appreciation.

This is where the "Now what?" comes in. This question arises, however, from at least two very different ideologies, representing dialectally opposed positions. One position very clearly sees the impact of power and of power relations as they operate within the socially constructed discourse communities, represented by different textual practices. Literacies marked as good or high are those that are practiced by those sociocultural groups who hold economic and political power, or capital. The literacies that are marked as deficient and low, and thus in need of remediation, are those practiced by sociocultural groups who exist on the margins and are considered "nonmainstream."

Those educators, researchers, and theorists occupying the other end of the dialectical continuum do not see this. This second perspective, which I suggest is the dominant one outside of academic structuralist/post-structuralist communities, constructs reality much differently. Admittedly hypothesizing, I posit that the research reflecting literacy as multiple is explained by those holding this position as simply focusing the spotlight on vernacular literacies that have heretofore been taken for granted. Within this perspective, these vernacular literacies, taken together, represent an incomplete construct of literacy, missing the all-powerful academic literacy. A complete literacy (or what one might presumably mean when using the term *fully literate*) would include vernacular literacies (however these play out in the different lives of different people and groups) plus academic literacy. Full literacy (vernacular plus academic), continuing this scenario, can be reduced for purposes of measurement and naming, to just *academic literacy*, much as one would reduce an algebraic equation by canceling out the equivalent terms (in this case, *vernacular literacies*).[3] Therefore, when one documents literacy level, or literacy development, one would by definition focus on academic literacy, because vernacular literacies can be assumed. From this perspective, the "Now what?" becomes the "So what?"

I only comment on a few of the problems that inhere in this approach, not the least of which is the fact that the definition of *literacy* has from the

---

[3]In this way, perhaps, the construct of *autonomous literacy* emerges from the teeming world of vernacular literacies.

beginning of writing included more real-life applications of literacy than what most people would identify today as academic literacy. In fact, in many countries of the world, up until the mid-20th century, whether or not one was considered literate relied on whether or not one could write one's name. Additionally, definitions of literate have at different times in different places referred to ability to read particular texts such as the Bible. Currently, *literacy rate* (a statistic that relies primarily on a simplistic definition of literacy) is measured along similar, nonacademic-literacy dimensions in most countries. For example, in Costa Rica, the literacy rate is determined by "the people over 15 who can read and write" (UNESCO, 2000).

Another difficulty with the assumption that academic literacy completes vernacular literacies to equal *full literacy* lies with the fact that currently we measure literacy level for adults (those who have supposedly finished schooling) with what can only be defined as skill with vernacular literacies. In fact, the National Adult Literacy Survey (NALS) and the International Adult Literacy Survey (IALS) define literacy, not with arbitrary standards like signing one's name, completing a particular grade level of school, or achieving a set score on a norm-referenced test, but in a functional, multi-textual way:

> Using printed and written information to function in society, to achieve one's goals, and to develop one's knowledge and potential. This definition of literacy ... include(s) a broad range of skills that adults use in accomplishing many different types of literacy tasks associated with work, home, and community contexts. (U.S. Department of Education, 2001, p. 3)

The NALS and the IALS are criterion-referenced assessments and scores fall within five levels. Test takers are asked to locate, match, and integrate information across different types of texts of differing lengths and complexities: newspapers, forms, advertisements, directions for taking medication, warranty instructions, poems, editorials, transportation schedules, graphs, and so on. Those whose scores fall within Level I are not considered illiterate, despite how these levels have been misinterpreted in the popular press. They are able to perform a number of literacy tasks that life requires. On the other hand, they "do not have the full range of economic, social, and personal options that are open to Americans with higher levels of literacy skills" (National Institute for Literacy, 1998, p. 5).

So, this is a complication for those who would equate full literacy with academic literacy, and thus assume the "So what?" response to the research that has recently documented the multiple faces of literacy and the ways in which literacy is integrally woven throughout the social lives of people. Current official definitions and assessments of literacy level incorporate the assumption that literacy is at least multitextual and socially and culturally functional. Of course, what is not recognized by these official stances are the essential relationships among textual practices and authentic contexts of use, contexts that reflect power and ideologies as well as individual agency and purpose (Perry & Purcell-Gates, 2005).

Now What? Multiple Literacies and Schooling

I turn now to the other ideological end of the dialectical continuum—that which sees the ways in which power and status play out in privileged and denigrated discourses and their literacy practices. This other quite different perspective on the "Now what?" question comes from a sense that this new recognition and validation of vernacular literacies should have an impact on the teaching of literacy in schools. One version of this suggests that academic literacy should be de-privileged in schools, leading to equal acceptance and privileging of vernacular literacies that reflect the lived lives of students. How this would actually play out within the discourse of schooling is currently almost completely unspecified, not to mention undertheorized.

Other more nuanced implications can be drawn from the work of researchers from the literacy as social and ideological perspective. As I mentioned earlier, several influential literacy researchers (e.g., Dyson, 2003; Hull & Schultz, 2002; Lee, 1993) are calling for teachers to document the vernacular literacy practices and abilities of their students and bring these into the classroom as foundations for learning more academic literacies. The sense here is that the literacies taught and assessed in school align more with those of students from mainstream, middle-class, educated families and less so with those of students from nonmainstream communities. Thus, activities like teaching literary devices through language forms like Rap, or using familiar popular culture forms like television graphics, graffiti, or cartoons will help the students move from what they know into traditional forms of print literacy and to read and write texts that are typically required in schools.

Another aspect of this perspective is the belief that nonmainstream students need to understand that they, and members of their communities, are already literate before they can be expected to expand their literacies in ways valued and rewarded by the schools. Validating the literacies within communities in school would go a long way toward motivating students to learn from instruction, according to this view.

Others within this frame believe that the role that power plays in how students are positioned as literate or not needs to be made explicit and opened up for reflection and action for nonmainstream students (Morrell, 2005). This essentially critical literacy approach (Freire, 1993) is the focus of several ongoing action research studies. This approach recognizes the value of academic literacy in the lives of marginalized students. However, rather than use vernacular literacies merely as a bridge to academic literacy, academic literacy practice—as it functions as a social and political tool for the powerful—is opened up as a focus of critique and study. Academic literacy is renamed as one of the literacies of power, and students work to take power through its acquisition in order to reveal and confront classism, racism, and other forces of marginalization.

COMPLICATIONS TO CHALLENGE US

I believe we have now reached a point in our theorizing and researching literacy as social, multiple, and ideological where we need to take stock of where we are and to speculate about where we need to go. We need to respond to the "So what?" and answer the "Now what?" I raise and address several complications that have arisen for me and many of my colleagues as we have worked within the literacy-as-social-practice paradigm. These complications arise from primarily two aspects of this more complex view of literacy: (a) literacy as practiced by different sociocultural groups in a globalized world, and (b) the nature(s) of the relationships between literacy as practiced outside of formal instructional contexts and literacy learning acquired within contexts of formal schooling.

Literacy Practices Across Sociocultural/Linguistic Contexts

The influence of Street's (1984) paradigm-shifting work on literacy as multiple and ideological has been deep and widespread, as discussed previously. The construct of literacy as social practice, historically situated, subject to power relations, and intricately bound up in the lives of people living and functioning within and across multiple and shifting social and cultural contexts has been convincingly demonstrated by existing research. However, I believe that this demonstration has provided but a few broad, and essential, brush strokes of an as yet unfinished portrait of lived literacy learning and practice.

The nature of the research that is required to fill in the picture—ethnographic and descriptive—is related to this unfinished state of the construct. Ethnography is time and labor intensive. It also, by its nature, focuses on only small samples at a time. Thus, we now have a corpus of relatively few studies that have explored the ways that individual communities construct and practice literacy. In other words, we have enough data to conclude that literacy is constructed and practiced differently by different culturally defined communities. Specifically, how literacy is constructed by different communities is still only sketchily known. To leave it at that, and to run the risk of generalizing to all sociocultural contexts from the findings of a relative few context-specific studies, is to violate the very basis of the theory of literacy as multiple, social, and ideological. The tendency to resist further exploration of contexts may very well stem from lingering structuralist tendencies in a poststructuralist world.

This issue becomes more urgent when considering the concerns of many regarding the ways in which the alternative model of literacy—as context-free, autonomous, technical, and unidimensional—is wielded by powerful institutions to maintain constructions of poor and minority populations as deficient and academically underachieving. Research within a literacy-as-social-practice frame has been conducted with only a relatively few communities who are thus impacted by official constructions of successful and unsuccessful literacy.

Luke (2003) raises similar questions and challenges in his call for more research into issues of literacy as economic capital in a globalized world—one that is constantly shifting as world capitalism breaks down old political, cultural, and linguistic borders. People are moving across borders at accelerating rates in response to issues of military conflict, the rise of nationalism and racial and religious fanaticism, and economic globalization. Children are growing up in vastly different cultural and linguistic worlds that often overlap and must be negotiated daily. For these children, texts that are written and read often differ among these worlds. They may differ in language, in form, in purpose, and by who reads or writes them. Increasingly, we are seeing in U.S., Canadian, and U.K. schools (Gregory & Williams, 2000) a polyglot mix of students who bring different languages, cultural experiences, and literacy practices with them to the classroom. Not only do the linguistic and cultural worlds of the students vary, but they often differ from those institutionalized and privileged by the schools the children attend.

Although perhaps we did not see this need for more research 20 years ago, the more complex view of literacy as multiple and social reveals it. I believe more basic research needs to be done before we can fully understand how literacy is patterned by and patterns the lives of adults and children in these different and shifting contexts. Research into literacy practices of different communities must include questions of languages, discourses, and texts. Whose languages are privileged within the different domains of schools, workplaces, legal institutions, media, and others? Which texts and discourses (and whose) are similarly privileged? Luke (2003) called for "rigorous sociological, demographic, and economic analysis of how literacy makes a difference in communities and institutions in relation to other forms of available economic and social capital" (p. 135). He posed the following research challenges, many of which guided the case study research included in this volume:

- Which linguistic competencies, discourses and textual resources, and multi-literacies are accessible?

- How, in what blended and separate domains and to what ends, are different languages used?
- How do people use languages, texts, discourses, and literacies as convertible and transformative resources in homes, communities, and schools?
- How are these resources recognized and misrecognized, remediated and converted in school-based literacy instruction? (pp. 139–140)

In sum, we now recognize that literacy is multiple and woven within the sociocultural lives of communities. However, we do not yet fully understand how it is multiple, or, rather, how this multiplicity plays out across and within differing sociocultural community contexts. Although some may argue that we have enough small case studies of social practice of literacy and now it is time to draw implications for practice from what we have, I disagree. Each of the case studies in this book investigates literacy through the social practice lens in new and interesting ways. The social and cultural contexts for each study are unique, having never before been addressed by research. These studies represent but a few of those waiting to be done to flesh out the empirical data that will continue to inform the theory. Now that we recognize the complexity of literacy, we cannot back away from fully describing it in all of its complexity. This is particularly compelling, not just as good basic science, but also because it will impact the ways in which we address the next complication of this complexity: What do we do with this in schools?

From Reproduction Theories to Subjecthood and Agency Frames

Although much of the early work with literacy as multiple and social was heavily informed by theories of social and cultural reproduction, the influence of poststructuralist perspectives has begun to influence interpretations of power and subjects' responses to it. With poststructuralism, we have moved away from deterministic notions of linguistic hegemony of dominant discourses to possibilities of resistance and agency. We need more situated research to allow us to better understand linguistic domination and acts of resistance within multiple sociocultural contexts. The constructs of multiplicity, hybridity, and fluidity as they relate to discourse domination, cultural and social reproduction, and literacy acquisition and practice need much more empirical study.

Implications for Instruction of Literacy as Social Practice Research and Vice Versa

Looking at literacy through this more poststructuralist lens allows us to ask more nuanced questions—questions that may lead us out of the dead end of

"Now what?" I am thinking particularly of the fields of activity where schooling and social practice overlap. If the result of hegemony is not inevitably the rendering of disempowerment, then we can begin to look for ways that subjects take from schooled literacy for their own purposes. This will provide a more balanced beginning in exploring relationships between power, literacy practice, literacy learning, and schooling.

Education, as a social venture tied to knowledge and training of social groups within political bodies, has always drawn eclectically from different disciplines to form synthetic philosophical foundations. For literacy education, those disciplines include linguistics, cognitive psychology, anthropology, sociology, rhetoric, and literary theory. Thus, as secondary users of discipline-specific theory and research, educational theorists, researchers, and practitioners often find themselves co-opting ideas in less-than-complete form, transforming these co-optations and creating unique and, in some cases, bastardized theories that use the same terms and propositions of the original theories but in new and specific-to-education ways.

So it is that educationists have viewed the theory and research on literacy as multiple, social, and political. They ask the question, "What does this say or imply for instruction?"[4] In asking this question, they co-opt a theory that was not originally derived with literacy instruction at its center of concern. By moving literacy instruction into the focus, those who ask this question must be careful that they do not make overly simplistic interpretations of the theory itself, or of the elements of that theory that might have application to the ways we teach reading and writing in formal institutional settings.

What Is the Relationship Between Literacy in Practice and Literacy Learning?

One presupposition to examine very carefully, for example, is that a description of the construct of literacy is also a description of literacy acquisition and development. There is no empirical or logical basis on which to draw this assumption. The relationship between the teaching of and acquisition of a skill or practice does not necessarily have any direct relationship to the ways in which people put the skill to use in actual practice following mastery or learning.

However, this is not to say there is no relationship. There is the issue of quality of instruction, for example. Are teachers teaching students what they need to allow them to practice the skill later? Are students learning and practicing the skills in school in such a way as to be able to generalize their knowledge to actual practice once schooling is finished? There is also the

---

[4]Actually, there are those who fail to first ask the question. They simply assume that these theories brought from other disciplines apply directly to instructional contexts.

issue of motivation. Does the instruction motivate the students to learn the skill so that they can engage in practice later? This last question, though, begs the question of whether or not the teachers know the practice(s) for which the students are building skills. If not, why not? If so, how does this knowledge inform teaching practice?

So, although ultimately complex, it is the *nature* of the relationship that is the compelling and more interesting question. What relationship does the social practice of literacy have to literacy learning?

Following the conclusion of two large research studies, I, along with co-researchers, recently authored a book presenting a theoretical frame that attempts to begin to answer this question and, in the process, unite the social practice and cognitive perspectives on print literacy development (Purcell-Gates, Jacobson, & Degener, 2004). The frame is built on empirical data from studies of emergent literacy through adult literacy learning and mirrors in many ways for literacy development the work of social psychologists who have posited a sociocognitive model of learning in general (Cole & Scribner, 1974; Lave & Wenger, 1991).

The overarching theme, or hypothesis, of the book is that print literacy development proceeds for individuals as school-based reading and writing instruction builds their cognitive skills needed to participate in the literacy practices of their social and cultural communities. Students will "take" from instruction that which makes sense to them and that which allows them to participate in the written genres that make up their literacy lives. They begin to develop early literacy beliefs, values, and linguistic knowledge about print literacy as they participate in the literacy practices of their communities during the years prior to formal instruction. This "literacy set" is the lens through which they initially filter and make use of formal literacy instruction. Thus, to begin to explain the literacy achievement gap as it relates to socioeconomic factors, we must—acknowledging that socioeconomic measures are rough proxies for sociocultural factors—look to the ways that literacy practice plays out in the home and community cultural lives of students. Further, to craft reading and writing instruction that leads to increased literacy achievement by traditionally low-achieving students, one needs to relate that instruction to the literacy lives of the students.

A compelling implication of this conclusion is that much more research is needed into the literacy practices of different sociocultural communities, specifically those of marginalized groups whose members persistently underachieve in school. Before we can craft instruction in response to the different literacy sets brought to school by different learners, we must know what those sets are composed of. What do people read and write in these different communities and why? What roles do written texts play in the communities? What are the values and beliefs held by community members of literacy, literacy practices, and literacy forms? As I have already argued, few answers exist in any depth to these questions, certainly not enough to begin to inform curriculum design for the millions of children and adults around the world who have failed to achieve literacy as defined by existing educational systems.

We also do not know with precision what it would mean to craft literacy instruction around, or in response to, the different literacy worlds in which learners live. It seems too simplistic to speak of seeking a "match" between out-of-school literacies and in-school literacies. As personal colleagues have confided, literacy in school does not completely match any group's literacy outside of schools. Although this is obviously true of in-school literacy practices designed to teach skills, such as worksheets, reading to perform well on a test, and so on, it is also undoubtedly true of many of the more academic essayist literacy practices such as reading and deconstructing classic literature or writing persuasive prose.

Also simplistic, and dangerously deterministic, would be curricula that taught students only what they needed to know in order to participate in the discourses of their communities—even if we knew them. Aside from the social and linguistic determinism implicit in such a course, it is in such suggestions that one does see the inherent fallacy of the notion that literacy instruction is directly related to literacy practice. Most vernacular literacies (as already mentioned) were never taught as practices in any sort of instructional context. Why start now? Lankshear and Knobel (2004) recently raised a similar question in relation to literacy educators' interests in social literacy research. In response to the educators' question, "What does this say for instruction?", they responded that social literacy research does not necessarily have to say anything for instruction. Rather, much of this research stands on its own as literacy studies research and is interesting and significant in its own right.

This brings us to another complication of this complex view of literacy as multiple and social. If vernacular literacies do not necessarily translate directly into instructional practice, what is the influence of school-based literacy practice—autonomous, privileged, academic, and technical-skills focused—on out-of-school literacy practices embedded in sociocultural contexts subject to power relationships? If there are influences, what are they?

To further develop the sociocultural–cognitive frame for print literacy development (Purcell-Gates et al., 2004), I believe that this relationship between in-school instruction and out-of-school literacy practice must also be examined from the other side—that of instruction. Surely, school-based reading and writing instruction affects individuals' literacy practices beyond providing the skills needed to engage in those currently in play. This is an area that is virtually unexplored by research and theory: the impact, or influence, of school-based, or privileged, literacy practices on individual's out-of-school socioculturally situated literacy practices.

CULTURAL PRACTICES OF LITERACY STUDY

I have tried to suggest some of the many complications that have arisen for theory, research, and instructional practice as a result of viewing literacy as multiple and social. I believe that this theoretical frame has much to offer that is exciting and promising for understanding our lives as language users. However, just as this frame has provided us with new ways of thinking about language and textual practices, it has also opened up new areas for inquiry, areas that must be addressed if we are to continue with this theoretical line of work.

The chapters that follow in this book are a beginning to this end. They are all case studies (Yin, 1994) and they all address one or more of the issues I have just raised. They are not to be taken as the definitive work on these subjects. The research needed at this stage must be qualitative and, at least, quasiethnographic. This means that each case is a "small whole" that should provide unique insights into the issues of concern. It also means that many such cases are needed in order to begin to draw general principles and conclusions valid enough to warrant more inferential studies.

Each case study reported in this book reflects certain common theoretical presuppositions. First of all, the chapters are all about literacy in practice. Across all of the chapters, we see literacy as it occurs in the lives of people within and across nation states in a world dominated by ideologies of globalization, economic, cultural, and linguistic hegemony, and power. Literacy is addressed in the individual case studies as multiple and as mediating social lives. It is considered a social semiotic system of discourses and assumed to serve essentially communicative ends (Halliday, 1976).

The case studies were done under the aegis of the Cultural Practices of Literacy Study (CPLS). I am the principal investigator of the CPLS, and I initiated it as a focused research agenda in response to my perception of the need for more research, detailed previously. Two basic goals drive this work: (a) to theorize marginality in relationship to schooling in ways that will suggest real possibilities for schooling; and (b) to design curricula that promise to disrupt the persistent, almost perfect, correlation between social status and/or marginality and academic achievement. My interest in this topic is global because I see it as the same phenomenon played out in specific and differing contexts.

The questions addressed across the case studies reflect many of those raised by Luke (see previous discussion). These are questions of linguistic and textual resources and capital and how these elements co-occur in a globalized world within shifting and fluid sociocultural contexts. Several of the studies also address the question I raise: How are the resources provided through school-based literacy instruction recognized and misrecognized, remediated, and converted by students in their sociocultural lives outside of schools?

The researchers were all members of the CPLS Research Group, located at the time at Michigan State University, under my leadership. At the completion of the studies, some members of the group had met for about a year (others for 4 months), discussing and reading about issues of language, literacy, social and cultural practice, linguistic hegemony, politics, and economic globalization.

Each researcher, in response to calls for more research into local literacy practices, identified one group for a case study. Each case was identified and bounded by dimensions that could be labeled *sociocultural*. *Sociocultural groups* are defined for our purposes as groups of individuals who share common, and often unrecognized or nonconscious, values, beliefs, social structures, norms, conventions, activities, and discursive practices. Sociocultural groups may be marked by race, ethnicity, language, gender, class, age, geography, history, occupation, and socially constructed dimensions in different permutations and with different dimensions bearing different sociocultural "weight." Individuals may participate as members in multiple sociocultural groups as they engage in different aspects of their lives. These may be nested, or they may overlap, depending on the context of situations, and individuals will move, more or less, fluidly among them. Adolescents in the United States, for example, may be considered a sociocultural group, and different adolescents may participate in such different sociocultural groups as high school football players, Rap musicians, cheerleaders, band members, Teens-for-Christ, Young Republicans and/or Democrats, and so on.

Within this collection of case studies can be found representatives of such sociocultural groups as Sudanese immigrants; academically at-risk, urban middle-school children; Botswana women graduate students; Cuban immigrants; Puerto Rican farmers; African American, urban-poor, middle-school students; college students participating in a technological environment; and middle-class undergraduates. Each chapter, then, provides rich and complex portraits of literacy in use. We see multiple literacy practices as they weave throughout and mediate the lives of people around the world—men, women, and children whose lives are situated in different economic, linguistic, political, and cultural contexts.

Taken as a whole, this collection of case studies of cultural practices of literacy addresses many of the complications I have raised in this chapter and help to fill in the gaps regarding basic research in social practices of literacy and as regards the relationships between literacy instruction and literacy as actualized instruction—literacy in use outside of school.

CPLS METHODOLOGIES

The CPLS is the name of a metastudy of literacy development as it occurs across cultural contexts and in and out of school. The case studies presented in this book constitute one part of that ongoing research effort. Each case study was informed by several methodological procedures that were held constant across studies. These will be detailed now rather than within each chapter. Those methodological deviations or specifications developed for individual studies are presented within the relevant chapters by the individual researchers.

Researcher Location

Each researcher for the individual case studies was required to assume an active participant role within the cultural community studied. This requirement stemmed from several different concerns. First, issues of reciprocity and ethical responsibilities of researchers to communities that inform their work seem to call for this move. Secondly, issues of validity (representing accurately the way it really is) are addressed by this requirement. Ethnographers and case-study researchers, working in cultures not their own, face tremendous challenges in the recognition and interpretation of data significant to their research focus. For long-term ethnography, these challenges are eased by the passage of time and increased familiarity. However, for short-term microethnographies and case studies, particularly those specifically focused on cultural difference and cultural practice, researchers from outside the community must become as much a member of the community as is possible within a short time in order to address issues of validity. In my experience, this can be accomplished by finding a role within that community that is real and that is appropriate to the researcher and to the talents the researcher brings. The researchers of the case studies in this book took such roles as tutors, community helpers, program staff, and, in one case, impending family member.

The difficulty, and challenge, of assuming an active participatory stance is to account for one's role in the interpretation of the data and the results. Although ethnographers always acknowledge the inevitable role that the observer plays in what is observed (LeCompte & Schensul, 1999), the careful researchers track their participation in ways that can be accounted for in the analysis and final interpretation.

Each case study in this book contains a section required of ethnographic research reports, often referred to as *researcher location*. In this section, the researcher describes for readers the role(s) he or she played during the collection of the data and a little history of themselves as people and/or researchers, through whose eyes the data was interpreted. In this way, readers, as consumers of the research, can judge for themselves the degree to which the data and the resulting analysis and interpretation seem valid and generalizable to similar contexts.

Procedures

Several common procedures were used for each of the case studies, reflecting the need for common data across studies for the CPLS project. These included (a) observations; (b) interviews, including narrative elicitations of literacy stories, values, beliefs; (c) artifact and document collection and analysis; and (d) coding textual practices for sociotextual domains.

Observations.   Researchers made personal observations of the community environments within which the participants lived and worked, read, and wrote. They noted texts, literacy events, participant structures of those events, and sociotextual domains within which the practices occurred. Photographs were sometimes taken to augment this data and incorporated into the field notes documenting the observations.

Interviews.   Each researcher had a semistructured interview protocol that guided both the observational phase of the research as well as the interview phase. The protocol, which can be found in Appendix A, asked about such things as current and past literacy practices, in and out of school, and texts read and/or written. It also asked about practices of people in their communities, family members, and so on. Informants were prompted by the mention of different purposes or domains within which texts may be used such as "at work," "while shopping," or "with your children, spouse, or friends." The taped interview was supposed to start with a narrative elicitation of what literacy means to the informant. The interview protocol also prompted thoughts of linkages among literacy practices encountered in school and those practices outside of school. A demographic survey was also completed for each participant. This can be found in Appendix B.

Artifact Collection and Analysis.   Researchers collected, whenever possible, sample written texts that seemed particularly representative of textual practices reported by their informants. These were either copied or photographed and several of them appear within the chapters. These texts were analyzed for what they revealed of significance to the research questions and used to triangulate data sources for the final interpretations.

Coding for Sociotextual[5] Domain.   Following the lead of several works on literacy practices (e.g., Barton & Hamilton, 1998; Barton et al., 2000), we coded each textual practice observed or reported into the social activity domain the practice seemed to mediate. The construct of *social domain* proved to be complex, as reported by others (Barton et al., 2000), and, after

---

[5]I wish to thank Kendrick James for his provision of this term.

struggling with this for awhile, we took a somewhat different approach. Reflecting our focus on textual practices and documentation of textual genres (Halliday & Hasan, 1985), we ultimately settled on the term *sociotextual* for the domains of social activity that contextualize *social textual activity that reflects social relationships, roles, purposes, aims, goals, and social expectations*.

Sociotextual domains may include common settings, but that is not their defining characteristic. For this reason, settings such as home, school, church are not viewed as sociotextual domains, particularly if they are conceived of simply as places for social activities. Therefore, when we used terms such as *school literacy, out-of-school literacy, home,* or *community literacy*, we are not necessarily ascribing the same meanings as regards literacy practices as others who conduct similar research (e.g., Hull & Schultz, 2002). When, for example, we use the term *school literacy*, we are referring to reading or writing activity that is conducted within, and often in response to, the activity of schooling and that reflect purposes and practices sanctioned by schooling, for example, writing essays, practicing spelling words, reading an assigned novel. Writing an essay or reading a novel (or, theoretically, filling in a work sheet) are not always considered school literacies within this operational definition of sociotextual domain and literacies. If a person, say, writes an essay as part of his work as a scholar, then the sociotextual activity domain within which this literacy event takes place is that of work. If an adolescent reads a novel for relaxation, or as part of a peer book group, then that literacy event would have been coded by us for sociotextual activity domain as *entertainment* (defined as social activity for the purposes of pleasure, relaxation, or entertainment; e.g., reading a novel, doing crossword puzzles, knitting); or as *social cohesion* (defined as social activity whose purpose is to promote social cohesion, which can include participating in an information network; e.g., reading baseball scores to discuss with co-workers).

We consider sociotextual domains to be dynamic and, within the lives of individuals, to be multiple, fluid, floating, and overlapping. They are not static, mutually exclusive categories of social activity. People live in complex social worlds and their literacy practices reflect this. Our coding of textual practices by sociotextual domain, thus, was not mutually exclusive. A specific literacy event, or textual practice, was often coded within several sociotextual domains. For example, a literacy event in which a father reads the Bible to his child as part of a nightly ritual would have been coded within the sociotextual domains of *parenting* and *religion*.

As you read through these various case studies, I hope you will, as I do, take from them insights and information that help to complete the complex view of literacy as social and multiple. I also hope, if you are primarily involved in research, that as you read the individual studies, they will raise for you the inevitable new questions waiting to be explored. If you are primarily involved as a teacher of literacy learners, I hope the studies initiate some interesting and promising ideas about where we may go in our quest to make literacy available and within reach to all who wish to incorporate literacy into their lives in fulfilling and satisfying ways.

REFERENCES

Althusser, L. (1969). *For Marx*. (B. Brewster, Trans.). London: Allen Lane.

Althusser, L. (1971). Ideology and ideological state apparatuses (Notes toward an investigation). In *Lenin: Philosophy and other essays*. London: New Left Books.

Bakhtin, M. M. (1981). *The dialogic imagination* (C. Emerson, & M. Holquist, Trans.). Austin: University of Texas Press.

Barton, D., & Hamilton, M. (1998). *Local literacies: Reading and writing in one community*. London: Routledge.

Barton, D., Hamilton, M., & Ivanič, R. (Eds.). (2000). *Situated literacies: Reading and writing in context*. London: Routledge.

Bourdieu, P. (2001). *Language and symbolic power*. Cambridge, MA: Harvard University Press.

Bourdieu, P., & Passeron, J.-P. (1977). *Reproduction in education, society, and culture*. London: Sage.

Brandt, D. (2001). *Literacy in American lives*. Cambridge, England: Cambridge University Press.

Canagarajah, A. S. (1999). *Resisting linguistic imperialism in English teaching*. Oxford, England: Oxford University Press.

Cole, M., & Scribner, S. (1974). *Culture and thought: A psychological introduction*. New York: John Wiley & Sons.

Cushman, E. (1998). *The struggle and the tools: Oral and literate strategies in an inner-city community*. Albany: State University of New York Press.

Dyson, A. H. (2003). *The brothers and sisters learn to write: Popular literacies in childhood and school cultures*. New York: Teachers College Press.

Foucault, M. (1980). *Power/knowledge: Selected interviews and other writings 1972–1977*. New York: Pantheon.

Freire, P. (1993). *Pedagogy of the oppressed* (Rev. 20th-anniversary ed.). New York: Continuum.

Goody, J. (Ed.). (1968). *Literacy in traditional societies*. Cambridge, England: Cambridge University Press.

Goody, J. (1977). *The domestication of the savage mind*. Cambridge, England: Cambridge University Press.

Gregory, E., & Williams, A. (2000). *City literacies: Learning to read across generations and cultures*. London: Routledge.

Halliday, M. A. K. (1975). *Learning how to mean: Explorations in the development of language*. London: Edward Arnold.

Halliday, M. A. K. (1976). *Halliday: System and function in language: Selected papers*. London: Oxford University Press.

Halliday, M. A. K., & Hasan, R. (1985). *Language, context and text: A social–semiotic perspective*. Geelong, Australia: Deakin University Press.

Hildyard, A., & Olson, D. (1978). *Literacy and the specialization of language*. Unpublished manuscript, Ontario Institute for Studies in Education.

hooks, b. (1989). *Talking back: Thinking feminist, thinking Black*. Boston, MA: South End Press.

Hull, G., & Schultz, K. (Eds.). (2002). *School's out! Bridging out-of-school literacies with classroom practice*. New York: Teachers College Press.

Lankshear, C., & Knobel, M. (2004, December). *From Pencilvania to Pixelandia: Mapping the terrain of the new literacies research*. Plenary Address given at the 54th Annual Meeting of the National Reading Conference, San Antonio, TX.

Lave, J., & Wenger, E. (1991). *Situated learning: Legitimate peripheral participation*. Cambridge, England: Cambridge University Press.

LeCompte, M. D., & Schensul, J. J. (1999). *Designing and conducting ethnographic research*. Walnut Creek, CA: Alta Mira Press.

Lee, C. D. (1993). *Signifying as a scaffold for literary interpretation: The pedagogical implications of an African-American discourse genre*. Urban, IL: National Council of Teachers of English.

Luke, A. (2003). Literacy and the other: A sociological approach to literacy research and policy in multilingual societies. *Reading Research Quarterly, 38*, 132–141.

Mahiri, J. (1998). *Shooting for excellence: African American and youth culture in new century schools*. New York: Teachers College Press.

Moll, L. C. (1990). *Vygotsky and education: Instructional implications and application of sociohistorical psychology*. New York: Cambridge University Press.

Moll, L. C., & Gonzalez, N. (2003). Engaging life: A funds of knowledge approach to multicultural education. In J. A. Banks & C. A. M. Banks (Eds.), *Handbook on multicultural education* (pp. 699–715). San Francisco: Jossey-Bass.

Morrell, E. (2005). *Critical literacy and urban youth*. Mahwah, NJ: Lawrence Erlbaum Associates.

Morrell, E., & Duncan-Andrade, J. M. R. (2002). Promoting academic literacy with urban youth through engaging hip-hop culture. *English Journal, 91*, 88–92.

National Institute for Literacy. (1998). *The state of literacy in America: Estimates at the local, state, and national levels*. Washington, DC: National Institute for Literacy.

Olson, D. (1977). From utterance to text: The bias of language in speech and writing. *Harvard Educational Review, 47*, 257–281.

Perry, K., & Purcell-Gates, V. (2005). Resistance and appropriation: Literacy practices as agency within hegemonic contexts. In B. Maloch, J. V. Hoffman, D. L. Schallert, C. M. Fairbanks, & J. Worthy (Eds.), *54th yearbook of the National Reading Conference* (pp. 272–285). Oak Creek, WI: National Reading Conference.

Purcell-Gates, V. (1996). Stories, coupons, and the TV guide: Relationships between home literacy experiences and emergent literacy knowledge. *Reading Research Quarterly, 31*, 406–428.

Purcell-Gates, V., Jacobson, E., & Degener, S. (2004). *Print literacy development: Uniting cognitive and social practice theories*. Cambridge, MA: Harvard University Press.

Purcell-Gates, V., Degener, S., Jacobson, E., & Soler, M. (2002). Impact of authentic literacy instruction on adult literacy practices. *Reading Research Quarterly, 37*, 70–92.

Street, B. (1984). *Literacy in theory and practice*. Cambridge, England: Cambridge University Press.

Street, B. (1995). *Social literacies: Critical approaches to literacy in development, ethnography, and education*. London: Longman.

UNESCO. (2000). Retrieved May 5, 2005, from www.unicef.org/infobycountry/stats_popup5.html

U.S. Department of Education. (2001). *Technical report and data file user's manual for the 1992 National Adult Literacy Survey*. Washington, DC: Author.

Yin, R. (1994). Case study research design and methods (2nd ed.). New York: Sage.

Language, Literacy, and Hegemony

Victoria Purcell-Gates

Language and literacy practices and policies are never neutral; they always exist within political bodies and, thus, reflect ideological perspectives that, themselves, reflect relations of power. The role of power in the patterning of language and literacy practices is, perhaps, never more visible than in cases of language imposition. Colonial languages, for example, reflect the power of colonizing forces to impose a foreign language upon the colonized. English, Spanish, French, Russian ... these are but a few of the languages imposed on subjugated and dominated peoples over the years. Currently, the hegemony of English is widespread, primarily reflecting the dual roles of economics, in this world of "free trade" and globalization, and of military might. The power of the United States is behind the current domination of English worldwide. However, traces of prior English language hegemony are still visible, reflecting the historical colonizing activity of England, and can be seen in Africa, Australia, New Zealand, Canada, and other colonized territories. Language practice, though, is complex, and reflects more than just the power of the dominator. Native languages have deep social and historical roots and do not just disappear. Further, textual practices reflect hegemonic language policies and, themselves, reflect complex social and political landscapes.

The interplay of spoken and written literacy practices within contexts of language hegemony are explored in the following case studies by Catherine Mazak (chap. 2), and Annah Molosiwa (chap. 3). Mazak's study of a rural community, with a focus on a family of land owners/farmers, in Puerto Rico raises issues of language resistance, agency, and transformativity.

Molosiwa opens the African country of Botswana for us and provides a view of the ways in which the hegemony of English carries on as a legacy of colonial days and as the current currency of power. With her guidance as an insider informant, we see the complexity that results as tribal languages, a relatively new official language, and English co-occur in practice in concert with cultural, social, and historical practices.

Both of these studies contribute new insights into the ways that language and literacy practices today reflect past and present social, economic, political realities in contexts that reflect historical relationships of power, domination, and linguistic hegemony.

Chapter 2

Appropriation and Resistance in the (English) Literacy Practices of Puerto Rican Farmers

Catherine Mazak
Michigan State University

The road from San Juan to Ramona is crowded and winding. As you climb up hillsides covered in green palms and plantain trees, the crazy traffic of the city falls away. It is replaced with small *tiendas*, selling fresh roasted pork, which hang close to the roadside, and with views down the valley to the Río La Plata. Although only 3,000 feet above sea level, the small town of Ramona seems to be on top of the world. From the schoolyard you can see the Atlantic, but the tourist beaches and high-rise hotels that Puerto Rico is known for are a world away.

The cruise ship crowd never makes it this far into the island, although many other signs of an economy driven by the United States do. There are a local Sears™ and a McDonalds™ in a neighboring town. Many local businesses have signs in English: for example, *Palomas Mini-Market* and *Zayas Cash and Carry*. The center of the *pueblo* of Ramona sits on the banks of the Río La Plata, deep in a valley surrounded by the green mountains. A sign for *Julio's Parking–50¢* means that while you conduct your business, Julio will watch your car, which you can park on the river bank, for a very reasonable rate. The streets of the town square, which has the Catholic Church at its center, are narrow and better suited for horses than for cars. But if you want to get your mail in Ramona, you have to find a way to navigate them, because that is where you will find a U.S. Post Office, Zip Code 00892.

But don't be confused by all the signs in English. If you are planning a visit to Ramona, it's a good idea to speak Spanish. Although you will find an occasional bilingual speaker in Ramona (usually a military veteran, or those who have participated in the reverse migration from the mainland United States), English will not get you very far. Inside all of those buildings with the English signs, business is conducted in Spanish.

PUERTO RICAN LANGUAGE HISTORY

The colonial relationship between the United States and Puerto Rico accounts for the signs in English and the predominance of U.S. chain businesses even in the most rural parts of the island. Language policy has been at the center of the power struggle between Puerto Ricans and the U.S. government since the United States invaded the island in 1898. Education was the battleground where the war over language was fought. In 1899, Victor S. Clark, appointed president of the Puerto Rican Board of Education, made this strategy very clear in a report to his superior:

> If the schools are made American, and teachers and pupils are inspired with the American spirit, and people of both races can be made to cooperate harmoniously in building up the schools, the island will become in its sympathies, views, and attitude toward life and toward government essentially American. The great mass of Puerto Ricans are as yet passive and plastic .... Their ideals are in our hands to create and mold. (Davis, 1899, p. 646, cited in Morris, 1995, p. 26)

It was clear to this military government that "the easiest path to the eventual Americanization and anglification of the population was thought to lie through the children of Puerto Rico" (Scheweers & Hudders, 2000, p. 64).

Not surprisingly, one of the first acts of the U.S. military government aimed at achieving these ends was to declare English the official language of education in Puerto Rico. This started a long battle for those Puerto Ricans who wanted to retain Spanish as the language of education. The struggle occurred both at grass roots levels and through legislation, and a Puerto Rican's opinion on this issue defined his or her politics (Morris, 1995). This very imposition of English, designed explicitly to Americanize, actually succeeded in strengthening Puerto Rican identity and rallying Puerto Ricans behind Spanish as an act of defiance against the colonizer (Morris, 1995; Scheweers & Hudders, 2000; Zentella, 1999).

The policies surrounding the language of instruction in the schools changed as Puerto Rican government and status changed. In the elementary schools, from 1915 until 1934, a mixed policy existed: Spanish was the language of instruction until fourth grade; in fifth grade, students spent half of the day being instructed in Spanish and half in English; from sixth grade on, English was the language of instruction (Ramírez-González & Torres-González, 1996).

It is important to note here that what actually happened in these classrooms was probably very different from what this policy mandated. Many teachers taught in English only when they were being supervised (Scheweers & Hudders, 2000). High school students were taught in English from 1898 to the late 1940s, mainly because the students attending those schools were from upper-class families who wanted English to be the language of instruction.

In 1946, a bill went through the Puerto Rican legislature that would make Spanish the language of instruction in both elementary and high schools. The bill was vetoed by the U.S.-appointed governor, and the veto was overridden by the necessary two thirds vote in the legislature. According to the law at the time, any bill that had been vetoed and overridden was then sent to the president of the United States for the final say: President Truman vetoed the bill. However, as soon as Puerto Ricans had negotiated their commonwealth status in 1952, a law was passed making Spanish the language of instruction in the schools (Morris, 1995). This law remains in effect today, and Puerto Ricans study English as a subject in school from first grade through college.

On April 5, 1991, Spanish was declared the official language by the new procommonwealth government, overriding the 1902 law that had made both languages official. In January 1993, the newly elected prostatehood government passed a law reverting back to declaring both Spanish and English co-official languages of the island. This is still the case today, although a pro-commonwealth government has been in power since 2000.

Knowing the language policy history, though, is not knowing the whole story. The real story of language in Puerto Rico must be seen from the ground up. The actual language of education and business, and of the citizens and students who must negotiate those institutions, is very different from what the policies imply. The belief that learning English leads to economic success is widespread in Puerto Rico. For this reason, there is the kind of mythological quality that surrounds English as a world language in other countries (including in immigrant and other language minority populations in the United States). English is seen as the key to financial success as well as scientific and technological advancement, which is the basis for teaching it in the schools. The aspirations of even the procommonwealth government that had declared Spanish the sole official language were to promote bilingualism with English, not because English was an official language but because it was necessary for participation in the global economy.

Thus, the language policy in Puerto Rico today is bilingual, and it is fairly well accepted among U.S. institutions that Puerto Ricans are bilingual. As an example, although the large Midwestern university where I taught tested all international students for placement in English, they did not test Puerto Ricans. The assumption was made that all Puerto Ricans were bilingual, and thus could handle academic classes in English just as any native-English-speaking student could. (Later, I will complicate the notion of what it means to "speak English" or be "bilingual.")

A close look at the island soon reveals a more complex picture. The ability to speak English is influenced to a great degree by social class and by location on the island. The higher your social class, the more likely you are to speak English. Those from the urban, densely populated coast are more likely to speak it than those in the rural, mountainous interior. Key exceptions to this rule include veterans of the U.S. armed forces, into which Puerto Ricans were heavily drafted after U.S. citizenship was imposed in 1917 and for which they are still heavily recruited. Those who have participated in the steady flow of Puerto Ricans migrating to and returning from the mainland United States as they seek economic opportunities are also likely to speak English.

To begin to understand the true story of language, literacy, and power in Puerto Rico, we need to look closely at the assumptions about the role of English on the island. What does being bilingual in Puerto Rico really mean? What are the uses of English outside of the populated coasts? How important is English, really? This case study explores the ways in which reading and writing in both Spanish and English are used by two farmers in the interior of the island. It is a study of language appropriation and resistance, where English is taken up by the participants to meet their own needs on their own terms.

CHUCHO AND JACINTO'S FAMILY

Ramona is a rural community in the fertile mountains of Puerto Rico. It has a long agricultural tradition and was once well known for growing tobacco. The participants in this study are Chucho and Jacinto[1], brothers who live on their family's farm with their mother and sisters, in the house in which they grew up. The farm, large by Puerto Rican standards, is a hilly, red-earth spot of about 80 acres. It was once owned by Chucho and Jacinto's grandfather, Don Luis, who gave out parcels of the land around the boundaries of the farm where his 12 children could build houses. Chucho and Jacinto's house is one of those. With the death of Don Luis, the farm was split into smaller parts and distributed among Chucho and Jacinto's aunts and uncles. The brothers are trying desperately to make the farm turn a profit so that the *tíos* won't sell off their pieces to developers. Chucho and Jacinto

---

[1]All names have been changed.

work the farm, doing the picking and planting themselves, with an occasional hired worker. They manage the business end of the farm as well, selling their products to local buyers, applying for loans, and doing everything that running a small business might entail.

They are also community organizers. Jacinto works with the local farmers as president of the "nucleus of production," a group of farmers who grow the same crops and manage a small store. The brothers won the Conservationist Farmer of the Year award for Puerto Rico, given by the U.S.D.A. national resources conservation service.

Chucho and Jacinto come from an educated family. Their father holds a bachelor's degree and worked in banking; now he is a real estate appraiser. Their mother was an elementary-school Spanish teacher and, in her spare time, a writer, who has published several stories and poems in local magazines. Both brothers have bachelor's degrees in agricultural science from the University of Puerto Rico at Mayagüez. Jacinto, the older of the two, began to work toward a master's degree, but never finished. Chucho and Jacinto are good informants because they provide a perspective from rural Puerto Rico. Although they have an extensive English education, they do not consider themselves English speakers. In this way, Chucho and Jacinto are typical of many educated Puerto Ricans from the interior of the island.

Researcher Location

I have come to know this family well. There are five brothers and sisters—Elías, Ana, Jacinto, Chucho and Alma—spanning across 10 years in age. Through my work as an ESL teacher at a large Midwestern university, I met Ana, the oldest sister of Chucho and Jacinto, when she was my student for an intensive summer English course. During that summer, she introduced me to her brother Elías, the oldest in the family, who was a full-time graduate student. We started dating soon after the summer session. In the course of my relationship with Elías, I have traveled to Ramona many times, always staying in the house on the farm.

I have come to know Chucho and Jacinto as well, over the years, despite my initial limited knowledge of Spanish. When I approached them about this project, I was very much aware of my identity as an American who could be associated with the colonial power that occupies their country. More significantly, I am an English teacher, one of the very people who reify the role of power in the teaching of English, a language that is presented to Puerto Ricans as essential to economic and academic success.

Despite these factors, the brothers were happy to talk to me. After the first interview, however, Elías took it upon himself to reassure Jacinto by explaining something about me as a researcher. Elías felt it was important that Chucho and Jacinto know that I do not think everyone needs to learn English, and that I understand the historical role of English in Puerto Rico as a tool of imperialism. He told them how I feel about globalization and the hegemonic role of English in that process. In other words, he represented me as "on their side" and "safe to talk to." For this reason, Jacinto seemed more eager to talk to me, perhaps because he might have regarded me as someone able to make some positive changes for farmers in the community. Although it certainly does not eliminate my positionality in this study, this endorsement does give me confidence that Chucho and Jacinto understand where I am coming from.

"EVERYTHING THAT FALLS INTO MY HANDS IN SPANISH, I READ"

Chucho and Jacinto are in their mid-20s, just one year apart in age. Because they are always together, they seem more like twins and are treated by the family as one unit: *los nenes* (the kids). On a typical day they can be seen working on the farm in mud-stained brown pants and long-sleeved shirts, even under the scorching Puerto Rican sun. They are quite a sight from a distance. Old T-shirts serve as lightweight head coverings for protection from both sun and dust. They put the shirts over their heads, with just their eyes showing through the neck openings of the shirts, and tie the sleeves around the backs of their heads. Despite these measures, the brothers are very brown. The hard work keeps them thin and strong, even though they seem to eat at least a mountain of rice each day!

Chucho and Jacinto's literacy practices in Spanish are what one might expect from the educated children of highly educated parents. They use reading and writing in Spanish regularly in their personal and professional lives. When asked what literacy meant to them, they answered very similarly. Chucho said that reading was, "The way we communicate … how we know everything that we know. And writing? Writing is how we interpret the things we read. It's a way to deal with experiences." Jacinto's answer was very similar, "For me it's a sort of knowledge. And writing is a way to transmit what I think, to communicate myself." Reading strongly indicates "knowledge" (*conocimientos*) to both brothers, and they referred to "knowledge" as a driving purpose behind their reading of texts.

Chucho reported reading many things, saying, "Everything that falls into my hands in Spanish, I read." This is perhaps because he comes from a family of readers. When asked about what his family read, the list was long:

> In Spanish, that I remember, my dad and mom had many novels—novels in Spanish—Garcia Márquez and those of other Puerto Rican writers, and always I remember that I have seen *Selecciones, Reader's Digest*, always it was around here in Spanish; and other things are newspapers and magazines and yes, many novels and books of stories and things like that.

He describes a world full of text in Spanish, an immersion in books and print.

Chucho and Jacinto's mother was a Spanish teacher and a writer of poems and stories. The family reveals their pride in the pieces that she has published in a local magazine about life in their town, pulling it out to show me and encouraging me to read them. Even Chucho and Jacinto's grandfather, who lived next door to them, would recite poetry in Spanish, although he was formally schooled through only the fourth grade. Their brother Elías wrote poetry and songs in Spanish as a member of a punk band that the brothers formed during college.

Reading and writing seem to provide real pleasure for this family. For the brothers, in the case of the songs written for the band, reading and writing brought them together and gave them an activity to share. The family routinely passes around different types of reading material. Texts, including newspaper clippings and books, are regularly mailed back and forth from the island to Elías in the United States. Books in Spanish are frequently given as gifts, perpetuating the family's culture of literacy and strengthening the bonds between them, even across long distances.

LITERACY AND WORK

Literacy in Spanish is also a key part of the work life of all the family members. To manage the farm, the brothers must conduct financial activities that involve reading and writing in Spanish, including managing finances (e.g., writing checks, depositing money into accounts) and applying for loans. For instance, they used the Internet to compare tractor models before purchasing one, and to purchase seeds from a company in Hawaii.

The brothers also get information about farming through reading and writing. The island agronomist publishes a newsletter with information about agriculture, and the brothers also attend information sessions given by agronomists, where they take notes. When they have a question or a problem about the farm, the bookshelf is usually the first place that they would consult for an answer, including questions about how to treat sick animals (more on this in the English section later). The continued use of textbooks from their college studies in agricultural science shows one way in which school literacy interacts with home literacy.

LITERACY AND POLITICS

To understand how literacy mediates the political lives of Chucho and Jacinto, one needs to understand the role of politics, which is infused into the everyday life of Puerto Ricans. There are three major political parties on the island, and all of them position their platforms around the key issue of Puerto Rico's relationship to the United States: prostatehood, procommonwealth, and proindependence. Party affiliation is a large part of social life, and political discussions are frequent and heated among family and community members. Politics also has a great deal to do with economic life, often playing a role in who gets hired across many sectors of the economy, including education, agriculture, and banking.

The salience of the political party in everyday life can be seen in many ways. Each party has a symbol and a color, and everyone is aware of them. For example, every time I wore a red shirt in Puerto Rico I would hear some comment that I was a *Populare*, a member of the procommonwealth party. In addition, each newspaper is controlled by a particular political party, so to some extent you can detect the political leanings of someone by their newspaper subscription.

Choosing a newspaper to read is one way that literacy and politics interact in Puerto Rico. For the family, however, their relationship with politics is also mediated through many other kinds of texts. Speeches by political leaders, such as those of Luis Muñoz Marín, the founder of the procommonwealth party, were available in text format and were often read by Don Luis, Chucho and Jacinto's grandfather, who was an ardent party member.

Within this political context, Chucho and Jacinto, although very political, claim no party affiliation, rejecting the three main parties that dominate Puerto Rico. This is reflected in their reading about politics. Chucho reads books by political activists like Eduardo Galiano and also uses the Internet to read information about alternative political philosophy.

For Jacinto, reading in Spanish is a place where his work and political life connect. "Almost everything I read is about agriculture and politics, international politics in relation with agriculture." Jacinto's uses for literacy in Spanish cross into his political activities as a community organizer. He is the president of a "nucleus of production," a group of local farmers who meet to discuss production as well as the fair pricing of their goods on the market. The purpose of the group is to market their products together in order to eliminate the middle man. For these reasons, Jacinto needs to read information about economics and agriculture, much of which is provided through the agricultural extension service.

Chucho uses writing in Spanish for political ends as well. When developers proposed putting a *McDonald's*™ in Ramona, Chucho wrote to the mayor and explained how this would hurt the local economy.

"IN SCHOOL YOU DID IT BECAUSE YOU HAD TO"

As already mentioned, both Chucho and Jacinto hold bachelor's degrees from the University of Puerto Rico. Although they went to different high schools (Chucho opting to go to the local public school rather than the private Catholic school), they were taught Spanish literacy in very much the same way. They report reading stories, novels, poems, and textbooks throughout their years of schooling. They also wrote stories, poems, and academic essays of different types. Always the rebellious one in the family, Jacinto struggled a bit in school. "At the beginning, I didn't care for Spanish [class], but once I got into middle school I started working harder on it and started appreciating it more."

For both, reading and writing in school gave them the tools they needed for reading and writing in Spanish in their adult lives, but now both feel the freedom to use literacy any way they want. When asked how their current literacy practices differ from the literacy they learned in school, Jacinto replied, "In school, you did it because you had to. Now you do it because you need to or to communicate, to do the projects that you have to do."

Similarly, Chucho said,

> Well, in school there was a project you had to read. Now you choose whatever theme interests you. But, in which way did those texts influence me? Well, I think substantially because with them I developed my taste, what I like and dislike. During that time and now I imagine that, yes, for example, there are novels like *Lautaro* that I like a lot, *La Llamarada*, *Relato de un Náufrago*, this is the type of writing that now I enjoy. However, there are a lot of other things that I really dislike, and now I don't read that kind of stuff.

This adult control over the texts they read and their uses of literacy in school is important to the brothers, and this theme reoccurs as they discuss their literacy practices in English.

"I READ ONLY WHAT I TRULY NEED TO READ IN ENGLISH"

The role of literacy in English in the lives of Chucho and Jacinto is very different from that of Spanish. Although they both studied English from elementary school through college, neither would claim to be an English speaker. (Even in the days when I spoke very little Spanish, they would not try to communicate with me in English, unlike their younger sister Alma.) When speaking of doing a presentation in English class, Chucho said that he imagined the goal of the teacher was to get the students to think in English. "But I don't think in English!" he said with a laugh. Jacinto reports, "I believe that after all these English classes that I took [before college], none of them helped me to understand it, really." Despite this, both brothers do read in English. When asked about what reading in English means to him, Chucho responded, "In English, well, there, it's more specific [than reading in Spanish]. In English I read what really interests me and what I have to read. What I don't find in Spanish, and, well, in English I can find it, then I make the decision to read it."

Similarly, Chucho writes in English only when absolutely necessary, when he must communicate with someone who doesn't speak Spanish, as when he bought seeds over the Internet from a Hawaiian company. During the first interaction with the seed company, he wrote in English, but when he found that someone there could write in Spanish, he switched. Jacinto asserts that he doesn't write anything in English.

Chucho and Jacinto use English in very specific domains. Jacinto explains, "In English, I mostly use reading to acquire knowledge. That's because most of the information is in English. But I never write in English. I almost never use it." Chucho reports similar purposes for English literacy, "Reading? Well, to get knowledge of, of other cultures that communicate in the English language. And, well, to incorporate it in my work and in my knowledge. Writing? Well, I have a little bit more of a problem with it, but, really, generally I don't write in English." Here, the ability to read in English is specifically characterized as a way to get something—knowledge or information—that they need. Jacinto goes so far to say that "most of *the* information is in English" [italics added], implying that most of the important information, the information worth knowing, is in English.

This emphasis on English, especially as a source of science and technical information, is consistent with the image of English presented in the schools. Chucho and Jacinto studied English as a subject in school throughout their academic careers. During English classes in school they read newspaper articles, poems, stories, essays, and an occasional short novel, but Chucho reports it was "very little." As for writing, the brothers reported writing and publishing a newspaper and a magazine in English as a school project. Jacinto expressed uncertainty about why they did this, saying that he guesses they did it to "promote the language." They also wrote out reports that they would then deliver orally as a presentation in front of the class. In the university, reading and writing in English was key to their degree programs in agricultural science. In English classes, they wrote essays, poems, and stories in English and read textbooks, essays, articles, and stories. Chucho remembers "writing essays about many things. The purpose was for you to develop fluidity in English." Almost all of their content-area classes required reading textbooks in English, but their writing in English took place primarily in the context of English language classes.

This emphasis on English in the sciences perhaps adds to the perceived difficulty of English and becomes a real obstacle for some students, like Jacinto. When I asked him how his knowledge of English affected his student life, he replied, "It affected me because it limited me from obtaining a lot of information ... because much of the information in the textbooks is in English, so it limited me in what I could read .... It limited me so much."

For Jacinto, who struggled learning to read in his first language, reading in English seemed especially difficult. Speaking of learning English in school, he reports:

> I always didn't care much for English. At the time I thought it was that I didn't have good teachers, they weren't good communicators, but now I think it was that I was learning two languages at the same time, one first language and one second. I was having problems learning [to read and write] Spanish so unconsciously I decided on one of the two. I learned one by my own effort and the other one I left behind. That's the attitude that I had in my early life and then I just kept with it. That's the analysis that I make now that I'm older.

The university changed things somewhat because it allowed him to read things in English that truly interested him. "Because English was difficult for me, I was just interested in things related to agriculture." Still, learning English was difficult. "I believe that after all these English classes that I took, none of them helped me to understand it, really. The university was different. I think that what I had at the university was worth it more than the nine years that I had before that."

Despite this, reading in English continues to be a source of frustration for Jacinto. In a recent phone conversation, Jacinto told Elías that he needed to find a good book about economics in order to participate more successfully in recent debates over the price the farmers in the nucleus were getting for their plantains. Elías asked him, "Don't you have an agricultural economics textbook from the university?" Jacinto replied, yes, but that it is in English and he needed to get the information fast, so he wanted one in Spanish.

Here the relationship between in-school and out-of-school literacy is clear. For Chucho and Jacinto, school and work literacy practices in English reflect the same purposes or functions as well as the same challenges. The fact that textbooks are in English means that in school students must read English to gain information/knowledge. When these textbooks then become the reference library of the students in their professional lives, they face the same problems of access to information that they struggled through in school.

Both brothers report that their use of English is limited to two domains: work and politics. Jacinto says he reads to "incorporate" knowledge into his work, and Chucho says, "I read [in English] really for my work." In addition to reading reference material in English, the brothers also have to read pesticide labels and other instructions in English that are vital to their health and work. They also use English to read about politics. Both said that reading in English was important in order to have access to political information. Jacinto reports, "Most of the information about politics is in English. Especially about world politics. Information is in other languages, but the one that I can most easily use is English." Because both brothers feel that their political perspectives are important in their lives, reading political information, and thus reading in English, is a crucial part of their lives.

The importance of English literacy in the domains of work and politics is clear in the home environment as well. In the family, Spanish is the preferred language, but texts in English are read in the domains of work and politics. Chucho reports that he remembers seeing his father read university textbooks in English for work. Occasionally their father brings home the Puerto Rican business newspaper in English, but this is not a regular practice. When asked about his father's writing practices in English at work, Chucho reported, "I imagine that almost everything that they do, all of this that they write for work would have to be in English, because it's an agency that works in English, really. Yes, I imagine that all the work in the office is in English." As for other family members writing in English, Chucho could only remember "two or three songs that my brother Elías wrote. Writing in English … I don't know, is for work or school or something." Elías' use of English literacy for pleasure (reading sports books, writing songs and poems) is the exception in the family rather than the rule. For the rest of the family, literacy in English appears in only the domains of work and politics.

APPROPRIATION AND RESISTANCE

When charting the domains in which Chucho and Jacinto use literacy in Spanish and English, two things are striking: the central role of reading in English (rather than writing, speaking, or listening), and how that reading is relegated to very specific domains. One interpretation of this finding is that Chucho and Jacinto are simply enacting the types of English literacy they learned in school. This would make sense from the perspective of learning English as a foreign language, where often reading and writing are emphasized over listening and speaking because of the lack of opportunities outside of the classroom for using the spoken language. This does not explain, though, the fact that the brothers do not write in English, although clearly they learned how to do so. From their reports, this was a focus of their language learning, especially during university study. We might look to the context, then, to explain the centrality of reading, given that students are unlikely to use any of the language they learn in the classroom if there are not sufficient opportunities for its use outside the classroom.

Although signs label businesses in English, Ramona is not a place where reading in English is necessary to function in daily life. (In fact, Elías confirms that these names of businesses are treated as any other name, without real awareness of their meaning in English.) Given that the two brothers never traveled outside of the Spanish-speaking world, why would reading in English be so central to their literacy practices?

Jacinto answers this question himself when he says, "All of the information is in English." He and Chucho both go on to talk about English reading in terms of appropriating knowledge or information. In their own words, they use reading to "acquire" and "incorporate" information into their own repertoire of knowledge in order to use it in their lives for their own purposes.

Not only do they have few opportunities to use writing in English, but writing will not get them access to knowledge in the same way that reading will. Similarly, the ability to understand and use spoken English gets them little. "The information" is not encoded in spoken English, at least not in Ramona; it is encoded in written text. Further, the use of productive skills in English—speaking and writing—would mean sharing some of their own knowledge with the very audience that seems to withhold information from them, encoded in a foreign language. As Chucho himself says of writing in English, "They wanted you to think in English—but I didn't think in English!" This appears to be a clear rejection of English, with all that it represents, and perhaps a defense against its control of his thoughts.

Similarly, Jacinto's suspicions about writing a newspaper in English "to promote the language" is an indication of how he sees writing in English as an act of Americanization, of language "promoting" rather than language learning. Thus, Chucho and Jacinto's proficiency in reading English and their rejection of other English skills can be interpreted as an act of resistance (Canagarajah, 1999; Pennycook, 1994, 2001). They resist English as part of their productive repertoire, rejecting the identity of "English speaker." Instead, they appropriate the literacy practices in English that support their farming and give them access to information about their political interests.

Literacy and Activism

In the spirit of community organization and activism, Chucho and Jacinto's reading in English becomes a resource for other farmers in the community. When farmers have questions about how to use pesticides, which are generally labeled exclusively in English, they go to Jacinto, who not only can read the instructions but is also an agronomist. They trust him as an expert on farming, which he is in part because of his access to information—in the form of texts—about farming. As president of the nucleus of production, he must access economic information through texts in order to be able to negotiate a better price—and thus a better standard of living—for the farmers whom he represents.

Complicating Notions About the "Need" to "Speak English"

The earlier argument calls for a complication of two commonly held ideas: the "need" to speak English, and what it means to "speak English." As English has become a global(izing) language, some have called for the recognition of global English(es) as legitimate varieties in their own right. Chucho and Jacinto's use of reading in English takes this notion even further, problematizing what it means to "speak English" at all. Although I would not say that the brothers speak English, it would be hard to deny the fact that they certainly "know" or have proficiency in English (Pennycook, 2001). So, has the language policy of the educational system succeeded in making them bilingual? At one level the answer is yes, but that should be qualified by saying that they have become bilingual on their own terms, for their own clearly defined purposes.

Statements about the "need" to learn English because of its status as a global language are also called into question here. At the very least, we must say that this need is dependent on context. Speaking English does not have much capital in the life contexts of the informants for this study, although reading English has some.

The informants' literacy in Spanish, however, has far greater capital (Luke, 2003). Through Spanish they negotiate their world: their work life, their political interests, their leisure time. Literacy in Spanish helps them to be community members, activists, farmers, and family members. Literacy in English, however, is part of a constant struggle to get information, in which the brothers participate because of their position as educated, concerned farmers and citizens. Although this does help them in their position as community leaders, it is not because English literacy, in and of itself, gives them prestige. Instead, it is because other farmers can access information in English through them, and thus can bypass the English language struggle themselves.

The Roles of Language Brokers

Chucho and Jacinto's position in the community can thus be seen as that of language "brokers." The farmers in the nucleus come to Jacinto for help in part because of his ability to negotiate texts and access information in both Spanish and English. Even Jacinto, with all his talk of difficulty with English, can use it well enough to help someone who has little or no English reading ability.

Between the two brothers, Chucho is the more proficient in English. Thus, he is positioned to act as a language broker for Jacinto in their farming business. When he needs to ask for help while reading English, Jacinto reports, "Yes, I ask Chucho. I also look in the dictionary." When I asked him if he thought Chucho was an expert in English, Jacinto said with a laugh, "No, but he knows more than me!" As the status of English as a global language continues to dominate, the role of these language brokers, those who have some proficiency in English and act as resources for community or family members who have less proficiency, is an area that deserves exploration.

CONCLUSION

The saliency of English in the domains of work and politics is not so surprising when viewed through the lens of colonialism. The United States dominates Puerto Rico economically and politically, and in those two domains English dominates as well. What drives Chucho and Jacinto to read in English is access to information. It is precisely that lack of access to information in the vernacular that a colonial system supports and, in fact, relies on (Mazrui & Mazrui, 1998; Pennycook, 1994). In order to maintain control of Puerto Rico, the United States must convince Puerto Ricans that they need the United States. This perceived need is reinforced in the educational system and even in the homes of Puerto Ricans where English is seen as the key to opportunity.

The status of English and its importance for economic success are not questioned, and it likewise remains unquestioned in countries throughout the world that are trying to gain access to the world market. Why does Jacinto need to turn to reading in English to get information about world politics, when Spanish is the first language of more countries in the world than any other language (Comrie, Matthews, & Polinsky, 2003)? Why does Elías have to send his brothers articles about tropical agriculture from a Midwestern U.S. university when his brothers live in, and were educated in, the tropics? Why are the textbooks used in agricultural science in English, when so many Spanish-speaking countries have well-developed agricultural science programs with texts in Spanish?

What is fascinating is the way this case shows the subtle alternatives that Puerto Rican individuals and communities employ to overcome the lack of access to information in the key domains of work and politics. They do not accept English, learn it, or make it their own; Spanish is not threatened in Ramona, Puerto Rico. Instead they take only the English they need and employ language brokers to access information that they cannot access any other way. As part of a long tradition in Puerto Rican culture and history, they resist.

REFERENCES

Canagarajah, A. S. (1999). *Resisting linguistic imperialism.* Oxford, UK: Oxford University Press.
Comrie, B., Matthews, S., & Polinsky, M. (2003). *The atlas of languages* (2nd ed.). New York: Quarto.
Luke, A. (2003). Literacy and the other: A sociological approach to literacy research and policy in multilingual societies. *Reading Research Quarterly, 38*(1), 132–141.

Morris, N. (1995). *Puerto Rico: Culture, politics, and identity*. Westport, CT: Praeger.
Mazrui, A. A., & Mazrui, A. M. (1998). *The power of Babel: Language and governance in the African experience*. Chicago: University of Chicago Press.
Pennycook, A. (1994). *The cultural politics of English as an international language*. New York: Longman.
Pennycook, A. (2001). *Critical applied linguistics*. Mahwah, NJ: Lawrence Erlbaum Associates.
Ramírez-González, C. M., & Torres-González, R. (1996). English under U.S. sovereignty: Ninety-five years of change of the status of English in Puerto Rico. In J. Fishman, A. W. Conrad, & A. Rubal-López (Eds.), *Post-imperial English: Status change in former British and American colonies, 1940–1990* (pp. 174–204). Berlin: Mounton de Gruyter.
Scheweers, C. W., Jr., & Hudders, M. (2000). The reformation and democratization of English education in Puerto Rico. *International Journal of the Sociology of Language, 142*, 63–87.
Zentella, A. C. (1999). Language policy/planning and U.S. colonialism: The Puerto Rican thorn in English Only's side. In T. Huebner & K. A. Davis (Eds.), *Sociopolitical perspectives on language policy and planning in the USA* (pp. 155–172). Philadelphia: John Benjamins North America.

Chapter 3

Language and Literacy Issues
in Botswana

Annah Molosiwa
Michigan State University

This study investigated current language and literacy issues in the African country of Botswana. Four students who are pursuing graduate studies in the United States provided data for this case study. This results of the study are contextualized by descriptions of the language and literacy contexts of Botswana, historically and today. Thus, the data came from the women's accounts, my own experiences as a scholar in Botswana, and through existing scholarship on Botswana. Through this investigation, I sought to uncover insights into issues of literacy practice and the educational system of Botswana.

Data for the study were collected through formal interviews that lasted for 1½ to 2 hours per visit at the informant's residence and at my residence for the informants who visited from states outside Michigan. The interviews were audiotaped and subsequently transcribed. The study lasted for a period of 4 months (from September to December, 2003). The questions were open-ended and some had a list of possible prompts to guide the interviewer to the information wanted. In addition to formal interviews, I visited some informants' homes once per week to observe the kind of literacy materials that were available as well as literacy practices in which they were engaged. Because I had a common language of communication (Setswana) with all the informants, I conducted the interview mostly in that language, although at times there was code-switching between English and Setswana. Data were analyzed in relation to the categories of questions that mainly covered out-of-school literacy practices, historical literacy practices, and school literacy practices.

The informants of this study and I are colleagues from the University of Botswana where we taught in various departments. We are in the United States on study leave pursuing postgraduate degrees at different universities. I therefore selected the informants who were within reach from my place of study. I wanted to compare the circumstances under which I attained print literacy with those of other professionals from my country so as to explore insights that might be drawn for literacy education in Botswana schools.

POSITION OF THE RESEARCHER

I am a 44-year-old woman who grew up in a rural village where I did my primary education. My parents were farmers who had attained very little elementary education. They had only the basic skills of reading and writing, not much education. The most common forms of literacy practices in my home and community that children were exposed to during my childhood days were storytelling by elderly people, play school that was conducted by our elder siblings who attended school, and traditional games. I went to one of Botswana's main cities for secondary education where I saw a library and book shops for the first time. Later on I ended up in the capital city (Gaborone) to attend university. I teach in the teacher education department at the University of Botswana and am currently pursuing a PhD at Michigan State University in the United States. All names given to informants in this study are pseudonyms.

Informants

Dineo is a 38-year-old teacher who grew up in a rural village with parents who had never attended school. She went to primary school in her village and later transferred to secondary school in a mining town where her father worked in the mine as a laborer. After secondary education, she went to the capital city to the university. She is married with one child. Dineo and her husband communicate with each other in Setswana in their home but in English to their daughter, whom they send to an English medium private school. The daughter speaks very little Setswana. The reason given for this scenario is that she was sent for babysitting at a very young age where she was taken care of by non-Setswana speaking caretakers who communicated with her in English. Following babysitting from an English-speaking environment, the girl was sent to an English medium school at age 6. She ended up acquiring more English than Setswana because she was denied the latter even at home by the parents. Dineo teaches in the Home Economics Department at the University of Botswana. She has been studying for a masters degree in Early Childhood Education in a large Midwestern university in the United States. She has once visited her family back home and her daughter also visited her twice in the United States.

Peo, 33 years old and also a teacher, grew up in the capital city. She was raised by her mother who is a secretary in a government department. Peo obtained all her education in Gaborone, from primary school to university. She teaches in the African Languages Department at the University of Botswana and is studying for a masters degree in a Western university in the United States. She is married but has no children yet. She has been in the United States for only 1 year and has visited Botswana once.

Tshidi, 34 years old, is a single parent of one child. She grew up in a semiurban village and obtained both her primary and secondary education there. Then she went to Gaborone for university education. Tshidi was introduced to reading and writing by her father who is an elementary school teacher. She remembers learning the word "equator" from her father. She also recalls how she got excited the day she wrote the number "8" as she had difficulty writing it among all the numbers she knew. Tshidi was exposed to many reading materials like books and magazines before she started school. Like Peo, Tshidi teaches in the African Languages Department at the University of Botswana and is studying for a masters degree in Theater/Literature in an Eastern university in the United States. She has visited Botswana once in the 2 years she has been in the United States.

Naomi, 39 years old, is married with two children. She also grew up in a big semiurban village where she obtained her primary and secondary education. She was introduced to reading and writing by her mother who is a retired teacher now. She went to Gaborone for university education after which she joined the teacher education department at the University of Botswana. She is studying in a Midwestern university in the United States for a masters degree in Curriculum and Instruction. Naomi has visited Botswana twice since she came to the United States.

The chapter starts with an overview of the language situation in Botswana. The next section briefly describes the nature of education that existed in the country (precolonial education) before the introduction of Western education by the missionaries. Thereafter I focus on the colonial education that brought print literacy to the country. The final section is a discussion of the findings, followed by the conclusions.

GEOGRAPHICAL, HISTORICAL, AND LANGUAGE CONTEXTS OF BOTSWANA

Geography and Language

Botswana is located in the interior of Southern Africa. It is bordered by Zambia, Zimbabwe, Namibia, and South Africa. The number of languages spoken in Botswana[1] is estimated to be at least 25 (Batibo & Smieja, 2000).

---

[1] Botswana is the name of the country.

Setswana[2] is demographically the most dominant language in the country, spoken by at least 80% of a population of 1,680,863 (Botswana in Figures, 2001) either as first or second language. It is the declared national language (Government of Botswana, 1985) and the *de facto lingua franca* of the country. It is sometimes referred to as the second official language in government circles. Setswana is offered as a compulsory school subject at primary and secondary school levels.

English is the declared official language (Government of Botswana, 1985), the language of government and administration, science and technology, educational and international relations. It is the medium of instruction for all subjects at primary and secondary school levels except for Setswana classes. The number of minority languages spoken in Botswana is estimated to be 23. According to Batibo and Smieja (2000), it is difficult to determine the exact number of minority languages because "many of these languages, particularly the Khoesan ones, form language clusters involving several linguistic or socio-cultural entities" (p. xv). Thus, for some languages spoken in Botswana, it is not easy to distinguish between a language and a dialect. The minority languages have no official status in Botswana. Setswana is also spoken in some parts of neighboring Namibia and South Africa.

Precolonial Education in Botswana

Botswana was a British protectorate for 81 years, from 1885 to 1966. During the precolonial era, Botswana had some traditional form of education that "was part of a whole system of belief, or religion, as well as a means of socializing children into the accepted norms of society" (Parsons, cited in Crowder, 1984, p. 22). Parsons classifies traditional education into three categories: *informal, formal*, and *vocational* education. There was informal education in the home, which was mainly parenting, and included relations among siblings, with special emphasis on the aged as repositories of wisdom.

Formal education was characterized by *bojale* and *bogwera*, adolescent initiation schools for females and males, respectively. In *bojale*, young female adults were formally taught matters concerning womanhood, sex, behavior toward men, domestic, and agricultural activities. *Bogwera* was formal instruction for young male adults where they were circumcised and taught skills such as kaross sewing for shields and clothing, and modeling cattle in clay to reinforce practical knowledge of livestock. They were trained to be responsible men, warriors, and fathers. Whereas women qualified for motherhood and marriage after *bojale*, *bogwera* did not qualify men for mar-

---

[2]Setswana is the language spoken by most people. Batswana refers to people of Botswana (in plural terms, the singular form is Motswana).

riage until after they had proved themselves as herders, hunters, and fighters. Vocational education consisted of part-time individual apprenticeships in trades such as medicine, mining, and smelting. Also, skills in agricultural and hunting techniques were imparted.

Colonial Education

Western education in Botswana was introduced around 1847 by David Livingstone, a missionary of the London Missionary society. This education replaced "traditional" or "heathen" precolonial education (Parsons, cited in Crowder, 1984, p. 22). The churches financed education and were therefore in full control of the curriculum and its content.

The curriculum consisted of Christian scriptures. A translation of the New Testament into Setswana came into being in 1840. The translation for the rest of the Bible was completed by 1857. Robert Moffat, a leader of the missionaries, provided the first translation of Setswana into the Roman alphabet and translated the Bible into written Setswana. In 1860, a school was established at Shoshong (then the Bangwato[3] capital) where children were taught reading, writing, arithmetic, and scripture in Setswana. The main emphasis was to instill in the students obedience and discipline.

By virtue of being tribal leaders, the chiefs were involved in the administration of the schools, so they had some input in educational matters even though very limited. In 1966, when the country became independent, the education policy shifted from colonial education to the kind of education that would meet the needs of the emerging society. Education was seen as a crucial aspect of economic development and the development of human resources. In this regard, postprimary education was emphasized and expanded during the early years of independence.

Education prior to the missionaries was oral. Print literacy began with the missionaries. Printed texts began with the translated Bible, and the reading of the Bible was the result of the Christian mission activity in Botswana. By the time schools were introduced, the majority of families had only the Bible and the church hymn book (that for the London Missionary Society) in their homes. Consequently, many children who started school during the early years of independence came from homes in which very little reading and writing occurred.

LITERACY AS MAKING MEANING

When asked what *literacy* meant to them, the informants for this study indicated an understanding that literacy means the ability to read with under-

---

[3]Bangwato is one of the ethnic groups in Botswana.

standing and to apply information read to the reader's situation, not just the technical aspects of decoding and encoding print. Literacy was associated with making meaning out of written material. Naomi defined literacy as being able to read using different genres, to be able to apply information read to the reader's situation, and to communicate one's thoughts through writing logically. Peo understood literacy to mean the ability to read comprehensively and critically as well as the ability to write grammatically correct sentences. One could attribute the definition of literacy as making meaning from textual material as related to the informants' level of education. Being graduate students and teachers by profession, the informants' understanding of literacy has moved beyond merely decoding words from printed text. Reading and writing are an integral part of their day-to-day lives due to the nature of their professions. Even outside of academic work, these highly educated women engage in the acts of reading and writing both in the United States and in Botswana in many domains for various purposes, including self enrichment and religion. They read magazines, newspapers, and use the Internet, varying their literacy practices according to the purposes and contexts within which they are operating.

HEGEMONY OF ENGLISH

Literacy practices of the informants and the materials they read revealed the degree to which English dominates in their lives, whether in Botswana or the United States. All of them report doing vast amounts of reading and writing in English for academic purposes in both countries.

Printed Texts

Examining the textual artifacts in their U.S. homes, it was clear that English dominates. Many of the artifacts, even those from Botswana, are written in English. In addition to formal interviews, I visited the homes of informants who were within reach once per week (a total of six visits per informant) to observe the kinds of literacy materials that were available as well as literacy practices in which they were engaged. I found documents such as newspapers, magazines, tourist guides, funeral programs, postcards, greetings and birthday cards, personal letters, calendars, and home decoration crafts.

The Botswana newspapers I found were *The Daily News, Mmegi/The Reporter, The Botswana Guardian, The Gazette*, and *Mokgosi*, and a magazine, *Kutlwano*. On analysis, I realized that of the newspapers, only *Mokgosi* is solely written in Setswana. This paper was founded in 2000 by a group of Batswana whose objective is to promote the national language because it is evidently dying. Most of the news in *The Daily News* is in English. Only one page, which comes towards the end of the paper, has a few articles written in

Setswana. That Setswana page appears hidden, as it comes just before the last page in all the papers I observed. In the past, many people have raised concerns that the Setswana news in this newspaper is news that had appeared on the previous day in English. *Mmegi/The Reporter* is also predominantly an English newspaper but has a column in Setswana and another one in Ikalanga, one of the local languages spoken in Botswana. The magazine, *Kutlwano*, is balanced; about 50% of the articles are in English and 50% or more in Setswana.

The distribution of the magazine *Kutlwano* illustrates the relationship between social class and textual practices and access (Luke, 2003). This magazine and *The Daily News* are produced by the Department of Information and Broadcasting, Botswana government. The newspaper is distributed widely at no charge; the magazine is sold at a very low price—the equivalent of less than U.S. $1 and is therefore popular among the low-income people and those in rural areas. The two are found almost everywhere in the country. Only two of my informants read *Kutlwano* and *The Daily News*. The other two seldom read newspapers. The women report that in Botswana, educated people seldom read *Kutlwano*. The daily news is read mostly by government employees because it is distributed in all government departments every working day. The private newspapers, *Mmegi, The Guardian*, and *The Gazette*, are more popular among the educated elite and have a wide readership. Some people argue that they prefer these newspapers because they present a variety of news, unlike the government paper, which is censored and is narrow in some respects.

Oral Language

The higher status accorded English in Botswana is also revealed in the choice of English as the medium of communication among people who have been to school or the educated elite. I explained the purpose of this research in Setswana and told the informants that they could respond in either English or Setswana. All the informants responded primarily in English, with code-switching between the two languages at times. Although this may have been prompted by the fact that the questions were written in English, in Botswana, most educated Batswana also communicate with each other primarily in English with some code-switching between their local languages and English. Data for this study confirmed that the informants use English, or code-switch, in many domains, including personal matters such as writing letters and e-mail messages and in telephone conversations with their fellow-country colleagues. By virtue of being in an English-speaking country (the United States), the tendency to use English with those who also know Setswana as a native language has, understandably, intensified.

The informants stated that even in personal domains like shopping, they use English. They use Setswana only for items that are labeled in Setswana. The common example cited by the informants was of *mabele*, meaning "sorghum," which is one of Botswana's staple foods. Sorghum is locally produced and packaged; for this reason, the retail label is the Setswana version—*mabele*. English has made fewer hegemonic inroads in the rural villages as compared to the cities. The informants pointed out that Setswana is mostly used at very local levels for social events like funeral programs mostly in villages. It is not uncommon, though, to find people in cities writing their funeral and wedding programs in English because they want to include the non-Setswana speakers as well. Most government materials in Botswana are also written in English. The women gave examples of documents such as driver's licenses, marriage certificates, and bank documents.

English and Power

English, as a foreign colonial language, is the official language in Botswana and associated with socioeconomic power. Most jobs require people who have done well in English at school. Everybody aspires to learn English or have his or her children learn English. Although public schools are funded by the government, increasingly parents strive to send their children to English medium schools where they pay tuition. Such parents tend to speak English to their children in their homes so that the children attain fluency. Nyati-Ramahobo (1996) reported that this hegemony of English is seen as also responsible for the demands of learners in literacy programs for English literacy and the subsequent training of literacy assistants and literacy group leaders in the teaching of English as a second language. In sum, literacy in Botswana, among the educated and the to-be-educated is associated with speaking and reading English. The language in education policy has elevated the status of English such that being literate in English is seen as a form of empowerment.

Given this association of English with print literacy and with power, one finds clear and definite differences in language practices among the life spheres of home, school, and work in Botswana. At home, people communicate in their local languages, most of which are not taught at school with the exception of Setswana. Thus, the disparity between home and school is greater for children for whom Setswana is not their mother tongue. For them, the school domain is different from their life world (Gee, 2000). They are encouraged to speak English around the school premises because it is the medium of instruction for all subjects except for Setswana. The reading and writing also are done mostly in English. Children are punished when they are caught speaking to each other in their local languages.

In the domain of religion, local languages or Setswana are used for services. In the rural areas, all churches use local languages for services. In the urban areas, religious services are conducted in either Setswana or English (or both). English is used only in those churches in urban areas that have mixed population of Batswana and foreigners.

At work, official matters like meetings are conducted in English though people speak to each other in Setswana or their other local languages. There are many more print literacy resources in English than in Setswana—texts such as books, magazines, newspapers, videos, movies, and the Internet. Most government documents (e.g., driver's licenses, passport application forms, national registration forms) used to be written only in English; some are now becoming available in both English and Setswana. Medical documents, such as records for patients including vital information such as immunization for children and labels on medicines, are written in English.

Overlaying this identification of life domain with language is the interplay of social relationships with language. In Botswana, the use of a particular language is often determined by the social relationships among the people involved. The informants for this study reported that they usually communicate with their family members and other Batswana students in Setswana in Botswana and the United States. For domains such as entertainment and personal expression, communication is either in Setswana or English, depending on the relationships involved. Because their fields of study are not available in Setswana even in Botswana, the informants do their academic work in English. The only Setswana materials they read are the few magazines and newspapers they brought with them from Botswana.

FAMILY AND COMMUNITY LITERACY IS PREDOMINATELY ORAL

With this association of print literacy with English, it is interesting to note that the informants agreed that there is no real culture of reading and writing in Botswana, as compared to descriptions of the United States (Taylor, 1983; Teale & Sulzby, 1986) or British (Barton & Hamilton, 1998) contexts. Many children grow up in homes that have no reading material, and not much writing occurs. The informants concurred that during their childhood days, most people in their communities did not read anything except for activities that had to do with work for those who were employed. Some elderly people read the Bible for religious purposes but did not engage much in writing. In most homes, books that were available were the Bible and children's school books. Children were introduced to print literacy by their siblings who attended school. Only a few became literate through the influence and/or teaching of their parents.

National Literacy Survey

This insight is supported by the first national literacy survey that was conducted in 1993, which reported that there was no reading and writing culture in Botswana.

According to the survey, 33.9% of people who could read Setswana never read anything, with females in the majority (76.2%). The majority of those who could read English reported that they were not interested in reading anything in English. Females (70%) expressing less interest than males. Reasons given for not reading or writing revealed the relatively limited life domains mediated by print literacy, for example, "nothing to read or write," "lack of time," "lack of interest," "could not read well," and "poor eyesight." Table 3.1 and Table 3.2 provide relevant results of this survey.

Responses by the four Batswana women illustrated this absence of a print literacy culture and the preference for oral communication. To announce social events like wedding ceremonies, birth of a child, or death, for example, certain family members are sent to tell people in other villages or in the neighborhood. This practice is such a cultural norm that, even today, some people do not attach value to card invitations or accept them as worthy, especially when they are from close relatives. People want formal invitations by word of mouth. Card invitations are regarded as impersonal and associated with Westerners.

TABLE 3.1
Eligible Population Who Could Read by Language, Reason for Never
Reading and Gender—1993

| Reason | Setswana | | | % of Grand Total | English | | | % of Grand Total |
	M	F	Total	Total	M	F	Total	Total
Nothing to read	56.6	43.4	752	23.4	83.0	17.0	88	9.6
Lack of time	49.0	51.0	363	11.3	53.6	46.4	28	3.1
Lack of interest	35.7	64.3	947	29.5	30.0	70.0	700	76.3
Could not read well	23.8	76.2	1,090	33.9	23.7	76.3	59	6.4
Poor eyesight	75.8	24.2	62	1.9	100.0	—	43	4.7
Total	38.8	61.2	3,214	100.0	38.7	61.3	918	100.0

Note. M = Male, F = Female.
From *Report of the First National Survey on Literacy in Botswana* (1993).

TABLE 3.2
Eligible Population Who Could Write by Language, Reason for Never
Writing and Gender—1993

Reason	Setswana			% of Grand Total	English			% of Grand Total
	M	F	Total	Total	M	F	Total	Total
Could not write well	43.4	56.6	2,085	53.6	53.0	47.0	610	68.0
Nothing to write	24.0	76.0	438	11.3	52.6	47.4	95	10.6
Nobody to write to	35.7	64.3	235	6.0	53.1	46.9	64	7.1
Lack of time	36.2	63.8	376	9.7	39.5	60.5	86	9.6
Lack of interest	23.6	76.4	759	19.5	64.3	35.7	42	4.7
Total	36.2	63.8	3,893	100.0	52.2	47.8	897	100.0

Note. M = Male, F = Female.
From *Report of the First National Survey on Literacy in Botswana (1993).*

Written documentations, although in official use, are still not integrated culturally in the lives of many Batswana, according to the informants. For example, documentation of such events as childbirth is attached more to certain historical events in people's lives than to written birth certificates. Dineo explained:

> Most of our parents do not know their exact birthdates but would tell that they were born during the war of Hitler, meaning that they were born during the Second World War. Some say they were born during the year of the great drought. Naming of children was also not done haphazardly but after careful observation of some important events in people's lives. We have people who have been named after certain events like during the year when locusts attacked the country. Children who were born at that time were given names like Tsie, meaning the locust (if it's a boy), or Mmatsie if it's a girl, which means mother of locusts. Those who were born in 1966 when the country gained its independence were named Boipuso which means independence or MmaBotswana—mother of Botswana.

Historically, Batswana learned about events that took place locally or in distant places around the world, not by reading books or newspapers, but through names given to children who were born during those times, or through songs that were composed about certain events and passed on from one generation to the next. Several informants acknowledged that the oral nature of Batswana culture is inherent in them even today. As an example, they relayed that, even though they try to keep things like personal diaries, they sometimes forget to record events or to refer to them on a daily basis. "The young generation is able to cope with such modern literacy practices but for people who were born in the 1960s, it is not easy. We are used to being told things verbally and keep them in our memories," said Dineo.

The Role of Oral Literature

Despite the absence of print literacy in Botswana homes, the informants stressed that children still acquire a high degree of education. They pointed out that they gained a lot of education from their elders. Traditionally, Batswana children used to learn folktales, riddles, proverbs, and idioms at home from their elders. Although stories considered as passed along by elders were previously told orally, they are now conveyed in school through books written in Setswana. Naomi explained:

> Setswana is one language that is rich with proverbs and idioms. To emphasize a point, my grandmother always used proverbs and I really enjoyed that. This is the reason I liked reading Setswana literature books at high school, to enjoy the language. I no longer read any Setswana books because my teaching subject is in a different field, and I really do not have time to do that. The folktales offered a lot in moral values. We learnt moral lessons like cheating is a bad thing.

Naomi believes that oral literature taught mental development and critical thinking skills. She described how, in their home, some evenings were devoted to competition of riddles between them and other children in their neighborhood.

> The competition was some form of a game to find out who could think fast and use imagination. Some Setswana riddles are questions which are in the form of a statement, for example: My mother's white house which has got no door (*Ntlo ya ga mme e e senang lebati*), the answer is "an egg." One group says the riddle and the other one supplies the answer. The aim is to test one's imagination of associating things within a short time. The answers have to be given quickly or else the group loses its chance.

The oral literature discussed is recognized and has been included in the Setswana curricula at all levels of the education system, from elementary school to university. As to whether the way in which it is taught impacts positively on the learners is a matter that needs investigation.

Emergent Literacy Experiences

Given this reported lack of print literacy culture in the homes of the informants when they were children, the question of emergent literacy experiences and knowledge construction arises. Western research on emergent literacy documents that young children learn critical early literacy concepts by observing and participating in many different literacy events in their homes and communities (Purcell-Gates, 1995, 1996; Teale & Sulzby, 1986). In the Botswana context, in homes where siblings are attending school, this type of learning occurs with the available texts, primarily school books. The informants for this study who had older siblings who attended school, and were therefore exposed to books at an early age, reported that they learned to read and write before they started school formally.

Tshidi was brought up by parents who had attained higher education of Standard 6. Until the 1940s, only primary education up to Standard 6 was provided in the country (Tlou & Campbell, 1984), and people who had gone to school up to that level were regarded as educated. This is no longer the case. Primary education is 7 years, followed by 3 years junior secondary education and 5 years senior secondary (high school) education after which people can go for tertiary education. Depending on who makes the judgment, ordinary Batswana people who are regarded as educated are those who have at least obtained a high school education. People whose parents had Standard 6 were exposed to print literacy earlier and this influenced their literacy practices later in life. Tshidi reads widely than others and has even written some Setswana short stories that were published a few years ago.

CONCLUSION

The literacy practices of the informants in this study highlight important factors that need to be considered in the design of literacy programs for Botswana schools. The study has revealed three major themes: (a) hegemony of English; (b) division/separation of domains of home, religion, school, work/official language; and (c) heavy influence of cultural preference for oral over written language. Most children in Botswana are exposed to various sources of oral literacy before they start school. Only a few whose parents are educated have exposure to print literacy before they start school. Language policy devalues the status of Setswana and other minority languages while promoting that of English. For this reason, people do not consider their languages as resources. In order for families to utilize their cultural and linguistic resources to contribute to their children's education, there should be a connection between school and home at the policymaking level. Gee (2000) posed, "school-based, specialist, academic, and public-sphere forms of language often require us to exit our life world ..." (p. 66).

He argues that in the process of being exposed to specialist domains, the minority and poor children are denied the value of their life worlds and their communities in reference to those of the advantaged children. The literacy practices experienced at school by children from minority groups are far removed from those of the mainstream children.

To promote adult literacy, the resources used in the adult education curriculum should draw content from the day-to-day activities and events adults experience in their lives. To inform the language in education policy and the school curricular, large scale research about cultural practices of literacy for the different ethnic groups in Botswana should be conducted.

REFERENCES

Barton, D., & Hamilton, M. (1998). *Local literacies: Reading and writing in one community*. London: Routledge.

Botswana in Figures. (2001). Central Statistics Office, Department of Printing and Publishing Services.

Batibo, H. M., & Smieja, B. (Eds.). (2000). *Botswana: The future of the minority languages*. Frankfurt am Main: Peter Lang.

Crowder, M. (Ed.). (1984). *Education for development: Proceedings of a symposium held by the Botswana Society at the National Museum and Art gallery, Gaborone, Botswana*. Gaborone, Botswana: Macmillan Botswana.

Gee, J. (2000). New people in new worlds: Networks, the new capitalism and schools. In B. Cope & M. Kalantzis (Eds.), *Multiliteracies: Literacy learning and the design of social futures* (pp. 43–68). London: Routledge.

Government of Botswana. (1985). *Botswana up to date*. Department of Information and Broadcasting, Gaborone: Author.

Luke, A. (2003). Literacy and the other: A sociological approach to literacy policy and research in multilingual societies. *Reading Research Quarterly, 38*(1), 134–141.

Nyati-Ramahobo, L. (1996). Challenges for improving literacy programmes in Botswana. *Mosenodi: Journal of the Botswana Educational Research Association, 4*(2), 49–60.

Purcell-Gates, V. (1995). *Other people's words: The cycle of low literacy*. Cambridge, MA: Harvard University Press.

Purcell-Gates, V. (1996). Stories, coupons, and the *TV Guide*: Relationships between home literacy experience and emergent literacy knowledge. *Reading Research Quarterly, 34*, 406–428.

Report of the First National Survey on Literacy in Botswana, Central Statistics Office, Department of Non-Formal Education. (1993). Gaborone, Botswana: Author.

Taylor, D. (1983). *Family literacy: Young children learning to read and write*. Portsmouth, NH: Heinemann.

Teale, W., & Sulzby, E. (1986). *Emergent literacy: Writing and reading*. Norwood, NJ: Ablex.

Tlou, T., & Campbell, A. (1984). *History of Botswana*. Gaborone, Botswana: Macmillan Botswana.

The Immigrant Experience: Languages, Literacies, and Identities

Victoria Purcell-Gates

The literacy as multiple and social frame makes clear the ways that language and literacy practices are woven within and weave together the different paths that people take throughout their lives. Whereas the previous two chapters provided insights into language and literacy practices within contexts of political and military domination, the following three case studies examine these issues as they play out within the lives of three different groups of immigrants to the United States.

These portraits of language and literacy practice reveal other faces of linguistic hegemony. Taken together, they also add detail and texture to the complexity of language practice by demonstrating the diversity of immigrant experience, a diversity that reflects the influences of country of origin, native language, purpose for migration, and historical practices and experiences.

Kristen Perry's study (chap. 4) of a group of Sudanese "Lost Boys" who have settled in the Midwest region of the United states explores issues central to the multiple and social literacies frame: (a) language gain and language loss as the result of political and military force; (b) the acquisition of new languages and literacy practices driven by cultural and personal agency and purpose; (c) the interrelationships of religion, schooling, culture, and history; and (d) language and literacy practices.

Gaoming Zhang (chap. 5) focuses on another group of immigrants to the United States—Chinese and Chinese American families living near a large university. The portrait provided by Zhang reveals a very different picture of language loss and gain. This group of immigrants, living and learning within the national hegemony of English, approach language and cultural maintenance in other ways, expressing different motivations and taking different steps. With radically dissimilar historical and immigrant experiences, the Chinese families and the Sudanese refugees present varied and culturally specific pictures of language and literacy practice.

Finally, Kamila Rosolová (chap. 6) explores the language beliefs, values, and textual practices of two very different Cuban refugees in the United States. This case study is an interesting addition to this grouping of immigrant studies for several reasons. First, it provides yet one more instance of diversity and variety to the emerging portraitures of immigration, demonstrating again the impacts of historical contexts, personal familial contexts, and conditions of immigration. Secondly, it provides a striking portrait of difference within the case. Although both informants were relatively recent refugees from Cuba (both having won lotteries held by Fidel Castro to allow migration out of Cuba), their experiences once in the United States reflected their different social and familial situations in Cuba, both as children and as adults.

Looking across all three of the portraits of immigration and language and literacy practice, one is struck, I believe, by the multiplicity of influences that impact and shape the literacy worlds of people. Immigration may be a common experience but it is not played out the same across or within groups, at least when looking at it through a literacy practice lens.

Chapter 4

Sharing Stories, Linking Lives: Literacy Practices Among Sudanese Refugees

Kristen H. Perry
Michigan State University

> *Ours is an oral tradition. My people told stories about the raids and slaves—*
> *they sang about slavery. But they did not write books or newspaper stories*
> *about their suffering. And they certainly did not file reports to international*
> *human rights organizations. That is changing, as Dinka refugees move to*
> *the West and organize.*
>
> —Bok (2003, p. 249)

This chapter presents a case study of the literacy practices of southern Sudanese refugee youth—the so-called "Lost Boys"—in Michigan. There are approximately 17,000 southern Sudanese refugees in the United States today (Bok, 2003); of these, approximately 1,000 live in Michigan, and about a quarter of Michigan's Sudanese refugees come from the group known as the "Lost Boys." These youth, primarily boys, were orphaned by the 20-year-old civil war in the Sudan, made a grueling journey on foot across Africa, lived for years in the Kakuma Refugee Camp in Kenya, and eventually were resettled in American communities. The purpose of this case study was to describe the literacy practices of these Sudanese refugees, both in their current lives in America and in their past lives in Africa.

In a recent article, Luke (2003) laid out an agenda for literacy research. He suggests that literacy researchers should focus their attentions on questions such as:

> Which linguistic competencies, discourses and textual resources, and multi-literacies are accessible? How, in what blended and separate domains and to what ends, are different languages used? How do people use languages, texts, discourses, and literacies as convertible and transformative resources in homes, communities and schools? How are these resources recognized and misrecognized, remediated and converted in school-based literacy instruction? (pp. 139–140)

Street (2001) likewise suggested that an important task of literacy research is to make visible the complexity of local, everyday, community literacy practices. Barton and Hamilton (2000) defined *literacy* as social practice with six propositions that seem especially pertinent to the context of this case study: (a) Literacy is best understood as a set of social practices, which can be inferred from events which are mediated by written texts; (b) there are different literacies associated with different domains of life; (c) literacy practices are patterned by social institutions and power relationships, and some literacies are more dominant, visible, and influential than others; (d) literacy practices are purposeful and embedded in broader social goals and cultural practices; (e) literacy is historically situated, and literacy practices are dynamic and changing; and (f) literacy practices change and new ones are frequently acquired through processes of informal learning and sense-making. Examining literacy practices within this framework can lead to insights about the ways in which literacy is practiced and valued in a community, and these insights may, in turn, help educators design literacy curricula and instruction that are more relevant and authentic to that community.

Language use is an especially important component of literacy practices in many communities and contexts. Previous case studies concerning literacies in developing nations have revealed that the various uses or functions of literacy determined the language used for that literacy, rather than vice versa (Herbert & Robinson, 2001; Maddox, 2001; Othman-Rahman, 2003; Rogers, 2001; Wright, 2001). Luke (2003) also suggested that the issues of language rights, language loss, and the redistribution of resources through literacy education are test cases for democratic education; these issues are also key aspects of identity and community, which have become increasingly important in literacy research.

The purpose of this case study was to illustrate just such a complexity among Sudanese refugees. The study was designed to answer several questions, derived from Luke (2003), about literacy practices among the Sudanese refugees: (a) What does literacy mean to the Sudanese refugees? (b)

Which life domains characterize literacy practices for Sudanese refugees? (c) How are different languages used across and within these domains? and (d) In what ways do school literacies align or fail to align with those used in the wider community?

Why ask these questions of this particular community? Africans often are stereotyped as illiterate and uneducated; adding the word "refugee" only heightens this misperception. This sort of research, then, is an important step in challenging "dominant stereotypes and myopia" (Street, 2001, p. 7). The answers and insights gained from asking these questions also may help educational institutions, social services, and international aid organizations better serve refugee populations. Refugees continue to come to the United States in large numbers from countries around the globe. Although each new community clearly will bring its own literacy practices, studying one refugee community in depth may provide insights about issues of culture, community, and identity in relation to literacies.

HISTORICAL CONTEXT OF SUDANESE REFUGEES

The Civil War in Sudan

According to one participant in this study, "Sudan has never been a peaceful country." There have been many internal wars in the Sudan; the current civil war began in 1983 when the southern Sudanese organized an uprising against the northern-dominated Sudanese government. The current war is the result of centuries of deep ethnic and religious divisions. Northern Sudan is predominantly Arab[1] and Muslim, whereas southern Sudan is predominantly comprised of African tribes who are either Christian or animist. The country's government is controlled by the North, and it has systematically worked to subjugate the African South by imposing Muslim *sharia* law, making Arabic the official national language, and turning a blind eye to the traditional practice of enslaving southern Sudanese (Bok, 2003; Deng, 1995). In 1983, the southern Sudanese rebelled against the atrocities of the northern-dominated government by creating the Sudanese People's Liberation Movement and Army (SPLM/A), which has since engaged the government in a civil war. Deng (1995) suggested that this stark North–South dichotomy is the key to understanding the "complicated racial, cultural, and religious configuration of the Sudan" (p. 26).

The war has completely devastated southern Sudan. Two and a half million people have been killed since the beginning of the conflict, and 5 million people have been displaced as refugees. Militias bomb, pillage and

---

[1]Northern Sudanese are not ethnically Arab, but they have been "Arabized" culturally, and they are lighter skinned than their southern counterparts (Deng, 1995).

destroy villages and crops, slaughter families, rape women, and capture women and children to be taken to the north, where they are kept as slaves and forced to convert to Islam (Bok, 2003; Yang, 2002). The conflict in Sudan has caused a mass exodus of southerners, many of whom end up in the Kakuma Refugee Camp near Lake Turkana in Kenya. Despite vast oil reserves, southern Sudan is one of the most underdeveloped areas in the world, due to the ongoing civil war (Matheson, 2002). There are no roads, no schools, and no hospitals. A recent news article noted that southern Sudan has "possibly the worst health situation in the world" (Ross, 2004a); diseases that have been eradicated in the rest of the world are making a resurgence in the Sudan, and mysterious new diseases are emerging (Ross, 2004b). The civil war does not only affect southern Sudan, however. One participant in this study reported, "Although there is no war in the north, the north also remains poor because of the war .... You have a population that is starving to death. There are no jobs."

The Journey of the Lost Boys

Tens of thousands of Sudanese children, mainly boys, began a mass exodus from the south in 1987. The group was comprised mainly of boys for two primary reasons: First, boys fled their villages in reaction to news that the armies on both sides were abducting boys and forcing them to fight. Second, many young boys were away from home, tending to herds of animals in remote cattle camps, when militias descended upon their villages, destroying the villages and slaughtering their families (Yang, 2002).

And so these Lost Boys—so called because they reminded a journalist of the orphaned boys in *Peter Pan*—walked. They walked over 1,000 miles:

> In the weeks and months of their journeys, traveling mostly at night to avoid being bombed from the air or captured by ground troops, lions were a constant threat. The boys began to form close-knit groups, a new sense of family following the loss of their own. They traveled across Saharan desert, into jungles, over mountains and through swamps—all studded with land mines (Yang, 2002).

After a treacherous crossing of a crocodile-infested river, where thousands of boys drowned, approximately 33,000 Lost Boys reached refugee camps in Ethiopia, where they remained for nearly 4 years. Following a coup of the Ethiopian government, the refugees were forced back into the Sudan. Only 7,000 of the original group survived to reach the Kakuma Refugee Camp in Kenya in 1992 (Yang, 2002). These refugee youth lived in Kakuma for nearly a decade, living either with Sudanese foster parents or in group homes with other orphaned youth. The United Nations High Commission for Refugees (UNHCR) opened schools, which all of the Lost Boys were able to attend.

Beginning in November, 2000, the U.S. State Department began to re-settle these refugees around the United States, from Phoenix, Arizona, to Omaha, Nebraska, to New York City. Over 3,500 Lost Boys have been reset-tled so far (Yang, 2002), and the United States intends to resettle the rest of the Lost Boys over the next few years. The resettlement program is the re-sult of an agreement between the UNHCR, the U.S. State Department, and the U.S. Immigration and Naturalization Services (U.S. Department of State, 2001). Several other countries—most notably, Canada, Great Britain, and Australia—are also participating in the refugee resettlement program.

The decision to come to America was not an easy one for the refugees, particularly because they knew nothing about the country or the culture. One participant, Chol,[2] said that the American organizer had to make sev-eral trips over 2 years to convince groups of Lost Boys to apply to come to America: "She went there [to the Kakuma Refugee Camp] and talked to us and said, 'American people need you to go there.' We said, 'No, we don't want to go.' "

Chol described the southern Sudanese community as distrustful of American motives for wanting the Sudanese to come, a distrust stemming from the Sudanese government's implicit sanction of the slave trade in their native country. "We said, 'Maybe you are going to sell us away.' The commu-nity said, 'No, maybe you are going to be given to the Arab people.'... Even me, I said, 'I don't want to go!' "

Focal Participants: Chol, Ezra, and Francis

Chol is approximately 19 years old. He doesn't know his birthday and does-n't know his exact age—none of the Lost Boys do. Like most southern Suda-nese, Chol's skin is a deep, deep black; at about 6 feet tall, he is considered short for someone from the Dinka tribe, who are on average the tallest peo-ple in the world. Like most Sudanese refugees, the intensity of his black skin and his rail-thin height cause Chol to stick out in Michigan. Chol graduated from a local high school in 2001 and now attends a local private university, where he is majoring in business administration. Like many Sudanese refu-gees, Chol works two to three jobs in order to help pay for his education; these jobs have included work in the state university's dining halls, janitorial services in office buildings, and employment in the private university's library. Although Chol is still a young man, he has gained a great deal of respect in the Sudanese refugee community. He is often asked to organize community events, and he was elected to serve as a representative to the Su-danese refugees' local governing board. This committee represents the

---

[2]Some Sudanese refugees prefer to be called by their Sudanese names, whereas others go by their Christian names, which are more American sounding. In assigning pseudonyms, I have honored participants' choices.

community, mediates disputes, and organizes community events. Chol's hard work has also helped him pay the traditional bride price to his fiancee's family, and Chol looks forward to the day, a few years hence, when his bride will be able to join him from Africa.

Ezra, approximately 26, is well over 6 feet tall, and he has a long scar running the length of the crease of his smile. Ezra's two lower front teeth are missing, a symbol of a traditional rite of passage in the Dinka tribe. He attends the local state university, where he is majoring in linguistics and public policy. He has also simultaneously taken courses at the local community college. Ezra is deeply religious, and he serves as a pastor in a local Christian church, where he often performs services in the Dinka language. In the Kakuma Refugee Camp, Ezra was trained as a Bible translator, and he worked with a team to translate parts of the Old Testament into Dinka. He also taught in the primary schools in the camp, where he was part of a team that wrote the first primary school textbooks in Dinka. Ezra also successfully wrote a grant proposal to fund a library at his church in Kakuma.

Francis, approximately 19 or 20, sports a shiny, bald head and speaks English with a crisp staccato. He also attends the local community college, where he is majoring in pharmacy. Francis says he enjoys science classes, and he has also enjoyed taking auto mechanics courses; he wants to keep his job options open. Like many of the Sudanese refugees, Francis has worked at a variety of jobs in order to pay for college and for his car. He has worked at McDonald's™ and an auto dealership. Francis is from the Madi tribe, the smallest tribe in the Sudan, rather than the Dinka tribe, the largest tribe, from which most of the rest of the Sudanese refugees in Michigan come.

In addition to these focal participants, much information about the Sudanese culture and the refugee experience came from the book *Escape from Slavery*, written by Francis Bok (2003), a southern Sudanese refugee from the Dinka tribe. Bok was captured in a slave raid at age 7 and taken farther north, where he was forced to care for his captor's livestock. He was also forced to convert to Islam and to learn to speak Arabic. Bok managed to escape after 10 years of enslavement; he was resettled in America, and he now works with the Boston-based American Anti-Slavery Group.

Refugee Camps Provide First Experiences With Schooling

For this group of southern Sudanese, their first experiences with formal schooling came in the refugee camps. They had had little access to schooling in Sudan, and what few schools were available in the south were taught in Arabic. As far back as the late 1930s, it was the government's official policy to promote Islam, the Arab culture, and the Arabic language in Sudanese schools. Deng (1995) described a memorandum stating that education in the Sudan should emulate the Islamic character, and that the Arabic language and religious instruction should receive the greatest possible attention in all schools. The educational institutions in Sudan also systematically discriminated against non-Muslims; Chol described the experience of an uncle who attended the university in Khartoum, and who failed all of his classes until he pretended to convert to Islam and took on a more Arab-sounding name. Suddenly, Chol's uncle found himself at the top of his class.

Opportunities for schooling were relatively more plentiful before the beginning of the current war. Ezra explained that many schools were established in the south prior to the war. "After 1972, the Addis Ababa agreement,[3] there was a relative peace for a period of 10 years, a decade, before the war broke out in '83. These schools were established either by the church, or church mission, or by the government." However, schools were still few and far between. Bok explains the situation in *Escape from Slavery*: "I did not go to school. No one in my family had any formal education; I don't think I knew what a school was or what happened there. I had heard the word 'school,' but all it meant to me was a place that some kids from the village had been sent to in Juba, the capital city of southern Sudan" (2003, p. 2).

Not surprisingly, literacy levels among southern Sudanese were quite low, due to such limited opportunities for schooling. For record-keeping, southern Sudanese rely on their memory, according to the informants for this study. "When I was young," Chol said, "I never read anything. Whatever has been told to me, I have to keep in my mind." He gave the following example: "In Africa, when an old man or a woman needs to die, he can mention all the things for his entire life since he was very young; 'I need my children to remind this person ... I have this many cows.' He don't forget the cows, all the things .... No paper written, but only in his mind." In fact, the participants in this study seemed to pride themselves on their memories: "I have a good memory," Francis stated during an interview about his past life in Africa. Chol explained, "When someone tells you something in my dialect, you cannot forget it .... If somebody talks to me here, we can talk until tomorrow. If you ask me what I'm saying yesterday, I can tell you from the beginning to the end. I [don't] write it down." In fact, participants suggested that southern Sudanese villagers sometimes took a rather dim view of the written word. "The [spoken] word is very important. They don't consider writing a lot. They are still talking, because whatever somebody said,

---

[3]The Addis Ababa agreement granted regional autonomy to southern Sudan, creating conditions of relatively peaceful and harmonious interaction between the north and the south for nearly a decade (Deng, 1995).

we accept as true, instead of writing," Chol explained. He estimated "about 95% don't read and write" in southern Sudan.[4] Ezra said, "Not very many people in the villages could read and write. No, the people who knew how to read and write were either civil servants or teachers. So, they live in the village, but they work for the government."

Language and Literacy Education in the Kakuma Refugee Camp

Yang (2002) observed that the southern Sudanese youth were deeply committed to their academic studies in the Kakuma Refugee Camp. The UNHCR set up schools in the camp, which were free for refugee children. The schools were based on the Kenyan educational system: primary school went from Standard 1 through Standard 8, with students taking a national exam to obtain their Kenya Certificate of Primary Education, and then high school culminated in another exam leading to the Kenya Certificate of Secondary Education. According to participants, the schools recently added preschool and kindergarten classes, which Francis says is a "very, very good program" because "kids are able to speak English right now."

Proficiency in English was very important for Sudanese refugee children in Kakuma, because English was the medium of instruction in the schools. Students were also taught KiSwahili, the national language of Kenya, as a second language. Because English and KiSwahili were the official languages of schooling, few southern Sudanese children had the opportunity to become literate in Dinka, the local language spoken by the majority of the refugees, or other local dialects. Churches in the camp offered the only opportunity for local language literacy instruction. Chol explains, "In the school, they taught us English and KiSwahili. At church, they taught us Dinka, not English."

Limited funding for Kakuma schools caused severe shortages of educational materials and supplies; often, there were not enough textbooks to go around for each student, and students could not take the limited textbooks home to study. However, Kakuma does have some libraries, which help support refugees' academic development. Chol said that his high school classes would go to the library "two times a week, during chemistry teaching or biology, because the biology books were very limited, so they were in the library .... The library is very big. It can take a lot of students." Francis

---

[4]Organizations such as UNICEF and the World Bank report that, as of 2000, the overall adult literacy rate in the Sudan was about 57%, with 69% of adult men and 46% of women considered literate. It is useful to remember, however, that these rates are averaged across the country as a whole; rates are likely much higher in the relatively more developed northern part of the Sudan as well as in urban areas, compared to rural villages in the southern Sudan. Organizations also report that literacy rates are currently on the decline in the Sudan, due to the civil war.

described the library as having "newspapers, magazines, all sorts of things. We have *Newsweek*." The large libraries were funded by international donor agencies, according to Francis. Individual churches also had libraries, which were intended to help students with their academic studies. It was this sort of church library that Ezra's grant proposal supported.

Due to limited resources, basic literacy instruction in the Kakuma Refugee Camp's primary schools typically took the form of repeating after the teacher and copying from the chalkboard. According to Francis: "The teacher may write something on the board and then pronounce it. That's the kind of reading, basically ... you repeat after the teacher, then you go and do some writing on the ground. You write on the ground because there is a lot of shortage of stationery."

Ezra described the high school system:

> The system is not like your system here [in America], where you take a certain course in a certain semester, then take another course. No, all courses are year-round courses. When you go to high school, in the first year you are required to take 12 subjects year-round .... The same in Form 2. That way, when you go to Form 3, the 11th grade, you choose the subjects that you want, and the minimum is always eight. Then, you take them continuously. Out of these 12, there are compulsory subjects that you have no option. Maths is one of them. English is one of them, and English as a subject is divided. There is comprehension part, there is summary part, there is composition part, and there is literature. So, you take English as a compulsory subject, maths, and KiSwahili .... Then, you have to take at least two sciences, either biology or chemistry or physics .... Then, you have to choose from the other groups of subjects, three at least.

ROLE OF THE RESEARCHER

I first began working with the Sudanese community in May, 2002, shortly after returning from 2 years of living and working in the tiny southern African kingdom of Lesotho as a Peace Corps volunteer. When I heard that Lutheran Social Services was looking for tutors for Sudanese refugees, I immediately volunteered my time. I wished to maintain my connection with Africa and Africans because I wanted to continue working with Africans in the areas of education and literacy. I also wanted to extend my Peace Corps service by continuing to work for the betterment of Africa and Africans because I believe they are all too often overlooked by the developed world. As a result, I have worked as a paid tutor with Lutheran Social Services since the summer of 2002, and in that capacity, I have officially been paired with three Sudanese students. However, due to the close-knit nature of the Sudanese community, I also found myself frequently volunteering as an unofficial tutor and community mentor for the roommates and relatives of my official students. In December 2003, Chol asked me to serve as a member on the board of the newly formed Southern Sudan Relief and Rescue Association, a local group comprised of both Americans and southern Sudanese who work together to help Sudanese refugees.

In my official tutoring capacity, I typically spend from 2 to 6 hours a week offering homework help, particularly in the area of English. In my unofficial role as mentor, I am often called on to help with various events such as driving members of the Sudanese community to doctors' appointments, helping them fill out job applications, providing limited technical assistance for computer technology problems, coaching Sudanese who are practicing for their drivers' licenses, or making phone calls to utility companies on behalf of the Sudanese.

My role as an academic tutor and community mentor was well established before this research project began, which allowed me to gain more genuine access to the literacy practices of the Sudanese community. Although I am clearly not a member of the Sudanese refugee community, I have a legitimate role in that community through my work as a tutor and mentor. I was able to enter participants' homes for reasons apart from performing research observations, and community members often invited me to participate in community events such as graduation parties, welcoming parties for newly arrived refugees, and the annual May 16th celebration, which serves as a memorial day marking the beginning of the current civil war in Sudan. This previous work within the community encouraged the Sudanese to participate in my research; they told me several times that they wanted to help me with my work because I had been so helpful in theirs.

CONTEXT, CULTURE, AND COMMUNITY SHAPE LITERACY PRACTICES AMONG SUDANESE REFUGEES

Literacy Means Access to Power, and Power Will Help the Southern Sudanese

Analysis of the data (see chap. 1, this volume, for analysis methods) revealed that literacy and education are highly valued among the Sudanese. The participants in this study tended to view literacy as something essential to their lives. They equated literacy with education and with access to power. To Chol, literacy "means writing, it means reading, it means learning. It means everything—a lot." For Francis, "Literacy basically refers to gaining access to education or to any other thing like that which is essential for one's living." For Ezra, literacy is more than just reading and writing; it means preserving his Dinka culture and identity. He says, "People have to know how to speak the language and how to write it in order to keep it, to make it a living language. If it exists as an oral or spoken language, without it being written, then chances are it will [become] extinct. But if it is written, then it is preserved, so knowing how to read and write is very important to keep the language alive." Ezra also explained that his generation of Sudanese refugees views literacy as an important tool in the struggle against inequality and injustice in the Sudan. "The young generation," he said, "especially people of my age who did not grow up in Sudan, who started their education outside of Sudan, who were victims of war, think that they need to read and write."

Sudanese refugees frequently expressed a belief in the importance of education. David, a nonfocal participant, believed that literacy and education are crucial for his future. "I pray to God to get an education," he reported. David believes the problems of Sudan are a consequence of having an illiterate, uneducated population. Many of the Sudanese participants equated education with improving Sudan's lot. Becoming educated, they believe, is one of the most important duties they have to those left behind in Africa. In *Escape from Slavery*, Bok (2003) described the two great dreams in his life as "to get an education and to do something that would help our people by telling my story" (p. 187). A speaker at a welcoming party for a newly arrived Sudanese family likewise urged the United States to bring over more young Sudanese refugees so that they can obtain an education. He said that it is difficult to fight a successful war without education, and that "being here is another part of the war." This speaker emphasized to the listeners that Sudanese refugees must learn as much as they can here in the United States so that they can return to the Sudan and help to rebuild their native country. "The only way we can help them is to have an education," Ezra said at his own graduation party. Speakers at every Sudanese celebration I attended emphasized the importance of education in their speeches.

From Storytelling to Writing: Transforming Literacy Practices

A link between the southern Sudanese tradition of storytelling and the desire to write memories of war, slavery, and the refugee experience emerged from data analysis. Storytelling is an important aspect of traditional culture in the southern Sudan, and this tradition shaped many current literacy practices among the refugees in the United States. In Dinka culture, storytelling is a form of traditional education in the Sudan. According to Ezra,

> Storytelling is an important aspect [of our culture] ... To keep the history of the community and the culture and the customs, you pass them from one generation to another through storytelling .... It was through storytelling where people came to learn about culture, the customs, about the traditions, about the norms, about the values. Because there was no way; you could not find them in a book.

Although storytelling is still an important part of the Sudanese culture for participants, most expressed the belief that it does not happen much in the

United States due to the lack of older generations. Francis explained that in Africa, storytelling happens in the evenings, when people sit together and share stories. "People tell a lot of stories," he said, "but here, now, we don't learn. We don't tell any stories like that." Ezra believed that this lack of traditional storytelling was a direct result of the war: "Most of these things were passed down from generation to generation, but due to the war, there is now a generation gap."

Although participants in this study did not tell many traditional stories, storytelling was nonetheless a powerful motivator for many of their literacy practices. Many times, Chol expressed the desire to publish the memories he had of his own personal experiences as a refugee, and he began to write down portions of his autobiography. Ezra explained that he sometimes gave speeches about his experiences and the situation in the Sudan, and he spent time in libraries researching material to include in those speeches. In *Escape from Slavery*, Bok (2003) described over and over again the powerful need he felt to share his story: "My story, however, was all I had with me, the only remnant of my past" (p. 105). Once Bok started giving speeches about his experience, "I began to understand how powerful words could be" (p. 198). For many of these displaced Sudanese refugees, storytelling is being transformed from a way of passing down cultural traditions within their own ethnic group to a way of educating the wider world about their experiences, both through speeches and written texts.

Schooling and Community: Key Sociotextual Domains Shape Sudanese Refugees' Literacy Practices

Five key life domains contextualize literacy practices among the Sudanese: school, religion, interpersonal communication, community information and news, and community organization. With the exception of school (the importance of which has already been described), each of these sociotextual domains is community-oriented in focus. Schooling in the United States typically is an individual pursuit, something that individuals undertake to better themselves or "get ahead." Although group work is encouraged in some situations in classrooms, students are largely expected to do their own work, and they are evaluated and assessed as individuals. It is interesting to consider that the participants in this study have transformed some aspects of schooling into a community-oriented domain; for the participants in this study, individual schooling has become part of a duty to the larger Sudanese community, particularly those left behind in Africa.

Religion.   Religion plays a central role in much of southern Sudanese culture (see Fig. 4.1). Deng (1995) suggested that there is a close link between southern Sudanese religious beliefs and identity, regardless of

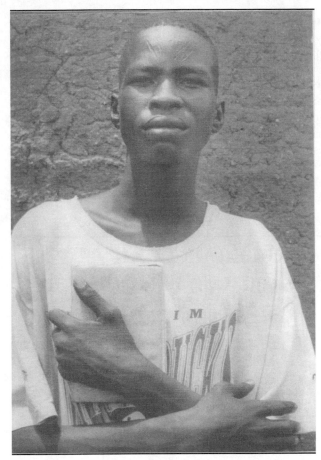

Figure 4.1. This boy holds his only possession from his homeland in Sudan. His cherished Bible made the journey with him through the battlegrounds of the Sudan and Ethiopia to Kenya's Kakuma Refugee Camp. Photo © Daniel Cheng Yang, *Kakuma-Turkana*.

whether those religious beliefs are Christian or traditional animist. In fact, he suggests that many southern Sudanese adopted Christianity precisely because it complemented their traditional cultural, spiritual, and moral values. Bok (2003) stated that approximately 20% of southern Sudanese identify as Christian, and he frequently cited God as the power which helped him to survive and escape enslavement.

The critical role of religion as it contextualized literacy practice was also observed among participants in this study. Participants read the Bible, the *Oxford Companion to the Bible* (Metzger & Coogan, 1993), church pamphlets, church bulletins, and other religious texts, and they wrote notes from sermons heard in church, the sermons themselves, and articles for church bulletins. During numerous observations, I noticed English Bibles lying on participants' desks or beds; Ezra, who worked as a Bible translator in the Kakuma Refugee Camp, had an entire shelf of religious texts, most in English. In separate visits, Chol shared Dinka religious texts with me—a passage from the Bible and a religious pamphlet (see Fig. 4.2). Participants' speech was also peppered with Biblical references, indicating their deep knowledge of that text. In one informal conversation, David asked questions about anthropology, world cultures, and current events that he related to Biblical history. For example, he talked about the fact that Iraq was once Babylon. Ezra referred to the Bible many times in a speech he gave at his graduation party, quoting several passages from memory. During interviews, participants also described a number of literacy practices that center around religion. For example, Chol has a little notebook that he takes with him to church, in which he writes down important messages from the pastor. Ezra reads the Bible for at least 20 to 30 minutes each day.

KUEER DE LUÄK
NË BËNYDA YECU
KËRÏTHO YÏC

Kä tö thïn – në ka cï gööriic

Cäŋ cïï Nhialic nhial cak ku piny
Yen ëcï rïööc guɔ rɔt thiaan
Ee Nhialic yenëke luel ëwëlkë
Aba cäk cɔk ye Yecu
Yïn bï beer dhïil në dhiëth
Gokë miet de piöu gɔl
Kake jieth de piöu
Abieny yic
Raan töŋ de we abï ya nyiëën
Gokë cööt ye, "Piäätkë"
Acïï tö ëtën ee rɔt jɔt në thou yic
Aköl de thiërdhiëc acï rɔt dhieel
Bëny yeeŋö buk looi?
Nhiëër de Yecu Kërïtho men kënë tïŋ guöp[Yecı
Nhial jöt kenë piny jöt

WËTDU EE LAMBA DE YEN
CÖK KU YE YEER DE DHÖLDIË

Figure 4.2.   This passage from a Christian religious pamphlet uses the Dinka script. Reprinted with permission.

Interpersonal Communication.   Interpersonal communication is another very important life domain for literacy practices among the Sudanese refugees. Participants used a variety of texts in this domain, including letters, e-mail, notes, and phone messages. In interviews, participants frequently referred to these texts, which they used to stay in contact with other southern Sudanese refugees, both in the United States and around the world, in the Kakuma Refugee Camp and in other resettlement countries. "I write people here," Chol explained. "I wrote to many people, like in the different states, different boys, guys who were in Kakuma. I write to them. Especially I use e-mail for that." Likewise, Francis stated that e-mail "is the easiest way to communicate at times, because to call a person in Africa costs $5, but the Internet is free of charge." Participants explained that although only government officials and NGO workers had access to the Internet in the Kakuma Refugee Camp, refugees sometimes traveled to Nairobi to use the Internet or to make phone calls. Indeed, I observed participants reading e-mails from refugees in Kakuma on several occasions. Often these readings were a community affair, with several Sudanese gathered around the computer screen or with the recipient reading the message aloud.

Community Information.   This community focus was also seen in the last two domains that contextualized print literacy practices for the Sudanese refugees: community information/news and community organization. The sociotextual domain of community information/news exhibited the greatest variety of texts used by the participants. Participants wrote texts such as newsletter columns, letters to the editor, letters passing on community news, and postings to discussion boards on Sudanese-oriented Web sites such as Sudan.net. Participants also read each of these texts; in addition, they also read listserv e-mails from organizations such as the UN News Service, international news Web sites, e-mails, community bulletin boards, and books about the situation in Sudan and the Kakuma Refugee Camp. Chol talked about his community writing: "I write also about Sudan. I write any information that I get from Sudan, and then I write many letters. Then, I take it to be corrected, and then send it to the Lost Boys. So then the Lost Boys, they can read it—what's happening ... information about the war." According to Ezra, the Internet has become a very important source of information and news about the Sudanese community:

> It is where I write a lot, because I read about almost every day, maybe two or three times a day, about Sudan and about the peace talks that have been going on in Nairobi. And I write a lot to the news media, and also I express my opinions, because we do have a website for the Sudanese who are outside Sudan in the West here. That website brings them together and shares their thoughts and ideas and experiences.

Like the other key sociotextual domains, the domain of community information/news was important both in the United States and in the Kakuma Refugee Camp. Chol explained that an important literacy routine for many refugees in Kakuma was to check the information board in the camp, where letters from displaced family members or other significant community information was posted: "I go there because maybe my brothers in Khartoum, maybe they send letters to Red Cross. So, you go there every day and check. Maybe someone sends you a letter ... it's the only means of communication with people around the world." Some participants also wrote for the local news media while in the camp. Ezra said that he frequently contributed to the *Kakuma News Bulletin*, where he "was just expressing myself on some issues that I think are pertinent to the community."

Community Organization. The final key domain for literacy practice, community organization, contextualizes reading and writing that revolve around community organizing, planning and implementing community events, and activism within the community. The distinction between the sociotextual domains of community information/news and community organization is therefore somewhat blurred; however, I believe that they are indeed separate domains due to their slightly differing intentions or foci. Texts used within the domain of community organization include letters, meeting notes, community newsletters, invitation letters, descriptions of committees, business ledgers, and organizational schemas. Deng (1995) suggested that Sudanese tribes highly value leadership in their communities, and this was exemplified by several participants in this study. Chol, for example, was viewed as a community leader, despite the fact that he is only about 19 years old. Many of Chol's literacy practices revolved around this leadership role. He was frequently nominated by the community to sit on organizational committees for important community events, and he also was elected to serve on the main Sudanese refugee governing board that represented the community, mediated disputes, and offered assistance to community members. Chol's leadership role required him to write notes during meetings (often retyped on the computer), write, and send letters to the refugee community, and to contribute columns to the local refugee newsletter (see Fig. 4.3). Similarly, Ezra described his dream of starting a nonprofit organization to organize Sudanese refugees and to provide assistance for those still in Africa; he explained that he had received help from a lawyer to get the organization up and running.

Community organization also involved literacy in the Kakuma Refugee Camp. Ezra successfully wrote a grant proposal that provided funding for a small library that was attached to his church. He also worked together with several other refugees to produce the first Dinka textbooks for primary

THE EFFECTS OF THE CIVIL WAR IN SUDAN

The war has had a huge impact on the people of the Sudan. The following conditions are caused by the war; dehumanization, destruction, traumatization, disruption of local commerce and lack of education.

Dehumanization: This involves lives of Sudanese lost due to the effect of war. Since the war started in 1983, approximately 2 million people have died. That is a great disaster to the Sudanese people. The war will continue to claim thousands of lives as long as it continues.

Destruction: This includes damage to and destruction fo the many towns and villages within neighboring countries. People have no place to build a house or cultivate crops vital to survival. The soil is damaged by bombardment from both sides.

Traumatization: The war has traumatized the people of Sudan. Some of the people suffer from mental ailments which gravely affect them, their families and their communities. Many people also suffer from nightmares and other problems related to the war.

Disruption of Commerce: This has occurred because of the civil war. Now it is very risky to move from region to region with food and other goods. The people may be arrested or even killed if they are caught. Without commerce, the Sudan is left far behind the rest of the world.

Lack of Education: Since the war broke out, very little attention has been paid to education. Especially in the south, where the war is very active, children have been unable to attend school because of the dangers of war.. Right now, about 95% of the children and adults are uneducated due to the conditions of war.

We, the citizens of the Sudan, are suffering terribly from the above-mentioned conditions. We need unity and peace in our country. We need universal human rights in all of the Sudan. We would like our country to be considered the same as other nations of the world. We would like to live free of persecution.

Would you like to have your thoughts and ideas published in this newsletter? Call Jill at ext. 117 for information about being a guest writer.

OTHER NEWS FROM AFRICA

KENYAN OPPOSITION ALLIANCE ANNOUNCES PRESIDENTIAL CANDIDATE

KENYA, OCTOBER 22
Kenya's opposition alliance has named Mwai Kibaki, a former Vice President, as their candidate for the presidential elections expected to be held in December.
Kibaki, the official opposition leader in parliament, heads an alliance of more that 12 parties known as the National Rainbow Coalition (NARC).
The ruling Kanu party has announced

BURUNDI PEACE TALKS DELAYED

DAR ES SALAAM, TANZANIA, OCTOBER 21
Talks to secure a cease-fire in the nine-year Burundi civil war were postponed due to the absence of the chief mediator, South African Vice President Jacob Zuma. Mr. Zuma is expected to arrive on October 22.
Most of the parties in the war-the Tutsi-controlled government and the two largest Hutu rebel groups, had arrived in the Tanzanian capital of Dar es Salaam on October 21.
Pierre Nkurunziza, leader of the rebel group Forces for the Defense of De-

government. "We must start real negotiations between the real belligerents," he said.
The assassination of Melchior Ndadaye, the democratically elected Hutu president, in October 1993 sparked off the civil war. At least 200,000 people, mostly civilians, have been killed in the war.

Figure 4.3. Chol regularly contributed columns to this monthly newsletter for the local Sudanese refugees. His columns typically focused on issues concerning the war and other problems in the Sudan, what that country required to resolve its conflicts and rebuild the nation, and other similar issues that were important to the Sudanese community. From *Sudanese Activity Newsletter*, December 2002, by Lutheran Social Services of Michigan. Reprinted with permission.

school children. Chol explained that community organizing occurred on a much larger scale in Kakuma, particularly in reference to the challenges of life in the camp: "A lot of people make a strike. They go in the road, shouting and what, and then the community writes the problem. They need food, they need water, they need clothes, they need everything." He said that community leaders often composed letters, which they sent to the UNHCR and to other NGOs.

Mismatches Between In-School and Out-of-School Literacies

The school-based literacies of the participants in this study often do not reflect those that exist within their community lives. School literacies, as experienced by the informants for this study, both in the Kakuma Refugee Camp and in the United States, tend to focus on purposes of certification and credentialing. For example, Ezra explained that the majority of the texts funded by his grant proposal in Kakuma were books to support academic studies that ultimately led to certification exams:

> There are other books, we call them learning books, written by experts who have experience on the subject matter of the KCPE (Kenya Certificate of Primary Education). So, if you want to excel, if you want to succeed on your national exam, then you go out of your area of the textbooks that are designed for your class and read wider outside. The same thing when you are in 12th grade, they call it—in high school, 12th grade, your last year—you sit for another exam. They call it Kenya Certificate of Secondary Education, KCSE. So, candidates for both KCSE and KCPE read other books that are not necessary textbooks for the class.

Likewise, Ezra reported that in Kakuma, exam-related materials received preferential treatment for limited typing and copying resources: "Especially during exams, the instructor would write the handwritten exams and then take it to the typist. In high school, they have only one typing machine, so the typist has to type each sample for each subject, and then they take it to the UNHCR compound where it can be reproduced with the machines there." Certification and credentialing played an important role in the participants' current experience of literacy in schooling in the United States. When asked about what he finds difficult about school literacy, Francis responded:

> General maths was hard. Organic chemistry, too, was very hard, but I passed it, but I did not do good in maths. I was having four classes or five … I did not pass my maths, so I have to take it to get associate's [degree] in chemical technology. Otherwise I can't take my two physics classes …. I'm trying to get an associate's degree in chemical technology … to go and work for a pharmaceutical company.

Ezra also indicated the importance of credentials in American education for the southern Sudanese refugees. He explained that shortly after he arrived in the United States,

> I passed the GED, and I was given my GED diploma right away. So when I came here, the same thing happened to me at [the local] community college. I did not get any remedial or developmental classes at LCC. I was tested and I was placed ... right away .... There are some of my colleagues who graduated with me together, who were my classmates, but now they are still—some of them are still taking remedial classes. Though we came together, and some of them came ahead to America, but they have not yet graduated from college. They have not yet finished their two-year program, and that has to do with their level of reading and writing.

Ezra's statement also suggests that many southern Sudanese refugees struggle somewhat when they enter the U.S. schooling system. Many are required to take what Ezra calls "remedial classes"—that is, basic English classes, despite the fact that they have been educated in and have communicated in English for about a decade. On many occasions, I observed Chol's roommate, John, struggling with worksheets for his ESL class. Sometimes, John asked me for help—and even I (a native speaker of English!) occasionally struggled to ascertain the answers these decontextualized skill-and-drill pages were looking for. Like many Sudanese refugees in this community, John was required to complete these "remedial" ESL courses, despite the fact that he could engage in lengthy, in-depth conversations in English. And, like many, John could not complete higher level courses until he had passed the ESL certification requirements.

Certification and credentialing are therefore of high importance to the southern Sudanese refugees. If students succeed in Kakuma schools, they receive Kenyan Certificates of Primary and Secondary Education; schooling in the United States results in high school diplomas and other degrees. In contrast, out-of-school literacies had a very strong community focus for Sudanese refugees, both in Africa and in the United States literacies in the domains of religion, interpersonal communication, community information/news, and community organization all involved methods of linking lives within the community.

Although analysis revealed that the participants used literacy in a rich variety of ways in their daily and community lives, they clearly equated literacy with education and schooling. For Chol, literacy "means learning." Similarly, Francis described literacy as "gaining access to education," both inside and outside of formal school settings. And Ezra explained, "It does help when you know how to read and write; things can be more easier for you. That can help you pursue your education."

The misalignment between in-school and out-of-school literacies can be illustrated further by the disparity in the types of texts used in each context.

Texts read in the sociotextual domain of school include textbooks, course syllabi, homework packets, newspapers, Internet Web sites, and reference books; texts written in this domain included class notes, research papers, e-mails, and essays. Participants used a much larger variety of texts in the four other, more community-oriented domains of religion, interpersonal communication, community information/news, and community organization. For example, texts read and written within these domains included the Bible and other religious texts, sermons, listserv and Internet discussion board postings, Web sites, e-mail, newsletters, newspapers, magazines, articles for various news media, meeting notes, a variety of books, and all sorts of letters.

A further mismatch can be seen in observations of Sudanese refugees who function quite well with English and who use English for a variety of authentic literacy practices in the U.S. context, but who struggle with decontextualized worksheets for required ESL classes. Schools in the Kakuma Refugee Camp, at the very least, appeared to do a slightly better job of incorporating community literacies in the school domain by allowing students to read the Bible in their local languages. Schools in the United States, unless they are church-supported, are not allowed to include religious material, thus depriving many students of a vital and relevant text in the course of literacy instruction. There is growing evidence of the effectiveness of including this sort of authentic text in literacy instruction as well as authentic purposes for reading and/or writing them (Duke, Purcell-Gates, Hall, & Tower, 2003; Purcell-Gates, Degener, & Jacobson, 2002; Purcell-Gates, Jacobson, & Degener, 2004).

LANGUAGE ISSUES SHAPE PRINT LITERACY PRACTICES FOR SUDANESE REFUGEES

Language, Literacy, Religion, and School Intertwined Into a Whole

The boundaries between language, literacy, religion, and schooling are blurred among the southern Sudanese refugee community. In many cases, religion determined opportunities for schooling for refugees, which in turn determined the languages and literacies refugees learned and practiced. For example, Ezra explained that "my academic work is all in English, because I started my education in English. But, I'm a teacher for Dinka, so if I'm teaching in the church, then I use Dinka."

Religion and schooling were clearly linked for Sudanese in Africa. Historically, schools in southern Sudan were built and run by Christian missions (Deng, 1995), and "southerners saw the Christian mission as a source of literacy" (p. 207). Christian missions not only taught English to the southern Sudanese, but they also provided the only opportunities for southern Sudanese to become literate in their local languages. Public schools throughout the Sudan promoted Islam and taught Arabic. Religion, therefore, often determined whether or not one could attend school, because Christian students were reluctant to attend the Islamized public schools. Religion also determined which language one learned; public Islamic schools taught Arabic and Christian schools taught English and local languages. As Ezra explained, "There were church schools where Dinka was taught, but not in public schools, only in church schools. In public schools, Islam is taught. Churches in general [teach local language literacy], even churches in Khartoum also teach how to read and write."

Language and literacies traveled both ways across the border between religion and schooling in Africa. Religious-oriented schools provided refugees with opportunities to learn languages and literacies, and public schools in the Kakuma Refugee Camp also brought religion into the daily routines of the school. Religious literacies played a prominent role at the beginning of the school day, according to Chol: "During the school prayer in the morning, for the whole assembly in the morning, then a student can—each student has a duty to read the Bible." Students took turns leading the morning prayers and reading passages from the Bible, and this was the only time during the day when students were allowed to speak in their native languages. Chol clarified that, for the morning prayers, the language "doesn't matter. People will just come and pray. She [the prayer leader] can pray in her language. After prayer, say 'amen,' then people say 'amen.' "

Print Literacy Is Tied to English

Lack of Dinka texts.   Print literacy for the participants in this study therefore is more closely linked to the English language than it is to Dinka or other local languages. The focus on English literacy exists for two primary reasons, according to the participants. First, the printed texts available to southern Sudanese in Africa were written primarily in English; few texts beyond the Bible and other religious writing were available in local languages. Ezra explained the lack of printed texts in Dinka: "There is nothing much done in the Dinka literacy development .... Now, attempts are being made to develop it, but at times that is met by limitation of resources and also lack of people who are competent or well-trained to read." Ezra himself believes passionately in the need to develop written materials in Dinka so that members of that tribe can be literate in their own language.

Low Levels of Local Language Literacy.   Second, although all of the Sudanese refugees who participated in this study are literate in English, few are literate in their local languages. This lack of local language literacy is due to the fact that schooling in the Kakuma camp took place in English and KiSwahili, rather than in Sudanese local languages. Churches offered night classes in local language literacy, but Chol explained that those literacy classes were primarily attended by "people who need to be the pastors, who need to read the Dinka Bible, who need to read to interpret some other languages into Dinka language."

Preference for English. Although the Sudanese participants in this study usually choose to communicate orally with each other in Dinka (or infrequently in Arabic), either in face-to-face conversations or over the telephone, they nonetheless typically choose to use English for written communication with other southern Sudanese. As Francis explained, "English has become the easiest way for me to communicate with people." Participants in this study preferred English as a means of communication for several reasons: (a) Arabic carries a powerful stigma among the southern Sudanese participants, (b) English is a *lingua franca* among southern Sudanese who may speak different local dialects, and (c) many southern Sudanese are not literate in Dinka or other local languages.

Arabic Carries a Powerful Stigma for the Southern Sudanese

Although many might wonder at the preference for a colonialist language like English among the southern Sudanese, participants revealed a strong resistance to Arabic, the alternative language used as a *lingua franca* in the region. Most of the participants are fairly fluent in Arabic, and some can read and write it, although they indicated that they prefer not to. For the southern Sudanese, Arabic carries a stigma of religious oppression, cultural assimilation, war, slavery, and genocide. As the official language of the Sudan, Arabic is the language of the dominant northern part of that country, and it has been systematically used to oppress and exclude southern Sudanese from full citizenship in the Sudan. As David explained, "If you don't know Arabic, you are nothing" in the Sudan. Northern Sudanese use Arabic as a method of affirming their Muslim identity (Deng, 1995), and it has also been used as a means of forcing southern Sudanese to assimilate into that identity. Ezra explained the government's language, religious, and cultural agenda thus:

> It [Arabic] has been forced on people. The government uses—it is the vision of the government of Sudan to Arabize the country. The government has persistently used Arabic as its policy to promote the vision. It has also used Islam to promote the vision. It has also used the culture, because the three go together—Arab culture goes together with language and also with religion, with Islam.

Because Arabic is the language of the northern Sudanese, it is linked in the minds of the southern Sudanese with slavery, oppression, and forced religious conversion. Bok (2003) described an incident where he attempted to speak to another enslaved Dinka boy: " 'Don't ever talk to me in Dinka,' he warned. 'Not even a 'hello.' It will get me in trouble. You, too. They will beat us if we talk Dinka. They think we're planning to do something wrong, to escape' " (p. 60). The participants in this study reflected the effects on the language attitudes of southern Sudanese who have been oppressed by the use of Arabic: "It's [Arabic] a bad thing. It steals our language away in our minds," said Chol. Therefore, participants viewed Arabic rather than English as the colonizing language in the Sudan, and they did not believe that English carried the same negative stigma attached to Arabic.

English Is an Important *Lingua Franca*

Although the majority of southern Sudanese speak Dinka, not all do. In this study, Francis was the only non-Dinka speaker; he speaks Madi. As already noted, he finds communication much easier in English, because he does not share a local language with most of the other refugees. English is therefore a particularly useful *lingua franca* for southern Sudanese. Not only is English the primary medium of communication for the southern Sudanese in America, but it was also the main language used in the Kakuma Refugee Camp, which shelters refugees from across eastern Africa: "I think the diversity in the group in Kakuma, and even within the Sudanese community itself, made it difficult given that there are different languages being spoken by different ethnic groups within the community," Ezra explained. "It was not possible for the groups to use any particular local language other than English."

Participants all expressed a belief that fluency in English is vital. Chol said, "English is important to communicate with many people around the world." He also stressed the importance of English as a medium of communication with other Africans in Africa: "Most of the eastern Africans, they speak English … It's better to speak English so that you can communicate with other African people." English is not only a *lingua franca* among Africans who do not share a local language, but it is also a medium of communication for southern Sudanese who speak the same language, but who are not literate in that language. As described already, many southern Sudanese are not literate in their own languages, and they must therefore use English in written communication with each other. Finally, English is an important *lingua franca* for southern Sudanese who are refugees because they have been resettled primarily in the United States, Canada, Great Britain, and Australia, which are all English-speaking countries.

Some of the participants in this study also expressed a belief that written correspondence must be conducted in English for reasons of national and international security. Chol believed that he was supposed to write letters in

"English because the people who are in the post office, they couldn't read things if I write Dinka …. Maybe there is another virus or what [in reference to the anthrax attacks of 2001]. If they have to open the letter, they have to know what it says in the letter." Francis similarly described the method by which the Red Cross mediated postal communication from the Kakuma Refugee Camp to the Sudan. He believed that the Red Cross required letters to be written in English:

> If you write in a different language, they may tear up the paper, the message, because the Red Cross is not allowed to—there are some conditions for them. If you write in a different language, they may consider this is like you are communicating maybe in some spy language. Some of these letters or messages may go to government-controlled areas … so, they don't allow people to write in different languages.

Ezra, however, indicated that these beliefs were false. He had both written and received letters in English, Dinka, and Arabic, all mediated by the Red Cross, and he explained that the Red Cross employed people who could translate in the event of a problem. It is interesting to note, however, that Francis' statement (as well as the vignette about the slave children) indicate a strong belief that communication is monitored and that language choices can help protect one from suspicion and danger.

The Need for Local Language Print Literacy

English is clearly important for oral and written communication for the Sudanese refugees, but some of the participants in this study also felt strongly about the need to develop print literacy in Sudanese local languages as a way of both preserving their cultural identity and resisting the northern-dominated Sudanese government. Ezra feared that the lack of print literacy development in Dinka would spell the end of his culture: "If you don't have the language, you don't have the culture. Your language is your culture." According to Ezra, "There are problems with oral communication or oral forms of keeping things, because if there are no experts or if the older people who are much informed about certain issues are no longer there, then the new people will not know anything, and they will be lost." The lack of community experts and elders is particularly difficult for the participants in this study, who are orphaned and who are therefore missing much of the cultural and traditional knowledge of prior generations. Deng (1995) explained that the Dinka people consider orphanhood to be an exceptionally deprived condition; it is therefore not surprising that the refugees might keenly feel the need to preserve their heritage in written form.

Some participants viewed local language print literacy as a means to resist the Sudanese government and to gain access to power in their native country. Ezra expressed indignation that the literate north of the Sudan was the one to write the history of his country:

> There is no illiterate history of Sudan [meaning that only literate people control what is historically documented in print]. The history written is the biased one, written by the northern part of the country, so they have written it from their perspective. They are the people who are victimizing the other part of the country, and they should not be the ones to write it.

As described, participants in this study believe that obtaining an education is one way of helping southern Sudanese left behind and of aiding the rebellion. Dinka print literacy is one very concrete way that the southern Sudanese can resist northern domination and assimilation. Chol explained that on the South's side of the war, "Everything is communication in Dinka. Everything. Radio, what. For the army, it's Dinka ... it confuses them [the government army] because they don't understand Dinka a lot!"

INSIGHTS AND IMPLICATIONS

This case study has used the literacy research agenda outlined by Luke (2003) as a framework to study the literacy practices among southern Sudanese refugees, and the results of this study paint a complex picture of literacy use in that community. Two of Barton and Hamilton's (2000) elements of literacy as social practice seem especially pertinent to this study: (a) Literacy practices are purposeful and embedded in broader social goals and cultural practices; and (b) literacy is historically situated, and literacy practices are dynamic and changing. Each of the key domains for literacy practices of southern Sudanese refugees, both in the United States and in Africa, are embedded within the broader social goals of maintaining community and were purposeful toward that end. These literacy practices are historically situated within the contexts of life within the Kakuma Refugee Camp and as refugees spread around the world. These practices are also dynamic and changing as refugees incorporate the relatively new communicative technology (new to them, at least) of the Internet, and as they transform traditional storytelling practices into print literacies.

Connection Between Language and Literacy

This study among southern Sudanese refugees also illustrates that the connection between language and literacy may be more complicated than previous studies indicate. Although the context for a participant's literacy practice often determined which language was used (e.g., an editorial column for a U.S. newspaper required the use of English), schooling also played a significant role in determining languages used, because many participants did not have an opportunity to learn literacy in their local languages, due to the language policy of the schools in the Kakuma Refugee Camp. English therefore is the "default" language for most participants' literacy practices.

Luke's (2003) suggestion that the issues of language rights, language loss, and the redistribution of resources through literacy education are test cases for democratic education seems especially pertinent in the case of southern Sudanese participants, who feel strongly about the need to protect and preserve their native languages. They want to tell their stories and their histories, and they want to do this in their local language—Dinka. One important implication from this is that curriculum and policy developers may want to consider that it is equally important to develop both local language and English literacies for Sudanese refugees. The UNHCR and other non-government organizations may want to investigate ways in which they can either incorporate local language literacy instruction into Kakuma schools or provide support for churches or other organizations that make such literacy instruction available. Refugee organizations in the United States may want to develop similar programs.

Issues of Identity and Community

This study also highlights the increasing importance of issues concerning identity and community in literacy research. The participants in this study feel a strong need to maintain connections with the larger southern Sudanese community, which is now spread across the globe. Literacies of interpersonal communication, community information/news, and community organization within the southern Sudanese community serve this important function. The emerging need among Sudanese refugees to share their stories with the larger world is also part of this issue of identity and community. As a cultural practice, storytelling has been transformed into a new literacy practice for the southern Sudanese refugees, and it is a transformation that has linked the southern Sudanese community to the global community.

Finally, this study addresses Luke's (2003) question about the ways in which school-based literacies interact and transact with out-of-school literacies. Although participants in this study have been largely successful in school, their overall literacy practices do not reflect those that are practiced in schools. Recent research in adult literacy programs indicates that matching literacy instruction to authentic,[5] real-world purposes for literacy leads

---

[5]Authenticity is defined as using texts that are either identical or very similar to those texts that occur in students' daily lives, and using those texts in purposeful ways that reflect students' actual uses of those texts outside of school. Examples of authentic literacy practices that easily translate to instructional contexts include reading a newspaper article or Web site for information, writing a letter, and reading instructions for how to do or make something.

to positive changes in students' literacy practices. Students in classes that incorporated authentic purposes for literacy into literacy instruction not only read more often, but they also read and write more complex texts (Purcell-Gates, Jacobson, & Degener, 2004). Although researchers are still exploring the ways in which in-school and out-of-school literacy practices interact, it appears to be generally beneficial for school-based instruction to incorporate authentic texts and authentic purposes for reading and writing whenever possible. Schools, both in the United States and in refugee camps such as Kakuma, therefore may want to pay greater attention to the local literacies practiced by the communities that they serve. In the particular case of the participants in this study, school literacy instruction could be more authentic and more relative to refugees' lives by incorporating community literacy practices such as interpersonal communication, community organization, and community information/news into literacy instruction. Each of these sociotextual domains contains powerful motivations for participants to practice various literacies, and incorporating them into school literacy instruction may help to make schooling a more meaningful and a more successful experience for refugees.

REFERENCES

Barton, D., & Hamilton, M. (2001). Literacy practices. In D. Barton, M. Hamilton, & R. Ivani (Eds.), *Situated literacies: Reading and writing in context* (pp. 7–15). London: Routledge.

Bok, F. (2003). *Escape from slavery*. New York: St. Martin's Press.

Deng, F. M. (1995). *War of visions: Conflict of identities in the Sudan*. Washington, DC: The Brookings Institution.

Duke, N. K., Purcell-Gates, V., Hall, L., & Tower, C. (2003, December). *Explicit explanation of genre within authentic literacy activities in science: Does it facilitate development and achievement?* Paper presented at the meeting of the National Reading Conference, Scottsdale, AZ.

Herbert, P., & Robinson, C. (2001). Another language, another literacy? Practices in northern Ghana. In B.V. Street (Ed.), *Literacy and development: Ethnographic perspectives* (pp. 121–136). London: Routledge.

Luke, A. (2003). Literacy and the other: A sociological approach to literacy research and policy in multilingual societies. *Reading Research Quarterly, 38*, 132–141.

Maddox, B. (2001). Literacy and the market: The economic uses of literacy among the peasantry in north-west Bangladesh. In B. V. Street (Ed.), *Literacy and development: Ethnographic perspectives* (pp. 137–151). London: Routledge.

Matheson, I. (2002, October–December). The battleground. *BBC Focus on Africa, 13*, 26–27.

Metzger, B. M., & Coogan, M. D. (Eds). (1993). *The Oxford companion to the Bible*. Oxford, England: Oxford University Press.

Othman-Rahman, M. (2003, December). *A report on family literacy practices of two Malay-Muslim families in Johor Baru, Malaysia*. Paper presented at the meeting of the National Reading Conference, Scottsdale, AZ.

Purcell-Gates, V., Degener, S., & Jacobson, E. (2002). Impact of authentic literacy on adult literacy practices. *Reading Research Quarterly, 37*, 70–83.

Purcell-Gates, V., Jacobson, E., & Degener, S. (2004). *Print literacy development: Uniting the cognitive and social practice theories*. Cambridge, MA: Harvard University Press.

Rogers, A. (2001). Afterword: Problematising literacy and development. In B. V. Street (Ed.), *Literacy and development: Ethnographic perspectives* (pp. 205–222). London: Routledge.

Ross, E. (2004a, February 1). Ghastly diseases converge in southern Sudan. *Lansing State Journal. (Associated Press)*, 17A.

Ross, E. (2004b, February 1). "Nodding syndrome" hits region's children. *Lansing State Journal (Associated Press)*, 17A.

Street, B. V. (2001). Introduction. In B. V. Street (Ed.), *Literacy and development: Ethnographic perspectives* (pp. 1–17). London: Routledge.

U.S. Department of State. (2001, June 11). *Fact sheet: Sudanese (Kakuma) youth*. Retrieved February 28, 2004, from http://www.state.gov/g/prm/rls/fs/2001/3398.htm

Wright, M. W. (2001). More than just chanting: Multilingual literacies, ideology and teaching methodologies in rural Eritrea. In B. V. Street (Ed.), *Literacy and development: Ethnographic perspectives* (pp. 61–77). London: Routledge.

Yang, D. C. (2002). *Kakuma Turkana*. St. Paul, MN: Pangaea.

Chapter 5

Multiple Border Crossings: Literacy Practices of Chinese American Bilingual Families

Gaoming Zhang
Michigan State University

This research examined the literacy activities, beliefs, and values in two Chinese American bilingual families. The families were chosen from a community of families involved in a weekend Chinese school. I was a teacher at this school and the position gave me access to families with children who could provide valuable insights into the complex relationships of influences among different life and sociotextual domains on literacy development.

The data I collected addressed three research questions: (a) What are the relationships between in school and out of school literacies? (b) How are different languages used across and within sociotextual domains? (c) What roles do these Chinese American bilingual parents play in shaping literacy practices of children? I used a case study methodology to examine these issues for a 7-month period of study. A case methodology was employed, including participant observation, semistructured interviews, collecting artifacts, triangulation, and participant checks. Results of the analysis revealed that the formal schooling for the children in both English-based public school, and their Chinese-based weekend school impacted their practices of literacy outside of school as did the nature of their families' involvements in their literacy activities.

THE RESEARCH CONTEXT

According to the United States Census 2000 (Barnes & Bennett, 2002), analyzed by the Social Science Data Analysis Network (SSDAN), Asians represent 11.9 million, or 4.2%, of the nation's total 281.4 million population. Among the Asian Americans, 39% hold professional jobs, compared with 31% of native-born or 25% of foreign-born ethnic workers. And 84% of Asian Americans have a high school diploma, or a higher degree, compared with 67% of all foreign-born residents.

According to the United States Census 2000, about 12% of Asians reported that they lived in the Midwest, compared with 18.8% in the South, 20.7% in the Northeast, and 48.8% in the West. Michigan, where the study was conducted, is one of the Midwest states. Although the Midwest is lowest in the percentage of Asian residents, the population of this ethnic group in this area increased from 1.54% to 3.60% in the last two decades, becoming the second fastest growing population in Michigan.[1]

The Community

This study was conducted in the Chinese American bilingual community close to Michigan State University, located near the Michigan capitol city of Lansing. Many Chinese American parents have come to the United States and to Michigan State University for higher education purposes. Families in the community are at different stages of their graduate study. Some have even settled in with employment after receiving their degrees. The native language for most parents in the community is Chinese and most can speak English fairly well. The children in the community were either born in China, the United States, or some other country. However, these children for the most part speak nativelike English, and many are taking courses in one of the weekend Chinese schools in the area.

Although the community is located in a typical nonurban midwest setting, Chinese-language texts abound. There are a number of Chinese stores in the area. Among them, the Great China (see Fig. 5.1) is a popular one where most Chinese American bilingual families regularly shop every week for Chinese vegetables, Chinese snacks, and other Chinese food. It is located very close to the university campus. On the window can be found a traditional Chinese paper cut,[2] posters for Chinese movies, and a few hand-written advertisements in Chinese. Videos for TV series and movies from

---

[1]The fastest growing ethnic group in the Midwest is Hispanic.

[2]The paper-cut is one of the traditional folk decorative arts in China. Chinese paper-cuts are brightly colorful and fine handicrafts with a long history, drawn from local customs and landscape scenery. With vivid and lifelike pictures and beautiful colors, Chinese paper-cut is an ideal craft for decoration and collection.

Figure 5.1. A local Chinese store.

China, Korea, and other Asian countries are available in the store. Customers can also pick up a free weekly Chinese newspaper from the store. There is another daily Chinese newspaper in the store costing 80¢ and it comes with a free magazine during the weekend. Figure 5.2 portrays a sample of a few of the Chinese-language texts available in the community.

The Weekend Chinese School

Starting as a school for Chinese language instruction only about 11 years ago, the school has been developed into a comprehensive school as the population of Chinese and Chinese Americans in the area has grown. At the time of the data collection, three classes were offered—Chinese, math, and drawing. The instruction for math was in English. The instruction for drawing was basically in Chinese and might have some clarification in English. The levels ranged from Grade 1 to Grade 9. The children in the school were either born in the United States or came to the United States when they were very young. They learned integrated Chinese language skills in the school, including listening, speaking, reading, and writing. It is the school's

Figure 5.2. The front page of a daily Chinese newspaper from a local Chinese store. The newspaper is circulated in all the areas in the United States. From *World Journal*, April 9, 2003 (*World Journal*, Publisher). © 2003 by *World Journal*. Reprinted with permission.

tradition to hold a Christmas party and a picnic respectively at the end of the fall semester and spring semester. As a member of the Association of Michigan Chinese Schools, the school participated in the annual Chinese contest for children in Michigan and the teachers' training program in the summer.

Researcher Location

I have worked as a teacher of Chinese in the weekend school for a year and a half. I am also visiting the United States to attend graduate school, as is my husband, and my home is in South China. Thus, I am a member of this community and in a good position to know it from the inside. I felt a strong connection with the people in the community. I knew from the experiences of my acquaintances and myself what it is like to study in an English-speaking country. My acquaintances in the community also shared with me their experience of having English-speaking children at home.

PARTICIPANTS

Two Chinese American bilingual families were recruited from the weekend Chinese school. When I chose them, I considered their family backgrounds, interests, literacy levels in both Chinese and English, and whether their varied in- and out-of-school experiences would provide a rich understanding of the literacy activities and interaction of other Chinese American bilingual families in the sociocultural context. My decision to conduct an in-depth investigation with Cindy and Jerry[3] was also based on some practical considerations, such as their willingness to let me visit for different lengths of time and their parents' interest and support.

Cindy

Cindy, an eighth-grade school girl, often wore her long hair down to her waist, and colorful sweaters and low-waist jeans were her favorite clothes. She was born in China and immigrated to the States 3 years ago when her mother married an American. Her stepfather worked as a technician, and her mother was one of my colleagues in the weekend Chinese school.

A variety of written texts, attesting to a variety of literacy practices were highly visible in her house. A large bookshelf stood in the living room of the house. Half of the books on this bookshelf were her father's collection of cooking books and newsletters from his company. These were all in English. Cindy's father explained that he used to be an editor of the quarterly newsletter. That was why he kept a collection of the newsletters. The other books were brought from China by her mother. Most of these were historical novels and bibliographies in Chinese. Some of them were English textbooks.

In the kitchen, the refrigerator surfaces held several written texts that reflected the family's bilingual, bicultural status. These included a health insurance card number, an emergency call list, a schedule of Cindy's math class in the weekend Chinese school, a coupon for pizza, a notice of an appointment, and the phone number of computer services. On the left side of the refrigerator, a Chinese calendar for 2003 was posted, with the location and phone number of a local Chinese store. Next to this, the directory of parents, teachers, and board members in the weekend Chinese school was displayed.

The first time I went into Cindy's room, I encountered a plethora of posters on the wall. The posters reflected the singers, actors, bands, and movies that she liked. She told me that some posters were cut from the magazines to which she subscribed. Other posters were purchased separately. On the wall, behind a 13-inch television in her bedroom, there was a list of Direct TV channels with some channels highlighted. Next to her single bed was a

---

[3]Pseudonyms are used throughout this chapter to ensure the anonymity of the participants. English names were chosen to reflect participants' use of English names in their real lives.

shelf with two photo albums, two collections of stickers, and a collection titled Pop Star Book. A collection of the *Harry Potter* books by J. K. Rowling
and the *Lord of the Rings* books by J. R. R. Tolkein also occupied the bedside
shelf. A small desk sat by the other side of the bed. Over this desk, on the
wall, was a certificate of education for babysitting. A large variety of labeled
videotapes filled the bottom drawer of a desk.

Jerry

Jerry was 4 years younger than Cindy. He was in the fourth grade while the
research was conducted. The first time I saw Jerry, he was playing basketball
with his younger brother in front of his house. My first impression was that
he was energetic, fast moving, and excited to play sports. He lived with his
father and younger brother. His grandparents lived right next to his father's house. His father was the owner of a computer store. Jerry's grandmother worked in the same store while his grandfather went to a continuing
education program for seniors. Every day after Jerry came home from
school, he and his younger brother would do their homework from their
American school at his grandparents' house. After finishing the homework
from the American school, Jerry spent around 30 to 40 minutes learning
Chinese. He might read aloud the text he had just learned, or do the homework on his own. Usually his grandfather supervised Jerry's work in Chinese. He corrected Jerry's Chinese pronunciation and checked his Chinese
homework. When Jerry's father came back from work around 7 p.m., the
two brothers ran into their father's house, playing on their own computer.

LITERACY PRACTICES IN A BILINGUAL/BICULTURAL WORLD

Literacy for School and Social Purposes

Cindy and Jerry both read and wrote a variety of texts for a variety of social
and school purposes. A wide range of literacy activities were found in both
families. Cindy read sale flyers that were sent to her home on Sundays and,
from these, made the weekly shopping list. Both Cindy and Jerry read the
packages in grocery stores and toy stores. Cindy also purchased books from
Scholastic frequently. Usually Cindy and her mom would read the catalogs
together and discuss which books were worth purchasing. Then, Cindy
would fill in the order form and send it out.

Both Cindy and Jerry read and wrote as they did their homework from
both American and Chinese schools. These texts included self-chosen
chapter books such as the *Harry Potter* books by Rowling, and assignments
from math or Chinese classes from the weekend Chinese school.

They both wrote for purposes of recording and documentation. Several times, I observed Cindy writing notes and posting them on the bulletin board in her room or writing in her personal planner, reminding herself of important dates or assignments. Cindy also wrote in her photo album to record contextual information for her pictures. She even maintained a check-out book to keep the record of her books, videotapes, and DVDs that she loaned to others. Both Cindy and Jerry wrote phone messages whenever they answered the phone for their parents.

Both Cindy and Jerry subscribed to *Disney Adventures*. They, as did many of their classmates, read the magazine issues to obtain updated information about movies or DVDs that were coming out soon or had been released recently.

Many of Cindy and Jerry's literacy activities centered on the domain of entertainment. When planning to attend a movie, Cindy would read updated information for movies and write down on a notepad the number of the electronic ticket that she had booked online. From time to time, Jerry read Magic cards that he had collected. The cards were used to play the game Magic. He told me that he needed to understand the strength and weakness of the warriors on the cards so that he was able to use them strategically while playing with others. Besides, it also helped him to make a good deal when he traded cards with friends. Both Cindy and Jerry played a number of videogames for fun. While playing, they were reading instructions, conversations between the characters if applicable, and typing information as requested in the game.

The Internet was another source of entertainment for Cindy and Jerry. Both of them wished to change their wallpaper for their desktops frequently. To accomplish this, they went to Web sites and downloaded newly released wallpaper designs. Cindy also read a lot of online information while she was searching for her favorite songs online.

English and Chinese Literacies for Different Sociotextual Domains

Both families enlisted English and Chinese literacy for different areas of their lives. For the children, most Chinese language literacy activities were oral. In both families, the children communicated in Chinese with their parents, siblings (they may also speak in English to siblings, though), grandparents, and other family members who spoke Chinese. They were encouraged to speak Chinese in their Chinese language class in the weekend Chinese school. They spoke Chinese in their American school only when they preferred to keep the conversation to themselves.

For the children, Chinese print literacy practices mainly emanated from the Chinese language school. As I mentioned before, they each received weekly homework assignments from the weekend Chinese school. These involved writing a number of short essays during the semester, the complexity of which depended on their grade level. They also wrote Chinese for purposes other than homework, but most of these writings were connected to the weekend Chinese school in some way. Jerry and Cindy signed their Chinese names on the pictures they drew for their drawing class in the Chinese school. Jerry also wrote Chinese when he helped his younger brother with his homework assignments from the school (see Fig. 5.3). Cindy typed in Chinese the directory for the Chinese school since her mother was in charge of that.

All these writings were derived from the context of the Chinese school. However, they had a few opportunities to write in Chinese for some other purposes. One of these was revealed when Cindy used Chinese words in her drawing. She said Chinese characters look cool and would be a good element in art design. In one of her prize-winning pictures, she wrote the Chinese word "Peace," which was also the theme of that picture. She also began writing Chinese poetry for her own purposes, as described in the following section. Compared with limited Chinese language practices, English-language practices in oral and written forms crossed a range of sociotextual domains in both families as already described.

School Literacies Imported and Transformed Into Home Practices

One of the exceptions to this revealed one of the ways that school literacy practices were imported into home practices. This resulted from Cindy's

Figure 5.3. Jerry and his younger brother's handwriting in Chinese.

love of writing poetry. She first learned about poetry in her American school, and thus in English. Cindy read poetry for her language arts class in the American school. She was required to read a number of poems and summarize them to enhance her comprehension of the poems. Then, she was instructed to write several poems as a homework assignment. It was while doing this that she became extremely interested in poetry. She tried to write more poetry on her own, writing one poem to each of her parents and one to herself. She even tried a few poems in Chinese. Thus, she transferred what she had learned about poetry in English to the writing of English and Chinese poems at home for fun.

Cindy's experience of learning how to make polyhedrons [a solid formed by plane faces] reflects a similar importation of school literacy practice into home. In her American school, Cindy learned the basic procedures of making a polyhedron. Fascinated, she decided to further her study of them on her own. At home, she tried different shapes, different colors, sizes, and connection strategies. She thoroughly enjoyed this activity and considered it both entertainment and an activity that produced decoration for her room. Figure 5.4 portrays a few of the polyhedrons that she made and then hung in her bedroom.

In both of these cases, school literacy was transferred to self-motivated learning. What was learned in school was supplemented and applied to after-school, self-motivated activities.

Figure 5.4. Polyhedrons in Cindy's bedroom.

Parents Play Roles in Children's Literacy Activities

The role played by parents in their children's constructions of literacy practice was clearly demonstrated in this case study. In both families, parents and other family members played active and important roles in their children's literacy activities. They gave dictations to the children as recommended by the teachers in both the American and Chinese schools; they double-checked their children's homework assignments, and they purchased books or materials required or recommended by teachers. Each family had at least one computer at home that children could use to access the Internet. Parents subscribed to the magazines that children liked; children were sent to enrichment programs; they were also encouraged to participate in all kinds of contests or championship events.

Research has shown that parents' beliefs about involvement in their children's education can positively affect educational outcomes (Seefeldt, Denton, Galper, &Younoszai, 1998). In this case study, parents in both families expressed their beliefs that independence and problem solving were vital skills for their children to attain. Through their interviews, the parents reported their habits of encouraging their children to develop these skills whenever the opportunity arose. For example, during a family moving sale, Jerry was completely responsible for his own used items. He was told by his father and grandparents to decide what to sell, how much to sell, and how to negotiate with potential customers. He was also told that he could keep the money he made and decide how to spend it. This encouragement of independent competence is similar to the time when, during a trip to another state, Jerry's father asked him to check out online information about available hotels in the area. As part of this particular activity, Jerry compared the price, the location, and the vacancy availability before he made the decision.

Cindy's parents also created opportunities for Cindy to act independently as well as to engage in literacy practices. Many of these opportunities and practices intersected with her parents' professional lives. During my time with them, Cindy was encouraged to make a directory for the weekend Chinese school, a responsibility often given to adults. She also participated with her mother's professional world in other ways such as the time she prepared a handout for her mother's speech in a teachers' training program by typing and printing multiple copies on the computer. Cindy also participated in the annual calendar drawing contest sponsored by her father's company.

In all these examples, parents' values and beliefs led the children to specific literacy activities. The children in both families appeared to truly enjoy these activities. They were proud of what they could do and also expressed the beliefs that they would build their knowledge and ability at the same time. When asked about his choice about the hotel, Jerry said, "Usually my dad will approve my decision though sometimes he says that I need to give some consideration to distance."

Bilingual, Bicultural Literacy Interactions Across Generations

The impact of the families' involvement in their children's literacy is also reflected in the bilingual interactions that took place within the homes. In both families, parents or grandparents, whose first language was Chinese, instructed the children in Chinese language learning while the children helped the adults with English in some way. Cindy helped her mother to read and comprehend the financial statements sent by the college where her mother was registered as a student. Cindy also explained to her mother the handouts she brought home from her college classes and illustrated for her how to follow the instructions and complete the assignments. Jerry would communicate with English speakers for the family in public spaces if he was with his grandparents. Sometimes Jerry also volunteered to tutor his younger brother in Chinese. As shown in Fig. 5.4, he taught his younger brother how to write "Dad" in Chinese. He also enjoyed reading Chinese stories to his younger brother.

CROSSING BORDERS OF LANGUAGE, LITERACY, AND DOMAIN FOR CHINESE IMMIGRANT FAMILIES

This case study of two Chinese American bilingual families working toward higher education degrees in a university town provides an up-close picture of language and literacy activity in such bilingual and bicultural contexts. Through this case, we can see the ways that Chinese and English reading and writing, were learned, appropriated, and used for social activity both in and out of formal schooling contexts. We also could see the ways that the beliefs and values of the parents in this study provided access and opportunities for their children to learn and use different literacy practices as they mediated different social practices deemed significant and relevant by the families. These findings contribute to an evolving theory of literacy development that accounts for both instructional and social influences (Luke, 2003; Ormerod & Ivani, 2000; Pitt, 2000). It is important to point out that, as in all case studies, these findings are specific to Cindy and Jerry in their particular sociocultural contexts. Therefore, generalization of these findings across contexts should be cautioned.

In the literacy activities in both families, different languages were used across and within a variety of sociotextual domains. Some of these domains were entertainment/pleasure, news/information, interpersonal communication, personal writing, memory/record-keeping, finance, shopping, school, and enrichment programs. Throughout the case study, in order to better understand their literacy activities, it was always necessary to document the contexts of their literacy activities as well as the activities themselves. This illustrates the interpretation of literacy as social practice and that literacy practices are purposeful and embedded in broader social and cultural nature (Barton & Hamilton, 1998; Gee, 1996, 2000; Street, 2001). Conceptions of literacy that are socially based suggest that children learn culturally appropriate ways of using language and constructing meaning from texts in their early years at home. It is found that parents (and grandparents) in both families are concerned about children's literacy activities and actively involved in the activities. This is supportive of researchers' findings that beliefs and activities regarding literacy differ across ethnic groups (Okagaki & Frensch, 1998). As a result, children who have been socialized in diverse contexts come to school differentially prepared and positioned to respond to the demands of school. Therefore, they experience school differently and formal schooling is only a part of the process if education is seen as a process of cultural transmission (Cadzen, John, & Hymes, 1972; Heath, 1982). Awareness of students' broader sociocultural backgrounds is crucial to connecting home and literacy. Therefore, educators "must understand individuals within the full context of their home and school lives" (Paratore, Melzi, & Krol-Sinclair, 1999). These tenets are meant to apply across sociocultural contexts. Thus, further case studies situated within carefully described contexts are needed to begin to specify the ways in which literacy development proceeds as sociocultural practice.

REFERENCES

Barnes, J. S., & Bennett, C. E. (2002). *The Asian population: 2000*. Retrieved October 12, 2004, from http://www.census.gov/prod/2002pubs/c2kbr01-16.pdf

Barton, D., & Hamilton, M. (1998). *Local literacies: Reading and writing in one community*. London: Routledge.

Cazden, C. B., John, V. P., & Hymes, D. (Eds.). (1972). *Functions of language in the classroom*. New York: Teachers College Press.

Disney Adventures. New York: Walt Disney Publications.

Gee, J. P. (1996). *Social linguistics and literacies: Ideology in discourses* (2nd ed.). London: Falmer Press.

Gee, J. P. (2000). The New Literacy Studies: From "socially situated" to the work of the social. In D. Barton, M. Hamilton, & R. Ivanic (Eds.), *Situated literacies: Reading and writing in context* (pp. 180–196). London: Routledge.

Heath, S. B. (1982). Protean shapes in literacy events: Ever-shifting oral and literate traditions. In D. Tannen (Ed.), *Spoken and written language: Exploring orality and literacy* (pp. 91–118). Norwood, NJ: Ablex.

Luke, A. (2003). Literacy and the other: A sociological approach to literacy research and policy in multilingual societies. *Reading Research Quarterly, 38*, 132–141.

Okagaki, L., & Frensch, P. A. (1998). Parenting and children's school achievement: A multiethnic perspective. *American Educational Research Journal, 35*, 123–144.

Ormerod, F., & Ivani, R. (2000). Texts in practices: Interpreting the physical characteristics of children's project work. In D. Barton, M. Hamilton, & R. Ivani (Eds.), *Situated literacies: Reading and writing in context* (pp. 91–107). London: Routledge.

Paratore, J., Melzi, G., & Krol-Sinclair, B. (1999). *What should we expect of family literacy?* Newark, DE: International Reading Association and The National Reading Conference.

Pitt, K. (2000). Family literacy: A pedagogy for the future? In D. Barton, M. Hamilton, & R. Ivani (Eds.), *Situated literacies: Reading and writing in context* (pp. 108–124).

Rowling, J. K. *Harry Potter series*. New York: Arthur A. Levine Books.

Seefeldt, C., Denton, K., Galper, A., & Younoszai, T. (1998). Former Head Start parents' characteristics, perceptions of school climate, and involvement in their children's education. *Elementary School Journal, 98*, 339–349.

Street, B. (2001). *Literacy and development: Ethnographic perspectives*. London and New York: Routledge.

Tolkein, J. R. R. *The Lord of the Rings series*. Boston: Houghton Mifflin.

United States Census Bureau. (2001). *Profile of the foreign-born population in the United States: 2000*. Retrieved October 12, 2004 from http://www.census.gov/prod/2002pubs/p23-206.pdf

Chapter 6

Literacy Practices in a Foreign Language: Two Cuban Immigrants

Kamila Rosolová
Michigan State University

This is a case study of the literacy practices of two adults—Lara and Enrique[1]—who both came to the United States as refugees from Cuba seeking a better life. Lara arrived with her husband and two small children in 1997; Enrique arrived in 2002, only 1½ years before the data collection for this study. Both were able to come to the "promised land" because they won immigration visas in a lottery set up by the Cuban and U.S. government in 1994. This lottery is the result of a treaty that was signed as a part of efforts to end the "boat exodus," a series of desperate and often tragic attempts of hundreds of Cubans to get to the U.S. shores on shaky rafts . Every year, the lottery raises hopes for thousands of Cubans who wish to qualify for the U.S. immigration visas and file their applications with the Immigrant Visa/ Parole Unite in Havana (U.S. Department of State, 2000).

My goal with this research was to explore the ways in which literacy and language intersect and are negotiated by immigrants such as Lara and Enrique. Through semistructured interviews and observations, I tried to capture a portrait of their lives in the United States in a different language and culture, and implications of their past and current life situations for their personal literacy practices. Both participants in the case study received 5 years of university education in Cuba and are literate in their native

---

[1]Both names used in this report are pseudonyms.

language—Spanish. When they came to the United States, they had to start their lives over in a language that was foreign to both of them.

RESEARCHER LOCATION AND CONTEXT

I first met Lara when I attended a monthly gathering of local teachers and international educators. The group was discussing refugee issues and Lara was invited to visit to speak about her experiences when she first came to the United States as a refugee. She delivered a passionate speech describing the oppressive political situation in Cuba that drove her away, the challenges of starting a new life in a new language and culture, and the language barriers that prevent many university-educated Cubans from fully using their potential and escaping the trap of unqualified, low paying jobs in the United States. As she was painting the harsh reality of Cuba and lives of crushed hopes, fear, and dual morality, I began traveling back in time to the communist Czechoslovakia where I grew up. Her words strongly resonated with my memories of the communist hypocrisy, in which I lived for over 15 years, and I began to grow curious about this woman, about her views, and the sociopolitical and educational context within which they took shape.

When I decided that the Cuban immigrant experience was worthwhile to explore in a study of literacy practices, I wanted to hear at least one other voice besides Lara's. That voice belongs to Enrique, a 33-year-old Cuban soccer teacher who had only arrived in the United States 1½ years previously. A friend of mine met Enrique and his friends in a bar one night when he overheard their Spanish and joined them in a conversation, eager to practice his own Spanish and to make new friends noticeably different from the usual crowd of college students.

My inquiry sought to explore Lara's and Enrique's past and present literacy practices, paying particular attention to the ways both participants negotiate their uses of English and Spanish in their new country. During the fall of 2003, Enrique and I met regularly once a week in English tutoring sessions that I started giving him. Lara and I met on six different occasions, during which I conducted four semistructured interviews to elicit information about Lara's use of English and its place in the kinds of reading she partakes in and the writing she does.

Communism and Education in Cuba

I was curious to hear what these two people would tell me about their lives in Cuba, their school experiences, and their literacy practices that accompanied their childhood and adulthood. I expected that they would attribute a great deal of their reading and writing habits to their education and the sociopolitical context, in which they both spent considerable chunks of their lives. I vividly remember Czechoslovakia during the communist times and the effects the political regime had on people's minds. The oppressive environment of omnipresent surveillance in a society where only certain kinds of knowledge were allowed drove people into various forms of escapism. Many found self-actualization through work on their weekend cottages and gardens in the countryside; some submerged themselves into a world of books that provided information otherwise difficult to access. I remember the long lines in front of bookstores every Thursday when new publications, usually in limited numbers of copies, arrived on the store shelves. People were hungry especially for translations of classic world literature and contemporary Western suspense novels that offered a view of envied modernity absent in the communist world.

Reading was a popular pastime, also, because it did not have to compete with TV or other possibilities of leisure activities such as movies or video games. Television had only two channels, few people had VCRs, and movie theaters would play one movie every week. Books were irresistibly cheap and other forms of entertainment did not appear as overwhelming as they are now[2] in the endless possibilities of choices they offer.

Communist regimes generally took pride in their educational systems, which were also admired by many Western researchers. This admiration was arguably deserved, at least as regards universal access to education, high literacy rates and relatively high achievement that students from former socialist/communist nations showed in international comparative studies. Cuban education in particular has been praised lately. In 1997, the United Nations Educational, Scientific, and Cultural Organization (UNESCO) conducted a comparative study of third and fourth graders in 11 Latin American countries. Cuban students in 100 randomly selected elementary schools outperformed their international peers by 2 standard deviations (UNESCO-SANTIAGO, 1998).

My conversations with Lara and Enrique naturally touched on schooling and politics, but these themes surfaced only occasionally. From my experience, political context does have some effect on what people read and write in terms of what is made accessible as well as what is denied. Additionally, schooling always plays an important role in the development of reading and writing skills (Purcell-Gates, Jacobson, & Degener, 2004). However, Lara and Enrique's responses to questions about their school literacy practices did not reflect their particular Cuban political and educational experiences in any clear-cut way. What did emerge from their reflections was the role that family literacy practices, including texts, values, and beliefs

---

[2]Communism fell in 1989 and the country was free to turn to democracy based on a market economy. In 1993, Czechoslovakia experienced yet another change, a peaceful political divorce that resulted in the creation of two sovereign nation-states, the Czech Republic and the Slovak Republic.

(Barton & Hamilton, 1998) played in shaping their current literacy lives. For the remainder of this chapter, I explore this theme, and the ways in which Lara and Enrique's literacy practices intersect with their lives in a new society dominated by English. It became clear that the complex issues of language, text, textual access, social and cultural domains, and power relations (Luke, 2003) all transact to contribute to a pattern of gains and losses for these immigrants who crossed linguistic and political borders in efforts to improve their lives.

LARA

Lara and her husband won the Cuban visa lottery and arrived in the United States in 1997 with an 8-year-old son and a daughter 11 month's old.[3] Eight years later, the family had adjusted well to the local urban lifestyle and culture of the United States Midwest. Lara is an intensely active person who always seems to manage several different activities at a time. She used to own a Cuban restaurant in this small Midwestern city, but Carpal Tunnel Syndrome and Raynaud's disease in her hands[4] made it difficult for her to carry heavy dishes and continue running the restaurant. Eventually, Lara decided to give up her business and focused her energy elsewhere. At the time of the study, she worked in a modeling agency, gave Latin dance lessons, and taught Spanish to elementary school children. She also managed to rehearse with her band in the evenings, and remain a devoted wife and a mother.

Literacy and Language in Lara's Family

Although the English language was a great challenge for Lara's husband, it had never been a problem for her. Lara explained that foreign languages had always played a role in her life, even as a little girl growing up in Cuba. This was due to the varied influences of her family, particularly her father and her godfather. As Laura told it, one of her talents and hobbies that she inherited from her father was singing. As a child, she wanted to sing songs from parts of the world other than Cuba, and her father insisted that she make attempts to go beyond trained repetition of foreign sounds and search for the meaning behind the words she learned to pronounce. "You have to understand what you are singing," he would say to her. So she did. She learned some Portuguese, Italian, English, and French, depending on the origin of the song she tried to learn. Lara's godfather also played a role

---

[3]Lara's eldest son from her first marriage stayed in Cuba where he is married, with children.
[4]Carpal Tunnel Syndrome is a condition characterized by pain and numbing in the hands. Raynaud's disease is an autoimmune circulatory disorder caused by insufficient blood supply to the hands, resulting in numbness and pain.

in her interest in other languages. He was a veterinarian and originally from Poland. He also had many "off-beat" hobbies such as wine making and Morse code. He spoke "many" languages and he was the first one to introduce Lara to English and French. According to Lara:

> I would read in Spanish or English. And then, I would read in French or Italian, it depends. What they taught me when I was a child was: you read the writer in his own language. My godfather taught me that, who was Polish … He made me very researchful. I was always investigating. I wanted to know the etymology of words all the time, so that I could figure better …

Lara grew up in an environment where books and knowledge were highly valued and respected. As a result, she claims, she acquired a passion for books and a yearning for more knowledge. According to Lara, her father loved informative, educational, and historical readings. Her mother enjoyed mystery novels and fiction of various kinds, although there existed within the family a hierarchy of good books and not-so-good books. "We didn't read pink[5] novels, or soap opera novels. It was serious reading. Either history, or educational, or informational books or magazines, depending on my age. I was given books: by my godfather, by my dad and by my mom."

The habits learned at home held strong in Lara's life. She claims to be a faithful reader who will read anything that she considers valuable. However, some types of texts enjoy more prominence in her life than others. When asked what she enjoys the most, without hesitation, she replies, "forensics"; "I read forensics for entertainment—it's my hobby. My father was a forensic investigator. It takes a lot of intelligence and awareness." Lara likes to read texts related to forensics, detective stories, or watch TV documentaries about the FBI, but she also enjoys other genres. Usually, two or three books at a time lie on her bedside table. She will read a bit from one, then switch to another. English and Spanish blend, but if she is looking to read for entertainment and pleasure, she will try to find a way to get books in Spanish.

Since Lara began her job with a modeling agency, she has begun reading different types of texts related to this position, and these texts are all written in English. They include such things as handouts, manuals, brochures, and informational leaflets. Lara experienced this reading practice as purely functional, required by her work to develop an understanding of studio photography, lighting, colors, and makeup.

All work-related readings for Lara were generally English. English may not be the dominant language at home but it certainly is everywhere else. Although Lara's English appeared quite fluent, it still remains a foreign

---

[5]Pink literature refers to paperback romance literature.

language to her. When she moves outside of the work domain to pursue her personal interests and look for reading for entertainment, she deliberately turns to texts in Spanish:

> I don't want to read in English. I refuse to read in English because I spend most of my day speaking and reading in English. So for my enjoyment I'd like to do it in Spanish. It's just like a matter of coming back to the basics. When you spend all day speaking in a language that is not yours, you want to go back home and say, "I am at home."

Lara makes similarly strong distinctions in language choices when writing is called for. All job-related notes in her daily planner are in English, but when it comes to written reminders that relate to home, the language switches to Spanish. A shopping list of supplies for her office would be in English, a shopping list for home in Spanish.

Lara only realized this when I asked her about her language preferences in keeping ordinary daily notes. Initially, she wanted to say that all her notes are in Spanish but then she hesitated, began to wonder about it, and eventually peeked into her daily planner to discover, much to her surprise, that most notes were in fact in English. Because Lara lives in the United States, English has become her strongest foreign language and she has no difficulties expressing herself in it, whether verbally or in a written form.

Writing, just like reading, is an inherent and important part of her life. As she declared, she cannot imagine life without it, whether it is writing for self-expression or communicating with her children by leaving messages on their doors, or doing a homework assignment for parents, sent home by Lara's daughter's teacher every week asking the parents to read with their child and fill out a form corresponding to this assignment. She describes herself as always with a pen, scribbling notes on the margins of newspapers or any suitable surface to comment on points she notices in the texts, or to emphasize remarkable ideas. Writing for self-expression can take the form of a short story, a poem, or a conference paper, but poetry triumphs. Previously, Lara was writing poetry exclusively in Spanish but with recent prospects for an English-speaking audience, she has begun translating her poems into English.

No Spanglish Allowed

Lara did not restrict the deliberate switching between English and Spanish, and the drawing of boundaries between the two languages to note keeping and book selection. She expressed a strong belief that each language represents a unique culture and must be preserved in its original form. Cuban and American cultures are distinct and they should not be muddled by language hybridizations. According to her, it is crucial to know one's own mother language and to know it well. It is also crucial to be proficient and fully competent in the dominant language of the host culture. But more importantly, it is essential to develop awareness of the two languages and cultures as separate and distinct, each with their own rules.

Lara asserts that mixing is unacceptable to her as a form of hybridization that lowers the status of each language and culture:

> Mixing, that's one of the things that I loathe the most, with cultures that come with inventing new words that are not necessary. Our language has a lot of words already; we don't need to invent any words. We need to preserve what we have even when languages are alive and they change, we don't need to prostitute them. And that's what I feel when I see this "I am going to *la marketa*." NO, *el mercado*, there is a word, you don't need to invent a stupid word that is not English or Spanish. Doesn't make any sense to me.

Clearly, Lara was making very conscious language choices. Her definition of literacy suggests her underlying values and beliefs that seemed to be related to these choices. In her own words, literacy is "education, empowerment, and cultural awareness."

Education, for Lara, occurs to a high degree at home, although schooling was also acknowledged as important. In Cuba, she told me, people talk about *educatión desde la cuna* [education from the cradle]. Lara's mother apparently did not have a lot of formal schooling, but, as Lara described her, she was well-educated:

> My mom was able to get only to 6th grade but she had better spelling than many doctors because she read a lot. She did a lot of puzzles ... She came to Havana after the revolution and she started alphabetizing people [teaching people to read] who knew less than her. She has always been reading. My daughter is like her; she will read anything, like for example the labels on the bottle because it's fun for her to do .... [for my mother] it was like a challenge to her. She was like "OK, I only achieved 6 grades but I want to know." My mom would talk about anything. If she was interested about Afghanistan, she would go find a book, and go into the dictionary, ask questions, and she would know what she was talking about.

Empowerment, according to Lara, comes with knowledge and cultural awareness. In Lara's case as an immigrant, what counted for her as invaluable knowledge were her excellent English skills. It was through them that she gained access to the host culture and developed essential understandings of how the U.S. culture works. Lara believed that without fluent English skills, she and her family would have been marginalized, unable to live as fully as they do. The language skills gave her access to the host culture and made it possible for her to learn about many of its unwritten cultural rules and taboos. She began to make sense of the local etiquette, and to comprehend more than words. This is what she meant by cultural awareness and consequent empowerment. Everybody needs to learn, and this learning can happen through explicit instruction, she asserted. She emphasized, that at the same time, this cultural awareness must not only target the host culture. Her children need to learn about their own heritage as well:

> How do people get in the mainstream without acculturating ... Most of these people [foreigners who come to live in the U.S.], what they do is that they show their children into the new culture and have them forget about their own heritage because they have to be in the mainstream. No, you don't need to do that. And I am a living proof. My children are all 100% Cuban but they can be 100% American too. And they have both etiquettes because I took my time to teach them both. It takes long, it's difficult, it's excruciating pain sometimes, because they don't understand: "Why do I have to ...?" "Well, it has to be this way." Sometimes they understand; sometimes they don't. They have adapted very well. My daughter speaks Spanish with a gringo accent and gringo with no accent. And she speaks Spanglish sometime. That's another thing that I am always correcting them. You either speak one language, you don't speak Spanglish with me. You speak either Spanish or English.

Lara, herself, attributes most of her own literacy practices to her upbringing, and tries to raise her own children in a way that she experienced herself, inspiring them to develop cultural awareness and love for books. As her godfather used to say, "Books are like windows. If you want to open the window to Egypt, you read a book about Egypt." Lara treasures what her parents and her godfather gave her and she wishes to do the same for her own children:

> Children need to see that as a natural thing in their environment for them to do this thing. There is nothing that you can force on people. My daughter likes to read because she sees me reading and studying and she knows it's important. She knows that I enjoy it. My son, the same. It's not a genetic thing, it might be. My husband is also a writer. He is always studying, always with a book in his hand. If they see you in front of a TV flipping a remote control, that's what they are gonna learn. Unless, they have some other influence outside of their house, which is very difficult in this country because everything is so expensive.

ENRIQUE

Enrique's situation is rather different. Like Lara, he received 5 years of university education in Cuba. He studied to be a physical education teacher, which he did for 9 years. Neither Lara's nor Enrique's credential counts in the United States, but Lara has managed to find various ways to do things she truly enjoys doing and that are fulfilling to her. She believes that this is because she has mastered English. For Enrique, English was still a great challenge. He had arrived in the United States only 1 ½ years before we met.

Single, with roommates and friends who are all Cuban, he reported that he was receiving only limited exposure to English. But he appeared determined to learn as much as his circumstances would allow. However, with two jobs as a dishwasher and cleaner totaling 80 hours a week, it was very difficult. Despite his obvious lack of time, he found ways to slip bits of English learning into his days. He noted down new words that he would look up in the dictionary when he came home from work. He also would try to learn from his English-speaking co-workers, according to his account. Nevertheless, all those learning situations related to survival skills and English vocabulary only. Enrique never learned anything about English grammar, and he developed a way of communicating in English that is mostly comprehensible, but clearly signals lack of any language education. At the time of the data collection, Enrique was in the process of waiting for a green card. Then, he believed, he would be able to make more thought-out choices about what to do with his life.

Literacy in Enrique's Family

Enrique was the only person in his family who went to a university. He grew up in a small town in western Cuba in a family of six children, with parents who had received very limited schooling. Consequently, according to him, he did not see much reading or writing take place in his home. In his broken, but comprehensible, English, he explains:

> My father, if you give one paper, he no write nothing. He go to the school for only 3 or 4 year. Only work work work work.

> [Does he know how to read and write?]

> A little bit. My mother write a little bit more than my father. She has problems in her eyes. She like listen music, news and *novelas* on the radio. In my family, little people, little family go to the school 40 or 50 year ago. Everybody go to work. In Cuba, everybody had 5 or 6 children and need to work work work. Not have time for a study.

The only exception to this was his uncle who came to live in the house with Enrique's family in early 1990s after he returned from Germany where he spent 4 years as a construction worker. The German work experience rewarded him with a new kind of life. His savings from Germany, and the electronics and clothes that he brought back to Cuba to sell, provided him with enough money to retire and live without a job. It also gave him the time to start doing things he otherwise would not have been able to do, such as extensive reading. Enrique remembers him as always with a book or a newspaper. "In Cuba the life is very poor and when he come back to Cuba, he bring back a lot of clothes and he sell a lot, T-shirt, TV, and never more, he say, never more I work. All time he only in Cuba listen radio and music and read a book."

However, this memory is only from Enrique's adult life when he was already in his 20s. Prior to the German endeavor, Enrique's uncle, similar to Enrique's father, worked manually in construction. It was only upon his return from Germany that his uncle developed a library at home and shared it with Enrique. Enrique's favorite readings included stories about ancient Egypt and its pyramids, Mesopotamia, and Babylonia. But his true passion was soccer, which came much earlier than his exposure to books and took priority over everything else. He discovered the sport as a 12-year-old boy and determined to never let it go:

> I play with my friend. Always in front of my home. Play without shoes. All day, very hot weather. And after, in my high school. The championship. Every week, I play with other school. And in my college, all day, every day, Monday through Friday, after 3:30 p.m., I play. That was one specialization. Every day. Sometime I feel very sick, but if you don't play, you don't pass to other years. You may have trouble.

Enrique's Education

The passion for sports led Enrique to university to study physical education. Getting accepted was not easy. He had to take many tests in different sport disciplines such as athletics, swimming, and ball games. The entrance examinations also included a test in biology, mathematics, and Spanish. As Enrique explained, out of some 200 students at his high school, only a handful was accepted into a university. He was one of the only two admitted to study physical education. Several other students were accepted into a medical school and yet another few into the humanities.

Enrique's drive to study was also motivated by the desire to better himself. "Always when I see the other people [with university education] talk and talk, I see the communication different [and I think] I need to learn, I need to learn. I need to go to school."

During the 5 years at university, Enrique read extensively and took notes in preparation for exams although he did not feel too strong about his writing skills. Direct face-to-face communication allowed him to express himself better so he always chose to take his exams orally. He successfully finished the studies and got a job as a physical education teacher in his home province where he had taught for 9 years prior to coming to the United States. Teachers in Cuba generally make very little money and, as Enrique explained to me, many leave the profession. But he was happy because he was doing what he loved to do.

> Sometime, teacher say I no work more in the school because if I sell bananas in the street, I make more money. Forget about my specialization. If you go

to Cuba, you see in the street, the doctor or maybe the teacher sell bananas, candy, peach, whatever.

[What is university good for?]

When you finish university, you have one job. You don't need looking for job. You have guarantee. In your province or in another province but always you have job.

Life in English

Enrique's credentials from Cuba had no use in the United States, and the fact that his English skills were limited did not help. He was caught in two manual jobs with little time to work on his English. But he still tried. Street signs, ATM machines, bills, letters from the insurance company, all provided opportunities for his learning of English. He had a dictionary at home and when he would come from work and inspect his mail, the dictionary was a great aid in helping him understand written English. It was also tremendously useful when he needed to write checks and spell English numbers, Enrique reported.

Enrique also found some assistance at work. Many of his co-workers were Cuban, but in his meat-packaging job, he had an American co-worker who taught him new words and sentences every day. Usually, he said, he would write them down on a sheet of wrapping paper that Enrique took home and spread on the wall or on the table to memorize the phrases.

In Cuba, Enrique liked to read the newspaper, and occasionally history books and suspense novels. In the United States, with 80 hours of work a week, there was no room for these literacy practices. Sometimes, he reported, he tried to read the newspaper, but it was a learning endeavor rather than reading for information (as he did in Cuba), because a good deal of the written text was not clearly comprehensible to him yet. He would appreciate a newspaper in Spanish, he said, but he had not yet found one.[6]

However, there was one thing that Enrique loved in Cuba and that he could also do in the United States. He could listen to music, and now he could even understand some English lyrics that made no sense to him before. Once in a while, he told me, when he had a free evening, he would go with his friends to a karaoke bar where he could read the lyrics and sing along.

Movies offered yet another opportunity for both entertainment and language learning. He possessed a collection of videotapes of mostly action movies, all but one in English. He explained that what he sees on the screen helps him understand what his ear does not catch. Enrique dreamt that one day when he spoke fluent English, he would be able to find a better job in an

---

[6]There are four bilingual newspapers in the region but they seem to target primarily Mexican immigrants and migrant workers, and thus do not appeal to wider Latino audiences.

office, or perhaps even go back to school and study toward a teaching certificate that would allow him to teach sports again.

CONCLUSION

Through this case study, I had hoped to increase my understanding of immigrants' literacy practices in a new language, and the way that the new language intersects with native language literacy practices. By *literacy practice*, I mean not only reading and writing habits but the broader social and cultural context (Street, 1993) that provides for such habits to develop, to be sustained, and to flourish even in a new linguistic environment. Lara's and Enrique's accounts point to the suggestion that their immigrant experiences as regards their English literacy practices vary and appear to be influenced heavily by family literacy practices in their native countries. These practices influenced predilections, values, attitudes and language knowledge of the participants—both in their native country and in their new country—and they intersect with the social, political, and cultural contexts in which both participants live.

Family Influences on Literacy Practices

Strong family influence is explicit in Lara's accounts of home, describing her parents' and her godfather's encouragement to read, to learn foreign languages, and to educate herself. Knowledge and books surrounded Lara's childhood and continued to play an important role in Lara's adult life, regardless of the language she used. Furthermore, what Lara also carried into her adult life from home was a strong political consciousness. Even in a supposedly classless and egalitarian society such as Cuba, education and intellectualism function as symbols that indicate one's social status.[7] As Lara watched her mother do crossword puzzles, read, and educate herself in order to be able to participate in conversations with people who had received more formal schooling than she, she learned that literacy is empowering.

Enrique was also aware that print literacy comes with social rewards. In part, the reason he wanted to study at a university was to be able to "talk like educated people," as he told me. But unlike Lara, he seemed to have acquired reading and writing skills as a secondary discourse, outside of his family environment (Gee, 1989).

Print literacy practices were not in the center of his family's pastime activities and they did not accompany Enrique's childhood as they did Lara's.

---

[7]In the Cuban context, social status is no indicator of economic status. Regardless of education levels attained, people do not differ much in terms of their income levels.

Enrique acquired the respective reading and writing skills through his many years of schooling, and he adapted them to his needs. As compared to Lara, his use of reading and writing can be described as more functional—a means to an end. In university, he read to pass his tests; in his private life, he read to obtain information he was looking for. Newspapers were fun to read because they had sports sections, which provided the information Enrique appreciated in his job as a physical education teacher. Enrique's definition of literacy as "reading and writing for information, history, culture, and sport" suggests practical use of print literacies different from Lara's notion of literacy where reading and writing is understood more as a form of fundamental self-actualization as well as a political tool that can help one to gain particular social goals (Gee, 1989).

Old Literacy Practices Intersect With New Environments

The literacy practices brought by both participants from their native countries intersect with the literacy practices in which they engage in their new linguistic environment, although these appear to be somewhat modified due to different life circumstances. Lara still pursues the kind of knowledge that she is hungry for, although not entirely through reading. "In Cuba, I read more because the books were there." Not only that, the books were also accessible, affordable, and—more importantly—all in Spanish. Spanish books are not difficult to find in the United States but one must look for them, and books in general are not inexpensive. However, there are alternatives to books. Access to the Internet and e-mail is widespread in the United States and Lara has been using it extensively. The Internet is where she reads the news, checks the weather forecast to see what clothes her kids may need to wear to school, shops, and seeks information relevant to her interests—all of which she could not do in Cuba. With a number of different channels, she can also find interesting programs to watch on TV such as those on the Discovery Channel or Animal Planet. I would argue that these literacy practices are not completely new. Instead, they present variations of activities that satisfy the same interests and that go along with Lara's values and beliefs.

For Enrique, the acquisition of English as a secondary discourse has been more problematic. He came unprepared for a second-language study with no prior foreign-language instruction. He was not able to establish closer ties with host culture members who could help him access the local culture and reach proficiency in the new discourse. Instead, Enrique's closest personal as well as work environment is composed of other Spanish speakers who similarly have stayed marginalized from the dominant discourse. His broken English has been sufficient for his survival, but attempts to improve his English skills have not been very successful so far. This is because there are not many situations that would require Enrique to use a different kind of English from the one he has already grown accustomed to using.

Street (1993) pointed out that literacies are situated and embedded in the broader social and cultural contexts. Enrique's case provides us with examples of this assertion. As a physical education teacher in Cuba, Enrique routinely read and wrote to keep up-to-date with relevant sports information and his job duties. In the United States, in his job as a dishwasher, there is virtually no purpose for reading or writing, and he does none related to his new job. However, there are other situations outside of his job in which Enrique needs to read and write, and within these contexts, he does read and write in English: He reads and acts upon an official letter from the insurance company, he writes a check for a service, he withdraws money from an ATM machine, and he fills out requisite forms. In addition, Enrique's basic predilections and beliefs, first emerging in Cuba, remain and continue to influence his literacy practices in English. Enrique always loved music and movies, and he continues enjoying both. In the United States, he subscribed to a music club and now receives CDs in the mail—CDs that provide lyrics in English for him to learn. In karaoke bars, he enjoys many of his favorite songs and sings along. Movies are also more accessible in the United States than they are in Cuba. Enrique purchased a VCR and a TV and watches as many movies as the time allows, both enjoying them as entertainment and, concurrently, learning more English. His passion for sports now takes a spectator form as he watches soccer games on TV. Enrique understands that better English skills will open more doors, but he finds himself in a vicious cycle. Without English proficiency, he cannot find a better job, but with the two jobs that he worked at the time of the study, there was no time to intensively work on his English or do much of anything else. Moreover, none of the jobs required that his English skills improved, nor provided many opportunities to practice more sophisticated English. Spanish continues to be the dominant language in Enrique's life, and English is a functional language that helps him to survive.

"Language and literacy are acquired and used, gained and lost," according to Luke (2003, p. 138). In this case study, there is some evidence for both losses and gains with respect to particular uses of literacy practices. But more importantly, this case study also suggests that literacy practices do not miraculously appear and disappear when one enters a new linguistic environment, but they seem to be closely linked to the social, cultural, and political contexts in which they developed and to the new context in which they are modified and sustained.

REFERENCES

Barton, D., & Hamilton, M. (1998). *Local literacies: Reading and writing in one community*. London: Routledge.

Gee, J. P. (1989). Literacy, discourse, and linguistics: Introduction and what is literacy? *Journal of Education, 171*(1), 5–25.

Luke, A. (2003). Literacy and the other: A sociological approach to literacy research and policy in multilingual societies. *Reading Research Quarterly, 38*(1), 132–141.

Purcell-Gates, V., Jacobson, E., & Degener, S. (2004). *Print literacy development: Uniting the cognitive and social practice theories*. Cambridge, MA: Harvard University Press.

Street, B. (1993). The new literacy studies. In B. Street (Ed.), *Cross-cultural approaches to literacy* (pp. 1–21). London: Cambridge University Press.

U. S. Department of State. (2000). *Factsheet: Cuba–U.S. Migration accord*. Retrieved December 3, 2003, from http://usembassy.state.gov/havana/wwwhacco.html

UNESCO-SANTIAGO. (1998). *Primer Estudio Internacional Comparativo sobre Lenguaje, Matematica y Factores Asociados en Tercero y Cuarto Grado* [First international comparative study of language, mathematics, and associated factors in third and fourth grades] (Unesco document). Santiago de Chile: Latin American Educational Quality Assessment Laboratory.

Literacies in and out of School and on the Borders

Victoria Purcell-Gates

Focusing on children still in school allows us to directly explore the issues of relationship between literacy practice in the world and literacy development in school. Unlike many adults, children are simultaneously living literacy in their lives and learning literacy in institutional settings, settings designed to direct and shape literacy development. How do these two spheres of action and influence transact? How does lived literacy for children contribute to, impede, or simply bypass literacy learning in school? How does school-based, and school-shaped, literacy development and practice contribute to, impede, or simply bypass lived literacy practice?

The following four case studies address these issues. Each uses the Cultural Practices of Literacy Study (CPLS) methodological protocol (see chap. 1, pp. 17–21) to look for heretofore unidentified links between the lived literacy spheres and the school literacy spheres of their informants. The researchers probe and observe, question and document, evidence of textual practice—current and historical. The authors also explore the borders between participants' school and nonschool settings and the multiple and diverse ways in which literacies are enacted to meet a variety of needs.

In chapter 7, Stephanie Collins, through the benefit of long-time association, provides an up-close, detailed portrait of the many ways that literacy mediates different domains in a young child's life. It is unusual to find this level of literacy environment detail for a child who is not succeeding academically. Collins goes beyond this description, though, and complicates it by exploring hypotheses that Penny seems to hold regarding literacy. These hypotheses impact her out-of-school literacy practices in ways that do not hold promise for future literacy development. Thus, Collins uncovers ways in which Penny imports her "lived-world" out-of-school-based literacy into the classroom, a model of literacy that does not align with school-based models of literacy.

Jodene Kersten (chap. 8), also working with inner-city elementary-age children, involved her informants in exploring their own literacy worlds. Armed with cameras and mutually arrived-upon data collection and analysis techniques, her small after-school literacy group documented, discussed, and interrogated the myriad ways reading and writing played out in their lives, the lives of their parents and siblings, and within their communities. In the process, the ways in which school literacy aligned with, and failed to align with, their literacy practices became clear. A unique insight is provided in this chapter into the ways in which children apprentice into adult literacy practices as part of authentic helping with adult tasks, complicating again the construct

115

of sociotextual domains as we think of them as age-related. The issue of agency is also raised in this chapter as the informants clearly state the differences between reading and writing assigned in school and literacy that is freely chosen when outside of school control. What is eminently clear for all of the children is the rich, complex, and varied landscape of sociotextual domains in their lives outside of school. Because Kersten's group included one child in the gifted and talented program, though, she was able to uncover a disjunction between this child and the others as regards the richness and variety of literacy practices engaged with *in school*. Kristen, as part of her gifted and talented classes, reported reading and writing many more different types of texts than the others as part of their instructional programs. The children were mixed in terms of how they saw the relationships between their in-school literacy instruction and practices and their out-of-school practice of literacy.

David Gallagher's case study (chap. 9) of a group of four "at risk" adolescents presents a complex picture of literacy-mediated social spheres for these students, considered by the schools as deficient in literacy ability. Gallagher carefully documents the multiple literacies the students engaged within the social spheres of home/community, youth culture, and the official world of the classroom, emphasizing the fluidity of these spheres that allow literacies to be imported and exported across boundaries. Through his analysis, Gallagher present us with some promising insights into the complexity of the relationship between in-school and out-of-school literacy practices. Literacy as learned within official school curricula enables and is sometimes exported into other social spheres, whereas literacies arising from outside of the official school sphere manage to penetrate and, at times, support school-based literacy events and practices. Although the teacher of this class, specifically designed for students at risk of school dropout, tried to connect school assignments with the lives and related literacies of these adolescents, he was, for the most part, unsuccessful in importing the authentic purposes connected to these literacies, rendering the curricular assignments unconnected to lived literacy. Gallagher suggests ways in which literacy researchers and literacy teachers might begin to think about connecting the rich literacy lives of students to literacy instruction in school as a step toward improving the school achievement of marginalized students.

The final chapter in this section, by Chad O'Neil (chap. 10), foregrounds the aspect of the CPLS study that explores the perceived relationships for adults among their current literacy practices and their in-school literacy practices while they were children and students. This is another lens on the home/school connections issue that I raised in chapter 1. While Kersten could examine home/school connections in "real time" with elementary students, O'Neil explored this from an historical perspective. The CPLS intentionally targets adults as reporters of their own literacy lives and histories, including those that emanate from their schooling. His analysis provides compelling suggestions of the possibilities of such methodology. Over time and conversations with two undergraduate students with whom he shared work experience and space, O'Neil reveals strands suggestive of both literacy conflict and literacy agency in the stories. In his presentation, we see home-based literacies imported into school spheres and vice versa, reminiscent of Gallagher's findings. We also are reminded of Kersten's finding of agency in relation to literacy practice and the ways that plays out within the home and school contexts. Both of O'Neil's informants relate their feelings, growing over the years, of experiencing out-of-school reading as more engaging, varied, and exciting as compared to the literacy presented in the official school social spaces. Also, over time, each assumed more agentive roles in terms of preferences, likes, and dislikes of particular literacy practices. This description provides a beginning view of possible relationships between social–emotional development, as it transacts with social spheres and networks, and literacy practice(s).

Chapter 7

Breadth and Depth, Imports and Exports: Transactions Between the In- and Out-of-School Literacy Practices of an "At Risk" Youth

Stephanie Collins
Michigan State University

Penny,[1] her mouth full of purple taffy, squinted at the printed plastic which had a moment before housed her sugary treat. "Steph, can I read ya a joke?" she asked me, fully aware that I would say yes but not yet so aware of why I would say it. Penny expected the "of course" with which I replied because she has long known that I appreciate her humor—original or aided by "Laffy Taffy™." Penny at this point did not, however, know that I additionally appreciate her everyday literacy practices, that in this instance I happily observed her use of wrapper as text and text as a vehicle for social interaction. Now Penny understands this in large part. Eleven years old, she has served as an informant to this piece of the Cultural Practices of Literacy Study (CPLS).

THE CULTURAL PRACTICES OF LITERACY STUDY

Ideologically situated alongside the New Literacy Studies, the CPLS employs case study to explore questions dually oriented toward literacy theory

---

[1] A pseudonym.

and practice; Luke posed a series of such questions in *Reading Research Quarterly* in the winter of 2003:

> Which linguistic competencies, discourses and textual resources, and multi-literacies are accessible? How, in what blended and separate domains and to what ends, are different languages used? How do people use languages, texts, discourses, and literacies as convertible and transformative resources in homes, communities, and schools? … How are these resources taken into communities and recombined with other kinds of social, economic, and ecological capital in consequential ways in which social fields and linguistic markets? Which children's and adolescents' pathways through and across social fields will be affected? (pp. 139–140)

Queries of this sort do not arise out of thin air; their appearance in rhetoric follows their neglect in educational policy—policy such as the Reading First component of the No Child Left Behind (NCLB) legislation within the United States (U. S. Department of Education, 2004). Marketed as a large-scale effort to rehabilitate underachieving public schools, NCLB directly affects the school literacy experiences of students often labeled *at risk*. A highly politicized (and perhaps dangerously determinist and essentializing) phrase, "at risk" seems to subsume many of the possible combinations and conflations of marginalized identity in the United States. Whether called "at risk," "disadvantaged," "underprivileged," or by her name, Penny, an African American girl of low socioeconomic status, acutely lives out current policy decisions and will acutely live out upcoming decisions. In working with Penny to create a portrait of her in- and out-of school literacy practices and the transactions between these literacy spaces—a portrait of the "blended and separate domains" in which she practices literacies and the ends to which she does so—I hope to help equip future policymakers with some of the information necessary to meet Luke's (2003) call:

> the redefined function of governments … is to provide access to combinatory forms of enabling capital that enhance students' possibilities of putting the kinds of practices, texts, and discourses acquired in schools to work in consequential ways that enable active position taking in social fields. These ways should enable some control on the part of these people over the shapes of their life pathways and, ultimately, over the shapes and rules of exchange of the places where they will put their cultural capital to work. (p. 139)

PROFILING PENNY

Currently, Penny's living situation requires her to put her own "cultural capital to work" in various spaces within a declining industrial city in the Midwest. The youngest of nine children, Penny resides in a government-subsidized townhouse along with her mother and three of her brothers, ages 13 to 16. Train tracks running behind it, abandoned warehouses to the south, convenience shopping to the north, the cosmopolitan part of town a hair to the east, this townhouse sits among its architectural clones in a low-income public housing neighborhood known as The Court. On days when the howling of cold wind drowns out most sound and the screeching of a passing train drowns out all the rest, The Court can exude a sort of dreariness—this visitor, perhaps projecting, has read gloom on the faces of residents. On other days, more gentle days, when children swarm The Court's playground, teenagers gather by its blacktop basketball hoop, adults congregate on its porches, and small groups of people make their way across the busy street fronting it for trips to nearby stores, The Court can emit excitement.

On the latter sort of days, Penny, her brothers, and their friends, many of whom also live in The Court, have pre-/early teen adventures in the neighborhood—they scheme about each other and about members of the opposite sex while crossing back and forth over front yards, ride bikes, practice cheers and dance routines on the pavement, and make grand expeditions to Shop 'n Save. On the former sort of days, Penny and friends sit inside each others' houses, chatting and watching television, doing "nothin'," as Penny would say.

Penny believes she understands why her friends spend such time with her, believes she understands her appeal to them. Penny does not locate this appeal in her academic self; in fact, she often dismisses other people's characterizations—her teacher's, her tutor's, sometimes her mother's characterizations—of her as smart. In her view, intelligence functions as the currency of school, and school, as an institution-seeming entity, has labeled her and her brothers *bankrupt*. Penny, now a fifth grader at an intermediate (Grade 5 through Grade 8) public school, repeated the fourth grade last year; her three brothers who live at home attend varying levels of special education programming within their schools. Unsure of her intellect, insecure in the "in-school skin" that she associates with it, Penny shows greater confidence in her sense of humor and her appearance, spirited in her "social skin." As evidenced already, Penny feels comfortable telling jokes and relating funny anecdotes. Additionally, she frequently plays at actor; in good fun, she deftly imitates children and adults around her, and, in trying to get her way, she puts on a remarkably believable (and knowingly cute) pouting face.

Penny does not solely pride herself on her skill in generating fun; she holds to certain values, loyalty the most apparent. Time and time again, Penny has stepped forward to defend certain capabilities (particularly relevant herein) of her brothers, doing so diplomatically before adults—"They *can* read," and hotly before peers—"SHUT UP! He can read!"—and to stick up for her tutor when adults playfully joke about her or other children disobey her—"Don't you be messin' with Steph"; "I'm tellin' your mama you're not listening to Steph!"

RESEARCH AND RELATIONSHIP: LOCATING MYSELF

I, Steph, cannot help but feel sentimental at such moments—the relationship Penny and I share, represented in a timeline below, has grown from peripheral to personal since we met nearly 3 years ago when I became her literacy tutor through a Housing Authority/University partnership.

- *Spring and fall academic semesters of 2001.* Penny and I collaborated as a tutee/tutor pair through this program.
- *Spring semester of 2002.* Penny worked with several other undergraduates while I studied abroad.
- *Fall semester of 2002.* Penny, sometimes her friends and/or siblings, and I met outside of the program on a weekly basis for silent reading and social activities as I worked as an administrator for the program and Penny did not participate in it.
- *Spring semester of 2003.* I maintained my position as an administrator, Penny rejoined the program and worked with a different tutor, our outside-the-program reading continued, and our social outings grew to regularly include Penny's siblings and friends and my own good friend, who now acts as Penny's unofficial tutor.
- *Summer of 2003.* Penny and I saw each other an average of a couple times a week for reading, and Penny, her brothers, friends, and my friend joined together at least once a week for eating, swimming, shopping, or going to the movies.

Through these experiences and over time, I have come to know, to some extent, important people in Penny's life other than her brothers and friends: Penny's new tutor and I recently began friendly face-to-face and phone communication with Penny's teacher, and I have, for some time now, made a point of chatting with Penny's mother and neighbors when I pick her up from home for outings. Sometimes Penny's mother reacts to me as "one of the family," as she once called me; other times she seems more restrained and preoccupied (and I feel certain I seem the same way to her).

Now that I have completed my undergraduate education and attend graduate school at a university 2 ½ hours (by car) from Penny's home, I have chances to interact with Penny's mother, neighbors, brothers, friends, and Penny herself about twice a month. When Penny and I get together, we socialize and work on the CPLS. Certainly, I cannot claim the role of a "fly on the wall" researcher (not that anyone truly can); rather, following some initial ethical pondering, I have come to embrace my overt embeddedness within the CPLS. In working with Penny to document her literacy practices, I enjoy more opportunities to see her than I would otherwise and also strive to maximize this research experience as more than simply "neutral" for

Penny. By interviewing Penny regarding her literacy practices, I not only recognize, and thus validate, all of her literacy practices—nondominant literacy practices[2] especially—but also invite her to assume the researcher role herself. Penny does not just answer questions; she asks them of me, of her family, friends, and neighbors, and of herself. I hope that acting as a researcher of her own "cultural creation" will empower Penny via investigation, celebration, critique, and the mainstream and nonmainstream competencies[3] such ways of doing and seeing engender—the (multi)cultural capital they produce. Ultimately, or, perhaps, until my next episode of ethical and ethnographic questioning, I have reconciled research and relationship.

BREADTH: PENNY'S TEXT USE

This research with Penny to date reveals that the literacy practices enacted within her social world(s)—enacted by Penny, her family, friends/peers, and neighbors—span many domains that themselves overlap and intersect, span many of these space/action/purpose/role combinations that help to define an individual's various selves. The sociotextual domains encapsulating the literacy practices of Penny and those around her include: bureaucracy, clubs/organizations, community organization, entertainment, fashion, finances, interpersonal communication, personal care/daily routines, personal writing, public display, school, shopping, social cohesion, and work. Now, I delineate these domains mainly in terms of the texts and purposes involved therein—only a couple facets of literacy practice; later, I expound on the larger relationship between domain and literacy practice in Penny's life. Although I suspend this full analysis until the section entitled Making Sense of Literacy: Penny's Literacy Practices, I urge the reader at this point to contrast the volume of the listing that follows with the potency and the concentration of its contents.

Bureaucracy

Bureaucracy as a sociotextual domain contains literacy practices used for official and/or enforced purposes—literacy practices such as Penny's mother's navigation of the paperwork of private aid agencies offering bill payment assistance.

---

[2]Barton and Hamilton (1998) described nondominant/vernacular literacy practices via contrast to dominant literacy practices—those practices "associated with formal organizations, such as ... education, law, religion and the workplace" and "given high value legally" and "in the cultural mainstream" (p. 252).

[3]For example, academic essayist thought and pop-culture expert knowledge.

Clubs/Organizations

Literacy practices that occur in and around organized nonschool and non-religious activities fall within the sociotextual domain of clubs/organizations. Penny's text use/exposure within this domain includes: her mandatory and frequently dodged reading and/or writing (often centered around story and chapter books) during the "reading hour" of the mentoring program through which I met her, as well as her mother's skimming and signing of permission slips and consent forms for her children's participation in this program and its related activities.

Community Organization

The creation (and general distribution) of birthday-party announcing fliers by teenagers in Penny's neighborhood and the reading of these fliers by recipients falls into the sociotextual domain of community organization, which describes reading and writing done concurrent with efforts to bring community members together in various ways and to varying degrees.

Daily Routines/Personal Care

Reading the signs on restroom doors for direction into the women's room, the numbers on digital clocks when she wants to know the time, and the text near the heating/cooling knobs in my car when she wants to adjust the temperature, Penny frequently (and quickly) accesses basic information from text for simple self-maintenance. Embedded in routinized personal care, these literacy practices fit within the daily routines/personal care sociotextual domain.

Entertainment/Pleasure

The sociotextual domain of entertainment/pleasure refers to reading done for relaxation or "for fun," as Penny would say. Penny's reading and writing within the domain of entertainment/pleasure includes: reading a few select chapter books and poetry books through her past involvement in the mentoring program or with me independent of the program (initially self-reporting on such books without the assistance of my memory, Penny referenced only *The Twits* [Dahl, 1982], which she encountered 2 years ago); reading a joke book bought at a school book fair and (as mentioned earlier) reading a joke from a "Laffy Taffy" candy wrapper; exchanging cards and/or letters with me and her current tutor (my friend) on infrequently interspersed occasions; writing labels, every once in a while, on pictures she has drawn; and searching the Internet (at the public library) for hip-hop lyrics, and printing and reading those lyrics.

Fashion

The at-a-glance reading of brand-name labels on clothing (bought and owned clothing, desired clothing, and other people's clothing) that Penny and her 16-year-old brother do fits within (though not exclusively within) the sociotextual domain of *fashion*, which applies to reading and writing done with the *style* of attire in mind.

Finances

Although reading clothing labels for brand-names belongs to the domain of fashion, reading clothing tags for prices belongs to the sociotextual domain of *finances*. Penny and some of her family members engage in this text use and others that similarly deal with money: Penny and her mother read prices when purchasing food; Penny's mother reads checks and bills.

Interpersonal Communication

Text use facilitating communication with family members and friends—text use within the domain of interpersonal communication—appears in Penny's life in her seasonal selection and signing of birthday and holiday cards for family members and in her exchange of letters with her mother's boyfriend (recently away) once and with tutors a couple times. While I studied abroad, Penny, assisted by a program administrator, e-mailed me such a letter, the text of which I have copied below: "dear steph, imiss you. hope to see you soon. I hop england is fun. you are very fun and I read with sharon but I like you more. bye bye. love penny."

Personal Writing

Around the same time she wrote this letter, Penny wrote a couple entries in a diary I gave to her as a gift, and these entries *seem* situated within the sociocultural domain of personal writing—writing not intended for an audience—and here *seem* proves key, for I must admit that Penny has shared these entries with me!

Public Writing

Penny's reading and writing within the domain of public writing—the converse of the sociotextual domain of personal writing—includes (or may, in fact, consist entirely of) the time she designed posters hung as party decorations.

School

Identifying the literacies that occur in or around school and receive institutional sanction, the sociotextual domain of school proves broad. Penny's mother's cursory reading and filling out of permission slips for her children's participation in school events falls within this domain as does her writing of letters to her children's schools to explain their absences. Up to this point in the study, Penny has compartmentalized her own text use within the school sociotextual domain into subdomains. The following subdomains and the example text uses therein correspond, in many (but not all) cases, with academic subjects: (a) reading musical notes and the letters designating them within band class; (b) acknowledging the denomination of play currency circulated via a classroom management reward system; (c) reading, writing, and correcting "Daily Oral Language" sentences as dictated by classroom routine; (d) reading and writing numbers and words on math worksheets; (e) reading short stories from a basal reading series and, on one occasion, reading a basal-related article from a local newspaper; (f) loosely "following along" as other students read passages aloud from a social studies textbook; (g) writing, correcting, and rewriting spelling words. While in school, Penny does not always stick to such sanctioned literacy practices. Quickly and covertly exchanging notes with friends right under her teacher's nose, Penny "border-crosses" (and thus blurs) the sociotextual domain of school and the before-mentioned domain of interpersonal communication.

Shopping

The sociotextual domain of shopping encompasses literacies directly—not simply coincidentally—connected to the act of shopping. The casual perusal of store fliers (for sales and product selection), food packaging (for prices and favored ingredients), and clothing tags and labels (for sizes, prices, and brand names) and the rare reading/writing of shopping lists done by Penny and her mother fit into several domains, one among them shopping.

Social Cohesion

For literacy researchers who adopt a sociocultural perspective, almost all text use functions within the domain of *social cohesion* as this domain highlights literacies that promote social interaction or testify to social solidarity. Overlap between domains admitted, text use by Penny and her 16-year-old brother within this sociotextual domain includes their reading of hip-hop lyrics and brand name labels on clothing—both forms of cultural capital among their peers, both vehicles for signifying community-appreciated style, be the community actual or imagined.

Work

Literacies that comprise the work sociotextual domain aid paid employment. As Penny lives in an impoverished neighborhood within a city with few job opportunities, it comes as little surprise that she cites the reading of labels on car-detailing cleaning agents by her mother's boyfriend (who does car detailing informally but for pay) as the one and only instance of work domain text use she can concretely recall among her family members, friends, and neighbors.

DEPTH: MAINSTREAM IN-SCHOOL TEXT USE AND LITERACY PRACTICES

True to its name, the central question of the CPLS focuses on the dynamics between in- and out-of-school literacy practices; I have already outlined Penny's text use and its purposes within certain sociotextual domains but have not explicated the literacy practices at play. Barton and Hamilton (1998) defined literacy practices:

> Literacy practices are the general cultural ways of utilizing written language people draw upon in their lives. In the simplest sense literacy practices are what people do with literacy. However practices are not observable units of behaviors since they also involve values, attitudes, feelings and social relationships .... This includes people's awareness of literacy, constructions of literacy and discourses of literacy, how people talk about and make sense of literacy. (p. 6)

While emphasizing the plurality of literacy practices present in mainstream schools, Gee (1996) gave particular attention to school-endorsed essayist literacy practice and creative writing/literature literacy practice. Gee (1996) characterized the former literacy as linearly structured, reportive, assumptive of the existence of objective facts and

> founded on the idea—often associated with "modernism" as opposed to "postmodernism" ... of people transcending their social and cultural differences to communicate "logically," "rationally," and "dispassionately" to each other as "strangers" (the basic assumption behind the essay) in a thoroughly explicit and decontextualized way. (pp. 156–157)

He positions the latter within a "print-based 'high culture' literary tradition, a tradition that ... has origins in oral-culture practices (think of the line running from Homer to Hesiod to Chaucer to Shakespeare, and beyond)"

(Gee, 1996, pp. 160–161). Valuing these literacies, Penny's school asks her to practice them—to do them and to accept their premises—at a novice level but a nonetheless engaged, involved level: "Daily Oral Language" exercises (categorized within the school subdomain of class routine/management) teach their conventions; silent reading and teacher "read-alouds" (e.g., of both biography and humorous fiction) teach their appreciation; small writing assignments here and there ("little bits of science writing" and "little bits of creative stuff," as Penny's teacher calls them) teach their production. Note that these activities, most mentioned to me by Penny's teacher, require extended time and/or focused attention for their successful execution.

MAKING SENSE OF LITERACY: PENNY'S LITERACY PRACTICES

Imports

Despite the presence in her classroom of literacy events[4] that demand time and attention, Penny, when interviewed, generally recounts in-school literacy events that do not make such demands. She revels in her speed in copying weekly spelling words and takes great interest in the fact that I recognize as literacy the quick numerical reading and writing she does to complete "Minute Math" and the scanning of letters (marking musical notes) she does to play her instrument in band. These examples of in-school literacy events acknowledged by Penny bear a striking resemblance to literacy events framed by many domains other than the school domain, as just shown. Comparison of Penny's reported school domain text use with her total text use helps to reveal a pattern—a pattern that speaks to practice, to how Penny "makes sense" of literacy.

Across sociotextual domains, Penny's use of text functions in a sort of immediate feedback relationship with the environment, exemplified by, but not limited to, her reading of food packaging while shopping: Penny wants to eat a candy bar with peanuts in it so she skims the wrappers of various candy bars on store display, reads "peanuts" on one bar, and buys that bar and eats it. Here, reading serves as a means to an immediate end and need not take more than a few moments and a passing glance to meet that end.

Although counterexamples to this sort of reading (and similar writing) exist, they number few and far between; although Penny admits reading and writing letters and writing diary entries she, in the same breath, admits the rarity—and the corresponding novelty—of such uses of text in her life. From data on not simply what Penny reads and writes but also why and how

---

[4]Note the distinction between literacy events and literacy practices; see Barton and Hamilton (1998) for explication.

she reads and writes in and out of school, I have come to see Penny's uses of text as literacy practices governed by a particular understanding of how reading and writing work, by a "shopping for a candy bar model" or "immediacy model"; I have come to suspect that Penny has imported this immediacy model of literacy "native" to her out-of-school life—rooted in the text uses therein—into school.

One might wonder why Penny has done this importing. Underscoring the dangerous circularity of Penny's situation, my speculative explanation proves rather circular:

- To preserve a positive sense of self, Penny chooses to define that self (herself) in terms of validating experiences.
- Penny has such validating experiences out of school; for example, she "fits in" when she keeps up with the dance routines she and her friends do on the pavement at The Court and she reaps smiles from friends and family members when she tells funny or dramatic stories.
- Penny does not typically have comparably validating experiences in school; at least for the past 2½ years, possibly for longer, she has struggled in school, repeating the fourth grade and now "standing out" (according to her teacher) as one of the children who have trouble reading, especially reading aloud.
- Penny copes with her feelings of frustration and diminishment in school by superimposing her usual out-of-school talents and capabilities, "ways of being" (Gee, 1996), and understandings of "how things work" onto her school experiences.
- Transplants—whether medicine or literacy related—do not always take; Penny's importation of her out-of-school ways of using text and beliefs about using text, of the immediacy model, into school proves "improper"; it does not lead to school success and perhaps hinders school success as great differences exist between the time and attention requirements of her out-of-school literacies and mainstream in-school literacies.

And so, Penny again comes to the beginning of the cycle—she craves validation and does not get it from school.

Exports

However, Penny has not written off school, so to speak. She has accepted an "export" from me, her new tutor, and perhaps others. Although Penny does not see many of the adults around her holding steady jobs (recall the economic depression at large in her city and concentrated in her neighborhood), she gravitates (perhaps in response) toward the idea of economic self-sufficiency. Hoping for this component of Penny's potential future along with her, Penny's new tutor and I have had several conversations with her about what sort of job one needs in order to attain financial stability and what sort of education one needs in order to obtain that sort of job. In discussing this path from education to job, Penny and I have "charted" how reading and writing in school in the Grade 5 connects to high school achievement, which connects to college acceptance and achievement, which connects to job opportunities, which connects, finally, to having the money to support oneself and a family and having the skills to help people outside of family (e.g., working as a nurse or volunteering as a tutor).

Though I have often wondered if these sorts of talks might "go in one ear and out the other" of 11-year-old Penny, she has memorized if not fully internalized the "Steph-exported" educational plan.[5] During one CPLS interview, I asked Penny why she read her music in band, expecting her to say "to play my instrument" and dropping my jaw when she spoke to her reasons for all school reading and writing and offered this answer: "to get good grades, get an education, be like you." Helping me to flush out the meaning of "be like you" (certainly a jolting and perhaps a problematic phrase), Penny fairly readily explained that she sees me as a "grown woman"—a self-sufficient woman—and a tutor, someone who helps people.

However, Penny did not tackle the meaning of the phrase "get a good education" with similar ease; Penny had no comments to make about what constituted an education until I asked her, "Does getting a good education mean getting good grades or learning stuff or both?" The "correct" (Steph-pleasing) answer clearly marked for her, Penny answered, "Both." It seems Penny brought conversation from months before to bear upon the CPLS interview without fully comprehending the meaning of her own words or, rather, the meaning of the words her new tutor and I had exported to her.

For Penny, "education" and in-school reading and writing function as tools devoid of instructions. Penny knows that she needs to use education, reading, and writing to reach certain life goals, but, operating via her immediacy model of literacy, she does not know how to use them to reach these goals. Penny's teacher describes her as a nonparticipant in much classroom activity, including reading and writing activity; Penny agrees with her teacher's assessment in content but not in framing, not in definition. Describing her behavior during social studies whole-class reading, Penny divulges that she sits with her textbook and notebook open, pretending to take notes in the latter, not following along in the former. Although Penny clearly states to me that she "acts out" concentration on this social

---

[5]Perhaps this plan proved easy for Penny to commit to memory as it takes the means–ends form similar to that of her immediacy model of literacy.

studies reading (and writing), she still deems what she does "reading in social studies." According to Penny's model of literacy, reading does not call for concentration—"faking it" appeases her teacher and does not disturb her own conception of what reading entails.

CONCLUSIONS: A PLACE TO BEGIN

Recognizing school success as a means to a desired end and thus working toward it, Penny applies an available, familiar, ego-sustaining, and (unbeknownst to her) inappropriate model of literacy—her out-of-school immediacy model of literacy—to school literacies and thus engages in them superficially and ineffectually. Penny truly believes that in pretending to read her social studies textbook she meets the literacy demands before her and, furthermore, truly believes that such an approach to school literacies will gain her the credentialing that I and others have sold to her—sold to her but not adequately explained to her; Penny means it but does not "get it" when she says she reads and writes in school to "to get good grades, get an education, be like you."

"Meaning it" without "getting it," Penny complicates literacy theory and practice, and I suspect she does not stand alone. "Nonmainstream" students, children dubbed "at risk," employ multiple strategies to weather incongruencies between in- and out-of-school literacy practices. Whereas some children choose certain "life worlds"[6] over others—shunning the practices of school and retreating into the practices of church, for example—other children, children like Penny, create consonance across in- and out-of-school abstract domains and actual spaces through the importation and exportation of certain models and valuations of literacy. Such children do not simply accept or reject; rather they "refashion." In some cases, this transformative agency reaps success in and out of school. In other cases, in Penny's case, it does not. These latter cases reemphasize that children require not only an explicit "what" or even a "why" to navigate literacy events but also a "how." Beyond informing theory and practice in this way, Penny's collaboration with me has informed our relationship and serves as a caveat and a call to others who take on the privilege of acting as tutors or mentors.

REFERENCES

Barton, D., & Hamilton, M. (1998). *Local literacies: Reading and writing in one community*. London: Routledge.
Cope, B., & Kalantzis, M. (Eds.). (2000). *Multiliteracies*. London: Routledge.
Dahl, R. (1982). *The Twits*. London: Puffin Books.

---

[6]See the New London Group's *Multiliteracies* for more on "life worlds" (Cope & Kalantzis, 2000).

Gee, J. P. (1996). *Social linguistics and literacies*. London: Taylor & Francis.

Luke, A. (2003). Literacy and the other: A sociological approach to literacy research and policy in multilingual societies. *Reading Research Quarterly, 38*, 132–140.

U.S. Department of Education. (2004). *No Child Left Behind*. Retrieved May 1, 2004, from http://www.ed.gov/nclb/landing.jhtml?src=pb

Literacy and Choice: Urban Elementary Students' Perceptions of Links Between Home, School, and Community Literacy Practices

Jodene Kersten
California State Polytechnic University Pomona

> *At school you just have to do what the teacher says but at home you can read and write whatever you want.*
>
> —Kristen[1], age 10

> *I guess reading and writing in school helps for home … but when the school day is done, it's like yay, carry on and go home!*
>
> —Katie, age 10

At the turn of the 20th century, Dewey (1902/1956) proposed a child-centered curriculum in response to rapid social changes from the industrial revolution, a worldwide market, and wider communication and distribution. He described the disconnect between the child and the curriculum as "the lack of any organic connection with what the child has already seen and felt and loved [which] makes the material purely formal and symbolic" (p. 24) and "the lack of motivation" (p. 25) in relation to a curriculum that was also "external, ready-make fashion, by the time it gets to the child" (p. 26).

---

[1]All children's names are pseudonyms.

Much of what Dewey discussed has become the accepted philosophy of education today.

Unfortunately, many of the "evils" he addressed are still present and impacting the academic success of children. The gap between the child and schooling is perpetuated by a prepackaged school curriculum, high-stakes testing, and failure to make connections between school and home life for children. In 1902 Dewey was speaking of all children. However, at the turn of the 21st century, the disconnect between schooling and children, predominantly those considered marginalized or without access to the dominant culture, has become a chasm.

In the introduction to Dewey's (1956) *The Child and the Curriculum*, Carmichael stated that during Dewey's lifetime, "it may be that the world changed more during this period of nearly a century than in any comparable time in history" (p. vi). Fifty years later, philosophers might agree that education has experienced yet another significant change due to rapid advances in technology and globalization. This begs the question of what schools are doing to prepare students for the 21st century. It is both timely and necessary to revisit Dewey's concern of whether schools are teaching the whole child, mind and body, by embracing the experiences and knowledge the children bring to the classroom.

Cope and Kalantzis (2000) describe the ways in which the world is changing and how "new demands are being placed upon people as makers of meaning in changing workplaces, as citizens in changing public spaces and in the changing dimensions of our community lives—our lifeworlds" (p. 4). They propose six design elements in the meaning-making process as well as four components of pedagogy to discuss how schools might address social change and prepare children. Schools can no longer adequately prepare students and ignore the variety of texts associated with information and multimedia technologies. Cope and Kalantzis (2000) acknowledge "… in the emergent reality, there are still real deficits, such as a lack of access to social power, wealth, and symbols of recognition. The role of pedagogy is to develop an epistemology of pluralism that provides access without people having to erase or leave behind different subjectivities" (p. 18).

In this case study, I explore these issues in the context of one elementary school with a group of children who would be considered marginalized in terms of their quality of education, socioeconomic status, and various forms of capital (Bourdieu, 2001).

This chapter is an attempt to examine the types of literacy events that occur between home, community, and school as well as the connections and disconnects. I address three questions: (a) Are the literacy experiences and knowledge of students valued in the educational system? (b) Are all students being prepared to participate in a society that is rapidly changing? and (c) Are schools addressing the gap between the types of literacies valued by schools versus those valued by students? Luke (2003) describes this divide as a result of the "increasing diversity of background knowledge and competence, linguistic and cultural resources, available discourses and textual practices brought to and through classrooms and schools" (p. 137). He further states:

> The use and value of literacy for learners—the available discourses, background knowledges, repertoires of practices and motivation structures for learning and using literacy—are as contingent on those extra-educational social relations and linguistic markets that they inhabit before, during, and after school. (p. 137)

This study is framed by my belief that to ignore the literacy practices elementary students engage in outside of school is a disservice to students and fails to prepare them for life after formal schooling.

CASE STUDY: THE LITERACY SOCIAL ACTION GROUP

Participants

The site for participation in this study was an after-school program at an elementary school with a group of students who met once a week for 11 weeks. The participants were 7 female fifth-grade students at an urban elementary school (K–5). Their teacher selected 12 children to receive a letter from me, inviting them to participate in a small group as part of the after-school program. She had known these children as their third-grade teacher. The school is fairly small, so many students from the third-grade class were together for fifth grade. They were selected for the study based on the teacher's belief that (a) they were likely to want to participate in a group focused on reading and writing, and (b) their parents would allow their children to participate in the after-school program. Nine of these 12 students chose to attend the weekly group. Of these 9 students, 7 returned consent forms and chose to participate in the study. We met for a total of nine 2-hour sessions over 11 weeks.

The children ranged in age from 10 to 11 and spoke English as both their native and home language. They were all in the same fifth-grade classroom and several lived in the same neighborhoods and spent time together outside of school. Ethnically, the participants closely reflected the elementary school student body with two European Americans, three African Americans and two self-identified as "mixed" African American and European American.

The elementary after-school program depends on volunteers primarily from the teacher education program at the nearby university. Due to budget cuts at the district level and a limited number of volunteers, less than half of the students at the elementary school were able to participate in the program. When I asked to work with a small group of children, the coordinator of the program was anxious to remove nine more students from the wait list, and several students shared with me that their parents were relieved because of difficulties they experienced with child care. As a result, one of the participants could only attend if her younger sister could sit in with the group, which she did.

Researcher and Connection to Research Site

My roles and responsibilities at the elementary school were multiple and varied. As a doctoral student, I was employed through the university as a field instructor. My primary responsibility was to act as a liaison between the university, six mentor teachers, and six interns working toward their teaching certification. I observed interns and mentors one to two times a week and led a 2-hour seminar for interns once a week. The students in the fifth-grade class were familiar with me because I spent several hours in the classroom supporting the intern and working with the mentor teacher.

As a field instructor and leader of the after-school group, I needed to balance several roles. Many of the project participants saw me as their teacher and occasionally mentioned this to the intern who was also my seminar student. When I was visiting and observing my intern, many of the participants wanted to talk and share ideas with me, but this was often a distraction to the intern learning to teach. As a result, the children soon recognized when it was acceptable to speak with me, such as during recess and after school, and that I needed to be the intern's teacher when in their classroom.

As stated in the beginning of the chapter, the purpose of this study was to learn more about the literacy practices in the participants' homes and communities as well as the literacy practices in the school. Four weeks into the school year, I was asked by their fifth-grade teacher for support in developing a balanced literacy program because of my prior experience as a literacy specialist in the district and years of elementary teaching. After several meetings, we developed a literacy program that was implemented approximately the same time I began the after-school group and collecting data for this project. Thus, several of the school literacy practices mentioned by the students were co-created by me and their fifth-grade teacher. Whether these same practices would have occurred without my intervention is speculative. Therefore, most of the school literacy practices are intended to represent the curriculum and pedagogy prior to the balanced literacy program co-created by me and the teacher.

Building Trust and Group Cohesion

For our initial meeting, we used a classroom that is typically reserved for small groups or special meetings. Immediately the students felt unique. They were told by the director of the after-school program that they would not participate in the "power hour," an hour reserved for homework, because we would be writing in our group. Because most students do not have homework, and there is a ratio of 20 students to one tutor, they typically don't find the "power hour" useful. Therefore, they viewed the group as a privilege from the beginning.

Several students shared their excitement around reading and writing during the first group meeting. They were anxious to receive composition books to record their own literacy practices at home, in the community, and at school. They were also excited to keep their papers organized in a folder.

During the first meeting, I explained the purpose of the group. I told the children that I was a student at the local university and I was trying to learn more about their reading and writing activities in school, at home, and in their community. I explained that there was a possibility of writing about our experiences in a book, but that their names would be changed. I said I was a researcher and they would also be researchers in our group. From that point forward the students referred to themselves as "college researchers," which created some curiosity and envy by other students in their fifth-grade class. This title appeared to boost their status among peers.

After school, the participants began sitting together and sharing their writing in their composition books with each other and other students before going to their assigned rooms for the after-school program. Initially, cliques within the group were evident by where students chose to sit in our room and the students with whom they wanted to work. After a few sessions of repeatedly using group-building language such as "we" and "our group," changes occurred in how students began to work together and support one another. They eventually supported each other to finish tasks and encouraged one another to do their best. Many of the students' demeanors changed from defensive and making snide remarks to sensitive and offering help. Occasionally the participants were reminded that they were invited to this group and were expected to work as a team, which they eventually took to heart.

Nearly all of our sessions included extensive writing in the composition books. For some of the students, this was challenging because they struggled with reading and writing. During the first few weeks, I spent a great deal of time moving between three children in particular to help with their writing. Eventually, other children began working with the ones who wanted additional support and the participant pairings and groupings were rarely the same. By the end of the sessions, participants saw themselves as a group willing to offer and accept help from others.

Participants as Researchers

During the first session, two students asked what we should call the group because every after-school group had a name. We decided to call ourselves the Literacy Social Action Group. I explained the role of an ethnographic researcher and how they would research their own schools, communities, and homes. Essentially I was asking them to think as researchers by noticing reading and writing in everyday activities, or as Erickson (1986) explains, to see the "invisibility of everyday life" and to "make the familiar strange" (p. 121).

As the children thought more about their reading and writing activities in school and home, they became increasingly engaged with the project by sharing their observations when we met and recording their observations in their composition books. They began to notice the writing and reading activities of family and community members and to document these when possible. Following our individual formal interviews I asked the students to bring in literacy items they had mentioned, such as papers from church and magazines they read with a parent. These were then shared with the whole group. We discussed the importance of artifacts for documenting our personal notes and adding another example of print literacy to contribute additional meaning to their written words.

To document print literacy in their communities and homes, each child received a disposable camera during our second session. Because the district follows a school-of-choice policy, many of the students live in different neighborhoods so we needed to define *community*. We decided that community was the area where their home was located, where their family shopped for food and other goods, and where they spent the majority of their time outside of school. Although they lived in different communities, it was evident that the communities were similar in terms of demographics and the economic status of its community members. After establishing an understanding of community, we discussed what counted as "print literacy" and recorded these in the composition books. I added suggestions not mentioned by the participants, to develop a list of 13 examples (see Fig. 8.1).

After a week of taking photographs, the students' film was processed and photographs were returned so the students could glue their photographs to lined paper and write captions to describe the image as well as its importance in either their home or community. We assembled these 48 photographs in a binder with three sections labeled *home, community,* and *school*.

The majority of the photographs showed signs such as parking laws, street signs, and billboards. Several students photographed signs associ-

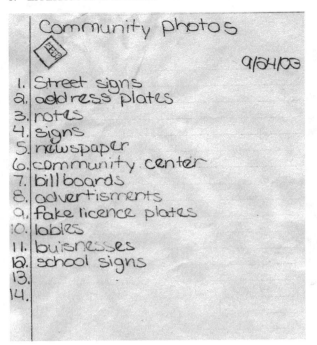

Community photos

9/24/03

1. Street signs
2. address plates
3. notes
4. signs
5. newspaper
6. community center
7. billboards
8. advertisments
9. fake licence plates
10. lables
11. buisnesses
12. school signs
13.
14.

Figure 8.1.   Kristen recorded the list generated by the group, of "what counts as print literacy" in her notebook so she could refer to this when taking photographs in her school, at home, and in her community.

ated with the hospital located less than 3 miles from the school and the nuclear substation near the school. They were extremely concerned with safety and shared narratives of their own experiences in the hospital. One student took three pictures of the substation and said the signs were necessary or else, "people could die!" By the end of the three sessions of assembling our photo journal, the children from the same communities helped each other write captions, thereby combining the photographer's and other participants' ideas of the importance of the print literacy in the photograph (see Fig. 8.2).

The children were also asked to think about all the places they visited on a regular basis, which we decided was at least once or more per week, and to record all the reading and writing that occurred while they were present. As they shared their lists, we generated more ideas of locations and discussed how each child engaged in reading and writing in those places. The most commonly visited locations were grocery stores and fast-food restaurants; however, none of the students took photographs of these places. This may have been an instance when making the "familiar strange" was difficult though they all created lists of at least 10 or more locations that were not captured on film. When I specifically asked what they read or wrote in these places, they were able to share various responses; however, it was apparently difficult to think of these on their own or when they had the cameras.

Figure 8.2. Participants took photographs of print literacy in their com- munity. For the caption, Ranecia wrote "It tells you wear [sic] all you can go in the hospital. You need to know where to go in case of an emergency." Reprinted with permission.

During the third and fourth week, we collected and represented all of their data on posters in a way that showed reading and writing at school, in the community, and in their homes. In groups of three, they gathered the data and thought about how to organize it into manageable sections. As the students prepared the three posters—(a) reading and writing at school, (b) reading and writing at home, and (c) reading and writing in our communities—they added new data prompted by the current data. The groups continually consulted one another for clarification and ideas and revisited their own notes to complete their posters.

While developing into researchers, the participants continued to coalesce as a group. The majority of our time was spent working together to generate ideas, to reflect on their own reading and writing practices, and to consider the reading and writing practices of others in their communities, homes, and school. There were certainly moments when relations disintegrated, and I found myself disciplining my participants rather than mentoring them as ethnographers, but this was to be expected when working with fifth-grade students with a variety of personalities and strengths at the end of a long school day. Often at the last moment, I was pleasantly surprised by their eagerness to help one another and refocus on our agenda.

OUT-OF-SCHOOL LITERACY PRACTICES IN THE HOME AND COMMUNITY

Religion

Church services and activities associated with church proved to be an important sociotextual domain for various literacy practices. Many participants were involved in several groups associated with church and had parents actively involved in their churches. When asked about reading and writing outside of school, Ranecia quickly listed all of her activities in church:

> Well, the thing is on Monday at church I have Young Women Rising, on Tuesday I have dance, Wednesday we have regular night service, Thursday we have choir rehearsal, Friday I don't do nothin' and I'm glad to have a rest! And then Saturday we sometimes have something and then on Sunday I have to come back!

When I asked Ranecia to think about all those days and what she reads, she quickly replied, "the Bible." When I asked her about specific groups, such as choir, she replied, "Yeah, we get these papers and we have to read them, and then in dance we have to read, um, the copy of the music but we have to make up ... things, then Young Women Rising she gives us a paper and we have to do all these skits and stuff ..."

Katie, who was also involved in several church activities, listed reading and writing practices primarily in Sunday school. These included reading directions and verses on worksheets as well as the Bible. Both participants have parents who are actively involved in church and who engage in a variety of reading and writing activities both in and outside of church. Ranecia saw her mother's role as a counselor for church members in their own home, which involved a great deal of reading and writing. Katie often observed her mother, who is one of the Sunday school teachers, reading in the classroom. Her mother also kept a chart for offerings or money and lists of visitors. Katie mentioned her father reading the words of songs printed on a piece of paper during the service and writing notes on the back. Her father was also responsible for recording the names of people who attended church on any particular day. At home, Katie saw her parents participating in a prayer group that involved writing, and her father often made labels for CDs for church.

Two other participants mentioned reading and writing in church, but with a lesser degree of involvement. Gabrielle spoke of reading church songs that were printed both in and out of songbooks and Kristen talked about reading music for choir. Their attendance appeared to be less consistent than Ranecia and Katie, but both girls found it worth mentioning in our conversations.

Shopping for Food and Clothing

When asked to make a list of all the places they visited regularly, which we
defined as at least once a week, all the students included shopping for food
and clothing. As a group they generated a list of nine grocery stores, which
included stores that also sell clothing and other items. In preparation for
the trip to the store, Katie and Gabrielle mentioned their mothers writing
lists. When discussing trips to the store and reading and writing practices
related to this location, participants talked about parents' reading and writing as well as their own. Jessica described the importance of reading at the
store to which she often accompanied her family, including her Mom, Dad,
and little sister. She explained:

> My dad has to read certain things at the store, like if he's trying to find a cer-
> tain meat or how much it costs, like this one time when we were shopping we
> were looking for good meat and I saw this meat that was 2 or something for
> $2.00 and they were both one pound and my dad read it and he said that was
> a pretty good deal and he liked it because it was honey ham, because I told
> him the good deal for ham over there.

To stress the role of reading while shopping, Jessica offered the following
example: "When we go to the grocery store we get cat litter and stuff like
that but our cat, we have to know what kind of cat food to get or else some of
them puke over it."

Jessica was not the only participant who was careful about reading labels
and signs at the grocery store. Kristen and Gabrielle also commented on
this important literacy function to make sure they were choosing the best, or
right, item. Nakita explained how she and her mother shop for a social service that provides housing and groceries for young, single mothers. They
receive a list and must refer to the list continually to make sure they are purchasing the right size diapers and correct type of baby food. Ranecia discussed how important it was for her to read the labels on the candy and food
so "you know what you are getting" as well as the cost and size of the items
when discussing purchases of clothing or shoes. Kristen and Gabrielle also
made reference to the signs above the aisles as a way to navigate their way
around the store and find particular items.

Eating Out

When asked to note all of the places they visit in a week and to record the
reading and writing associated with each place, the children generated a list
of 11 fast-food establishments, including McDonald's™, Kentucky Fried
Chicken™, and Burger King™. No writing, according to my informants, occurs at these sites, but much reading does. When asked to discuss what they

read at fast-food sites, they produced an impressive list. All of the participants said that they read the menu to decide what they wanted to eat.
Kristen and Ranecia discussed reading the price to calculate the final cost.
Kristen said she would read the amount on the cash register and always kept
her receipts in case she was given the wrong food. She then explained the
importance of having a receipt in case she got food poisoning and needed
to sue the fast-food restaurant. When I asked how often she kept her receipt,
she replied, "always!"

Journaling and Creative Writing

Many participants wrote for pleasure outside of school. Their pleasure
writing typically fell into one of two categories: *journaling, creative writing*
or a combination of both. Jessica spoke in great detail about how she wrote
in three different journals on a regular basis. She recorded stories in her
diary and "personal things" in her composition book. Her father installed
a program on her own computer, which was a Christmas present and located in her bedroom, so she could keep an electronic diary. When asked
about the reading and writing practices of family members, she discussed
her mother's Internet "life story," which is about Jessica's family. She
spoke with pride about this and how guests can visit and read the ongoing
story. Her computer diary sounded similar to her mother's activity. Like
Jessica, Ranecia kept more than one journal or diary. She described her
journal as an outlet to "write free-willing," her diary as "more personal,"
and a journal at church.

Many of the participants enjoyed writing various genres at home. Nakita
described her writing as "chapter books" rather than stories but did not
provide an explanation as to what the chapter books were about. She also
mentioned writing songs and poetry. Katie talked about writing poetry and
"writing about what people were doing, like my mom, sister and dad." Gabrielle, Jessica, and Katie shared their enjoyment of writing scary stories,
which Katie compared to Stein's *Goosebumps* books and Jessica explained as,
"Stories, like I was writing a Frankenstein story so I was using other people's
theory of that ... but this time, I used the mad scientist, well actually the scientist was just lonely and he wanted his brother from the dead ...."All three
emphasized the importance of making stories scary.

When Kristen described her story-writing process, she said, "I like to
write stories about animals, because I have these little toy animals and dogs
and stuff and I act them [the stories] out and then afterwards I write them ...
Um, I actually have a couple books of them, well not books, real books, but I
made like covers and stuff."

Kristen would then share these stories with her family members. She described three stories as one about teachers and kids, another about three

horses fighting for power, and the last one about an abandoned puppy. When asked what she reads outside of school, she mentioned the chapter books *Pony Pals*, by Betancourt, and *Puppy Patrol*, by Dale, which are similar to the themes of her own stories.

CHILDRENS' CONNECTIONS TO FAMILY MEMBERS' LITERACY PRACTICES

When asked about family members' home literacy practices, all the participants shared various and extensive activities of parents and siblings. The most common practice involved reading the local newspaper; however, only one participant had a daily newspaper delivered and her father is a journalist for that particular paper. Several other participants mentioned seeing family members reading the paper, as well as themselves reading sections such as the front page and comics, occasionally, but this required some effort to buy a copy from a local store. Katie's family bought a Sunday edition from the same local convenience store after church and the whole family read sections individually and together.

Many participants described their parents and older siblings as avid readers. Katie talked about her Mom and Dad reading books sent from her grandma and commented on how small the writing was, which led me to believe these were long chapter books. Kristen was able to share specific titles of books her mother was currently reading as well as the genre (historical fiction and nonfiction about sports) and the topics such as the Underground Railroad. She knew that her mother read these at night before she fell asleep and that this was a regular habit. She also knew her sister's favorite series were *Dear America* and *American Girls*. When asked what her family reads, Ranecia replied, "Books and books!" and explained her sister's voracious reading of chapter books. Gabrielle knew her mom had an office with many chapter books that she reads for fun. Both Ranecia and Gabrielle mentioned seeing an older sibling reading and writing essays as well as producing narratives for enjoyment, which they shared with their family. All the participants observed acts of reading and writing on a regular basis and engaged in similar practices to read a great deal of text and produce various text.

Entertainment: Media and Technology

All participants reported having at least one television in their home. When asked what they read outside of school, Katie, Nakita, and Gabrielle mentioned "reading" the television. When asked to clarify, Katie replied "the magazine (guide) and the one on TV." Both Katie and her dad read the summaries or captions to "find out about sports and movies," whereas

Nakita and Gabrielle read the closed captions. Katie and her dad also read video-game container cases and instructions to decide which game to play on Thursdays, or what they call "Daddy/Daughter" day when they spend the afternoon together playing video games. Ranecia mentioned "reading the television" by watching the news with her mom to learn about the weather.

It was not surprising that all the children mentioned having a television; however, I was surprised by how they did or did not use computer technology. Six participants reported having computers in the home but only three had access to the Internet. Ranecia mentioned reading e-mails on the computer with her mom and sister as well as proofreading e-mails before sending them. Each day, according to Ranecia, she was expected to spend 20 minutes using the computer for math, reading, and typing games. Jessica also used the computer regularly for her journal. Her mother writes an Internet "life story," pays bills and taxes electronically once a month, and "buys things off the Internet." This was the most extensive use of the computer compared to the other participants.

When asked if she uses a computer, Kristen replied that she has one in her home but is not allowed to use it. Her father, who is a newspaper journalist, uses the computer for "extra credit" at work. When at her grandma's house, Kristen uses the computer for The Print Shop® program to make brochures and create pictures. This was mainly for enjoyment and showed limited connections to school or to using the computer as a tool for acquiring information. Katie talked about having a computer but not being able to use it because of "power problems." However, she then stated that her dad makes stickers for her new books using the computer.

Literacy With Siblings

When asked about reading and writing outside of school, most participants focused on individual activities such as reading chapter books or writing their own journals, stories, and poems. However, when I asked about reading and writing in relation to others, all five of the seven participants with younger siblings talked about reading and writing with younger siblings, often while playing school. Two participants had a younger sister or brother who currently attended preschool. When I asked them to explain exactly how they "play school," their activity sounded like a replication of their own experiences in a very structured setting with a white board, homemade desk, and teacher as authority and keeper of knowledge. After 4 years of formal schooling, the participants had clear concepts of what school is supposed to look and sound like. Ranecia described her pretend school: "Regular writing ... like when you play school, I have a little sister and I play school with her. I write down like numbers, like I have a fake chalkboard, then I write down numbers and letters, and then I write down their names and do attendance and stuff."

Kristen's description sounded very similar to Ranecia's when she talked about playing school with her 4-year-old brother and third-grade sister:

> I read to my little brother. We play this little game, preschool is what we call it, and I teach [brother] letters and [sister] acts like she's in preschool too, like she doesn't know the letters ... Yeah, I teach him letters and I read books to him and then I take out things, like I make these little words and say what's this letter, what's this letter, what's this letter.

Kristen and Ranecia each assumed the role of the teacher and saw it as their responsibility to teach their siblings their "numbers and letters" in this manner.

Three participants discussed reading aloud to younger siblings and spoke in great detail about their siblings' genre preferences. Gabrielle talked about her 4-year-old sister's preference for fairy tales, especially ones with princesses. Katie talked about reading picture books about Barney™, from Mayer's *Little Critters* series, and alphabet books to her 2-year-old sister. She was not sure if these had been her books when she was younger. Jessica discussed her role in teaching her 4-year-old sister to read in an extremely serious manner. The participants who both played school and read aloud to younger siblings regarded this activity as valuable. They saw themselves as having important roles in preparing their siblings for school and showed pride when discussing these literacy activities.

Literacy Within Adult Roles

Several participants shared their enjoyment of mimicking parental literacy practices, particularly of their mothers. Gabrielle often wrote grocery lists for her mom without consulting with her. Whether or not her mother used the lists was unclear. However, she mentioned seeing her mother write lists of things she needed to do as well as grocery lists. Ranecia mimicked her mother in terms of profession. Ranecia's mother is a counselor for church members but conducts many of her sessions in their home. Ranecia giggled as she talked about sneaking past her to go to the kitchen and listening while her mother was counseling. On her own, Ranecia liked to "counsel" people by asking questions about their "issues," then writing the answers down to "help them solve it," similar to the literacy practices of her mother.

Besides playing school and mimicking professional work, several participants engaged in reading and writing activities that mimicked family members' literacy practices associated with leisure and relaxation. Nakita and Ranecia talked about reading the magazines that their mothers read for fun for beauty tips, such as *Sister 2 Sister* and *Jet* magazines. Ranecia enjoyed reading the directions, similar to Map Quest® directions from the Internet, while traveling to a new place and checking off the specific directions as they passed. Only one participant described an activity that involved the type of writing adults might do for a more utilitarian purpose. She explained how her mother, an athletic director and coach, has Kristen write to "help her." Kristen discussed how she: "Writes stuff for my mom, like sometimes she has me write lists of her students in her class and their attendance and stuff … and then I also … at cross country meets, my mom has me write things on the people names and what place they came in and stuff."

Whether or not Kristen's mother uses what Kristen has written is unclear; this type of writing mimicked what an adult might do and may have had real-life practical use as well.

SCHOOL LITERACY: BIMODAL EDUCATION IN ONE CLASSROOM

The literacy practices of school, described by the children, differed from their home literacies. Perhaps what is most interesting to note is the difference in the types of education the participants are receiving. Kristen participates in two gifted and talented programs intended for academically high achieving students in math, language arts, and science. Students are selected for this program based on standardized test scores, teacher recommendation, and grades. She was the only student in the group of participants who was in this program. When discussing the type of reading and writing practices in school, Kristen's list far exceeded the other participants' and the type of reading and writing she was exposed to in school was noticeably different from that of her classmates.

When asked to respond to the question, "What do you read in school?," the five participants who are not enrolled in the gifted and talented program stated the following: science, math, and social studies textbooks; worksheets; silent reading; the teacher's writing on the board; and the calendar. Two participants mentioned reading the print on the walls and posters "when you are bored." When asked which school reading activity they liked the best, four stated silent reading. Jessica said this was her favorite time because she "really enjoys reading fiction and biographies" and summarized a biography of Beatrix Potter that she recently finished. Gabrielle reported that her favorite reading activity was the time spent in her small reading group when they read books aloud, thought about predictions, summarizing and retelling what they read, and had time to read their own individual books. Kristen explained that her favorite reading and writing activities were related to the degree of choice. Other participants mentioned a preference for activities that they were able to choose and tended to be more authentic. When asked what their least favorite reading activity was, two said textbooks, one said worksheets, and one said biographies.

Kristen's reading experiences varied a great deal from the other five participants, reflecting her attendance 4 days a week in the gifted and talented program. She discussed reading a passage about Archimedes and his contribution to science, investigations about heat and materials related to science, the novel *Old Yeller* by Gipson (1990) and self-evaluation charts as part of the academically highest book club group. Similar to the other participants, her favorite activity was silent reading but her least favorite activity was music because, "the music is complicated to read."

The participants varied in what they wrote, as well. The five participants who were not enrolled in the gifted and talented program discussed writing on worksheets and copying what the teacher wrote on the board. In contrast, Kristen discussed writing about experiments, plot graphs for an autobiography, and stories when she completed the assigned work. Four participants, including Kristen, shared that their favorite writing activity was journaling in the morning. Two stated their favorite writing activity was anything related to math.

The type of education Kristen is experiencing is markedly different than the other participants who are not in the gifted and talented program. One other student in the group, who was not part of the study, also participated in the gifted and talented program. She and Kristen were the only ones in the group with two parents with college degrees, suggesting a tracking system with social reproduction results (Bourdieu, 1986; Oakes, 1986).

FROM THE PARTICIPANTS' POINT OF VIEW: CONNECTIONS BETWEEN HOME AND SCHOOL LITERACY PRACTICES

One focus of this study was to look for connections between home and school literacy practices. Responses to three questions in the semistructured interview as well as informal conversations provided a great deal of insight as to how the participants viewed the home/community and school literacy connections and disconnects. In response to the question, "Does reading and writing in school prepare you for reading and writing outside of school?," the answers varied from an enthusiastic response by Nakita, who happens to struggle a great deal with in-school reading and writing, to Katie's nonchalant, flat response, and Jessica's focus on practicality. Nakita's response sounded practiced, as if she were repeating a mantra, when she said, "When you learn something in school you take it into your life and you remember it forever!"

Kristen, Jessica, and Ranecia could identify the usefulness of reading and writing at school and its connection to life outside of school. Kristen said, "Yeah, in Kindergarten I learned the ABCs which helped me to do reading and writing later." Jessica related school literacy to daily activities and economics by stating, "Yeah, I think everything revolves around reading and writing because if you didn't know how to read you couldn't write checks or you could never read how much money you have and you couldn't pay for what you want." Jessica talked about money frequently and saw reading and writing as a tool to deal with financial dilemmas. Ranecia also saw reading and writing as a way to acquire goals beyond elementary and high school. She replied:

> Yes, because when the summer was getting to an end ... well, I don't know because after I do work at school I have to go home and do it at home ... it's going to help me be a doctor ... like learning hard words like *facetious* and *expeditiously* ... I don't know how to pronounce them, but ... what do they mean?

Katie did not see a strong connection. She was ambivalent when I asked if reading and writing in school prepares her for reading and writing outside of school. Her response was, "It helps me remember. I guess reading and writing in school helps for home ... but when the school day is done, it's like yay, carry on and go home and play with my dad and sister."

I also asked each child if reading and writing at school was similar or different from reading and writing outside of school to learn whether they viewed a connection between home and school. Again, their responses varied tremendously. They stated:

Nakita: Like in school you learn how to count your money, so if you like go to the store and you give a five dollar bill and it costs something, then you say, oh and I know I get back this amount of money.

Kristen: At school you just have to do what the teacher says but at home you can read and write whatever you want.

Jessica: Everything has to do with reading and writing ... it's possibly the same, like reading labels or books and stuff like that ... numbers too, math ...

Ranecia: Mmm-hmm, it's mostly the same type of writing, like mostly in school we're working in cursive and at home I'm working on cursive at home and that's the main focus.

Katie: Similar? Kind of hard, no ... I think, I don't write anything about math when I get home or reading, just what people are doing or stuff like that.

Unlike the other participants, Katie did not see a connection between the reading and writing she did at home and school. Katie's experiences and perspective of school is similar to what Lareau (2000) described in her research as the separation between some working-class families and school.

She found that many families "saw schooling as something that took place on the school site. They drew a clear line between school and home." (p. 115). Katie engaged in a tremendous amount of reading and writing at home and in her community such as reading chapter books, writing poetry, and participating in Sunday school. She saw her parents reading chapter books sent by her grandmother, as well as her mom teaching Sunday school, and both parents having an active role in church that required reading and writing. However, Katie did not identify a connection between her home and community literacy practices and those associated with school.

Learning to Read and Write

The participants have only been in school for 5½ years, but maintain vivid memories of learning to read and write. One question was intended to learn more about their personal experiences with learning to read and write. The responses to the question, "Do you remember your feelings about learning to read and write?," were surprising.

Kristen, who participates in the gifted and talented program, remembered the letters she had difficulty with and how she felt when she thought she was the only one who did not understand what was happening in Kindergarten. She stated, "Learning to read and write was hard at first because I felt like I didn't know what other people were doing ... like I remember being frustrated in kindergarten, like with the letters *g* ... and *k*." Jessica remembered details of reading with the reading specialist and seemed embarrassed when explaining how, "I had a tutor for reading ... at school and that helped me figure out writing. We started off small like with *Curious George* books, by Rey, in Mrs. B's room." Both Kristen and Jessica, who struggled with learning to read and write, are now avid writers and readers. In fact, they view themselves as competent readers and writers and proudly discuss their textual production. Kristen writes stories at home and plays preschool with her younger sister and brother to teach letters and numbers. Jessica keeps three journals, has read all of the *Harry Potter* books by Rowling, sees her mom engaged in a variety of writing practices, and is helping her sister learn how to read and write. The two participants who struggled the most with learning to read and write appeared to engage in more reading and writing outside of school than the other participants and were currently doing well in school. It's impossible to know whether the struggle to read and write strengthened their desire to read and write more, but it is an interesting pattern to consider.

Ranecia, who mentioned her professional goal of becoming a doctor, shared a great deal about her past as it related to the question. Since she changed caretakers at the time she learned how to read and write, this was a challenging question at first, but she quickly became adamant about her response. She stated, "Oh, I love reading and writing. Was it then … or was it, I don't know. I think I learned it at home. I know for a fact it was my mom!" She connected this important phase in her life, of learning to read and write, to a personal relationship, and whether or not this was the one person who taught her to read and write was less important to her than her needing this to be true. It was evident that Ranecia knew the value of reading and writing and linked this to a very special person in her life, her adoptive mom.

Katie, who saw very little connection between home, school, and community literacy practices, shared an interesting analogy to how it felt to learn to read and write. She said, "I think I learned to write in preschool or before that, but I learned to read then, but I'm not sure. I learned how to read more in Kindergarten or first grade. When I first started I felt excited, just like when I was at lunch (and) Jessica was right there and I helped Jessica go across the monkey bars!"

This was surprising since most of Katie's discussions about school were not at all animated. She observed a great deal of reading and writing at home and engaged in reading and writing on her own, but school did not seem to excite her. She mentioned on several occasions that school is sometimes boring, which may explain her sense of disconnect between home, community, and school.

CONCLUSION

Most of the children in this study are experiencing disconnects between home and school literacy practices, which Dewey (1902/1956) discussed a century ago. This leads one to question how much schooling has changed to meet the needs of children. It is not surprising that the favorite reading and writing activities of the participants were related to choice. The children found the most satisfaction in silent reading at school because they could choose what to read. Their favorite writing activity was 20 minutes of journaling each morning because they were producers of their own text for their own purposes and they were relating this activity to what occurred outside of school. Kristen's statement, "At school you just have to do what the teacher says, but at home you can read and write whatever you want," rang true for all of the students.

As stated earlier, the purpose of this study was to gain insights into the personal meanings and values assigned to literacy in different contexts by young children who are attending an urban elementary school in an after-school program. There seems to be a common belief both inside and outside of formal education that certain children are not succeeding in school because they are unprepared (Snow, Burns, & Griffin, 1998). The belief is that children who underachieve in school do not experience many literacy events in their lives outside of school. For the children in this case study, nothing could be further from the truth.

The nine fifth-grade students from an inner-city, low-achieving elementary school were engaged in a wide variety of reading and writing in their homes and communities, many of these events reflecting the vast array of literacy events they experienced in their homes and communities. Five of the seven students read and wrote with younger siblings and saw their parents encouraging read-aloud activities with preschool age siblings. It is unreasonable to assume that five of these seven children are academically behind because they live in environments that do not include literacy use or because they are not engaged in literacy practices of their own outside of school.

In a chapter titled "Home, Learning and Education," Barton and Hamilton (1998) considered the connections or lack of between various domains. They state, "There is a distinctiveness to many home literacy practices, but what is more striking is the range of different literacies which are carried out in the home, including work and school literacies which are brought home where they mingle together" (p. 188). Playing school, keeping a journal, participating in Sunday school and church, were all examples of the different home and community literacies engaged in by the participants and look similar to schooling literacy practices.

Barton and Hamilton (1998) also discuss the types of modeling parents or caregivers provide, which in this case study happened frequently (e.g., writing e-mails, counseling for church, reading novels and magazines, and writing for a variety of purposes). They go on to claim that the term *family literacy* is part of a deficit model because it focuses on what low socioeconomic status (SES) families and children lack as compared to middle-class ones rather than on their strengths. Unfortunately, the construct of family literacy has taken this turn, a turn away from the original focus of family literacy research exemplified by that of Taylor and Dorsey-Gaines (1988), who documented similar rich literacy lives of low-SES families.

Purcell-Gates (1996) found a wide range of frequency and type of literacy events in low-SES homes and cautioned against essentialist claims. Some homes had virtually no reading and writing events and others had a great deal. It seems clear that for the children in this case study, it is not enough to believe that the participants were not doing well because they failed to read and write outside of school or experience literacy use before beginning formal schooling. Family literacy was entrenched in these participants' lives, suggesting the cause of their academic struggles lies beyond the individual and their families.

After conducting this study and learning more about the out-of-school literacy lives of these nine children, it becomes increasingly difficult to ignore Dewey's (1902/1956) philosophy about the school and the child. We need to "consider the relationship of the school to the life and development of the children in the school" (p. 31) in order to value the knowledge and literacy practices they bring to the classroom. In the district in which this study was situated, the children who appear to struggle most attend the least resourced urban schools with the highest rates of student mobility. In these schools, little choice is offered to teachers or students. High-stakes testing and prepackaged curriculum in this district, particularly the elementary school featured in this case study, limit the freedom of the teachers to shape pedagogy to the needs of their students, and the students are afforded less time for authentic textual production and authentic activities related to reading. This was blatantly obvious when comparing the reading and writing practices of the few children in the gifted and talented program with those who were not part of the program. The results of this analysis reveal that the children in the Literacy Social Action Group were highly engaged in a rich array of literacy practices in their homes and communities. I conclude that the onus is on schools and educators to acknowledge the values and literacy practices children are bringing to the classroom and use these to inform and shape pedagogy to move toward academic achievement for all students.

REFERENCES

American Girls series. New York: Pleasant Company Publications.
Barton, D., & Hamilton, M. (1998). *Local literacies: Reading and writing in one community.* New York: Routledge.
Betancourt, J. *Pony Pals series.* New York: Scholastic.
Bourdieu, P. (2001). *Language & symbolic power.* Cambridge, MA: Harvard University Press.
Cope, B., & Kalantzis, M. (Eds.). (2000). *Multiliteracies: Literacy learning and design of social futures.* New York: Routledge.
Dale, J. *Puppy Patrol series.* New York: Scholastic.
Dear America series. New York: Scholastic.
Dewey, J. (1956). *The child and the curriculum & The school and society.* Chicago: The University of Chicago Press. (Original work published 1902)
Erickson, F. (1986). Qualitative methods in research on teaching. In M. C. Wittrock (Ed.), *Handbook of research on teaching* (3rd ed., p. 121). New York: Macmillan.
Gipson, F. (1990). *Old yeller.* New York: Harper Trophy.
Jet Magazine. Chicago: Johnson.
Lareau, A. (2000). *Home advantage: Social class and parental intervention in elementary education.* New York: Rowman & Littlefield.
Luke, A. (2003). Literacy and the other: A sociological approach to literacy research and policy in multilingual societies. *Reading Research Quarterly, 38*(1), 132–141.
Mayer, M. *Little Critters series.* New York: Random House.
Oakes, J. (1986). *Keeping track: How schools structure inequality.* New Haven: Yale University Press.

Purcell-Gates, V. (1996). Stories, coupons, and the *TV Guide*: Relationships between home literacy experiences and emergent literacy knowledge. *Reading Research Quarterly, 31*, 406–428.

Rey, H. A. (1973). *Curious George*. New York: Houghton Mifflin.

Rowling, J. K. (1998). *Harry Potter and the Sorcerer's Stone*. New York: Scholastic.

Sister2 Sister Magazine. Washington, DC: Sister 2 Sister Publishing.

Snow, C., Burns, M. S., & Griffin, P. (1998). *Preventing reading difficulties in young children*. Washington, DC: National Academy Press.

Stein, R. L. *Goosebumps series*. New York: Harper Collins.

Taylor, D., & Dorsey-Gaines, C. (1988). *Growing up literate: Learning from inner-city families*. Portsmouth, NH: Heinemann.

Chapter 9

"You Have to Be Bad or Dumb to Get in Here": Reconsidering the In-School and Out-of-School Literacy Practices of At-Risk Adolescents

J. David Gallagher
Michigan State University

For the last period of the day, 22 ninth graders enter the classroom, half of them looking tired and ready to take a nap, while the others already have their coats on to leave school at the end of the period. Each time they enter through the doors, the same six students run for the two couches dispersed at opposite ends of the room. The students who are not lucky enough to find a seat on the couch find themselves at one of the desks pushed together in the middle of the room, facing the whiteboard nailed to the wall at the front. These 22 students represent a diverse group of ethnic communities. They are all recognized by various school personnel as being greatly at-risk for failing and/or dropping out of school. For this reason they are placed in this particular school as an opportunity for them to "get back on track" in their schooling. The school is part of a districtwide initiative to recognize and provide a proactive intervention for the students who are on a downward path in their schooling (e.g., poor attendance, grades, behavior) and act as a springboard for their future years in high school.

As a result of this unique set-up (for adolescent students recognized as "at-risk" of dropping out), the class provided a promising context within

155

which to address Luke's questions for language and literacy-in-education policy: "Which linguistic competencies, discourses and textual resources, and multiliteracies are accessible ... [and] how are these resources recognized and misrecognized, remediated and converted in school-based literacy instruction" (2003, pp. 139–140). The purpose of the study was to explore the texts and purposes for literacy in the lives of the students who are "struggling" in a classroom at an urban school, and to come to an understanding of how these practices come into contact with the school practices in one English classroom.

RESEARCHER LOCATION

My past work in urban schools (as a teacher, tutor, and researcher) influenced and informs my interest in understanding how to reinvent the classroom experience for students who have given up on school (and on whom, quite often, school has given up). These students move from class to class, often apathetic to classroom activities, struggling to stay awake in class, and disconnected from most teachers. Such students have always interested me because, although they seemed unengaged with reading, writing, and speaking in the classroom, they seemed to be quite engaged (and adept) at reading, writing, and speaking when in the hallways between classes and outside the doors of the school. This phenomenon has led me to explore the relationship between the in- school and out-of-school literacies in the lives of students (Alvermann, Hinchman, Moore, Phelps, & Waff, 1998; Moje, 2002).

I met the classroom teacher of this case study the previous year, and I was intrigued by the way he encouraged his students to engage in the curriculum by forming personal relationships and individualized instruction for the variety of interests and abilities in his classes. Therefore, for this new class, I volunteered to tutor while undertaking this research to learn more about the ways students such as these use literacy in their lives.

For two periods a day, 2 days a week, I served as a classroom tutor, helping students with their daily class tasks and activities. During a few of the classes, I read with from one to three students in the hallway. To the students, I was seen as a "university tutor," someone who cannot and would not "get them in trouble," but who could provide a helping hand when they were struggling with their assignments.

Although I was not a teacher and wouldn't tattle on them, my looks, role, and demeanor in the classroom led them to believe I was "one of those guys." During one of my participant interviews, one girl, in response to a question about the texts she reads in school, asked with a smile, "Besides the books that you guys give us?" Understanding that the students saw me as a tutor in the classroom, I was aware that this role might influence the data that I would receive in the interviews. However, I felt that it was important that I be helping out when I could. When students called me over to help them with an activity, I was willing and able to provide models and suggestions for them.

THE CASE: ONE CLASSROOM OF "AT-RISK" ADOLESCENTS

To be a student in this particular classroom was to be identified as being deficient and/or resistant of academic literacy. "Constructing" the students as deficient of literacy, the school's goal was to give the students literacy tools (proper grammar, vocabulary training, essay structure, canonical texts) to succeed in future classes. This intention could be seen, as an example, in the degree and quality of the attention given to vocabulary words. In response to the districtwide pacing guides, each week the teacher listed a group of the words on the board (e.g., *discretion, affliction, reckoning, innocence*), and throughout the week, the students would be directed to engage in a variety of activities intended to teach them the new words.

Inevitably, the students in the class concurred with this construction of deficiency. As one student explained to me so succinctly, "You have to be bad or dumb to get in here."

Four Focal Students

The four focal students for this case study represented the diversity of this ninth-grade urban classroom (e.g., two African American students, one European American student, and one Mexican American student). Three of the four focal students attended consistently and participated in class to the extent that any of the other students in the classroom did. Allessandra (all names are pseudonyms) was one of the top students in the class. She passed in most of her work (e.g., essays, daily writing assignments) and was actively engaged in class. Self-identifying as Mexican, Allessandra was born and had lived in the same city for her entire life. She enjoyed traveling with her family, and she wrote about herself in an essay, "I basically just like to be simple and have fun." She understood school as a pathway for going to college and having a successful job.

Loving hip-hop music and cooking, Lashon (African American) is a mother to a 1-year-old boy, and was still involved in a relationship with the father at the time of the data collection. She dreamed of getting her high school diploma, going to college, and becoming a judge, in order "to send people to jail." She, like Allessandra, was born in the same urban city she had lived in all of her life, living with her large extended family. In class, Lashon participated when asked but she often forgot and failed to turn in her assignments.

Marshon (African American) also refused to work on assignments, and he repeatedly told me that he dislikes reading and writing in school, especially reading aloud in class. When discussing his past school experiences, he stated that he failed to do anything last year in school. "That's why I'm [in this class]." He would rather play role-play and video games, Monopoly™, hang out, and listen to music with his friends.

Living in and out of three different homes—with her mother, father, and grandparents—Carlee (European American) attended class only about one quarter of the time that I was there. When she did attend class, she usually spent much of the time chatting and passing notes to her friends in class, or asking to visit the nurse. She mentioned to me that when she began to read any book, she would become quickly bored; however, she enjoys writing poetry and hanging out with her friends. During one of her interviews, she expressed her anxiety about her father's opposition to her dating an African American student, something she often wrote about in her poetry. Carlee's attention to this dilemma reminds us that each of these students was an actor in a variety of situations played out in a range of different social and cultural contexts through their school and nonschool lives.

I selected these four students because (a) they were fairly typical of the students in the class, and (b) they were the only ones to return signed permission slips.

THE DIVERSITY OF OUT-OF-SCHOOL LITERACY PRACTICES OF "STRUGGLING" ADOLESCENTS

Although the students in the ninth-grade English class were often seen by the school as students who were deficient in literacy, the students revealed to me the many ways in which literacy mediated their lives outside (and, in unexpected ways, inside) of school. The students reported a wide variety of reading or writing activities that were part of their everyday lives. To help them think about the texts in their lives, at various times during the interviews I prompted them with a variety of possible sociotextual domains (e.g., fashion, enrichment activities, church, sports, entertainment) in which written texts may have been involved. With this prompting, each student elaborated on a variety of texts that they considered essential and that mediated their daily lives, as well as the vast array of social and cultural purposes for engaging in each of the literacy practices. Although there were textual commonalities among the four focal students, each of them reported diverse textual worlds.

LITERACY AND PASSION

What I began noticing during my time with all of the students is that they not only used literacy to navigate their everyday lives (e.g., reading the T.V. guide, making shopping lists, checking the news in newspapers), they each passionately read and wrote texts as a means of participating in activities that were entertaining, important for a means to some end, and/or for understanding one's part of their social world. Both the texts and functions of literacy for these students were determined by the activities that were structured for identifiable sociocultural purposes . For these students, culture-specific practices were embedded in three fluid spheres: in the home/community sphere; in the sphere of youth culture (i.e., what it means to be a teenager in the city); and in the "official" sphere of the classroom. Each of these *spheres*, defined as social and cultural networks of social practice, provided opportunities for the students to engage in literacy for (culture-specific) sociocultural purposes. These broadly defined cultural networks of social practice generally have their own ways of participating, within a social network, with their own particular shared understandings (Dyson, 1993). A better understanding of the spheres that literacy mediates and how the students negotiate the boundaries of these different spheres, will afford literacy researchers a better understanding of the nature of literacy in the lives of adolescents youth (Moje, 2002).

"I COULD JUST SIT THERE FOR HOURS, AND WRITE EVERYTHING DOWN": LITERACY IN THE HOME/ COMMUNITY SPACE

Each of the students engaged in certain literacy practices because of particular practices in place specific to some dimension of the home or community social networks. One of the activities in the home community that the students used literacy for was cooking. Marshon said that his father's friends would often tell him and his father of different ways of cooking common things, like Ramen Noodles™, that he would write down and try at some point.

For Lashon, cooking was more than simply a necessary activity that she did when she came home from school everyday. Cooking was a hobby and passion of hers. While discussing her fascination with TV cooking shows, she exclaimed, "I could just sit there for hours, and write everything down." Lashon would watch shows dedicated solely to cooking, surf the Internet looking for new and innovative recipes, and follow written recipes that had been passed down in her family. One instance in which literacy mediated Lashon's passion for cooking was when, after an episode of *Emeril Live* (Katz, 2003), she became excited about the appearance of a lime cheesecake Emeril had just made. She wrote down the required ingredients for the recipe, "and made one just like how [Emeril] did." When her mother needed to work late, Lashon would step in to prepare the dinner meal for the family. This family role provided the context within which Lashon learned to cook and to enjoy it. Understanding that the family recipes were important to her and the family, Lashon created a family recipe book consisting of the many recipes that had been passed down in the family.

The networks that were sustained through the home/community sphere became a major source for literacy for these students. As pointed out by Barton and Hamilton (1998), reciprocal networks of exchange are a prime medium for literacy engagement as people support and communicate with one another. Carlee used letter writing to correspond with members of her family who lived in all parts of the country. For Carlee, the purpose of these letters was to inform family members "that I'm staying off the streets and keeping busy."

Likewise, the role of support in social networks became evident in Allessandra's correspondence with her older brother who was currently serving time in jail. Recognizing that she had a social and family responsibility to write to him when other people in his life were not, she continued a correspondence through mail with her older brother. Negotiating this relationship with her brother, as a sister and a supporter, is a sophisticated and socially valuable literacy skill that is shaped by relationship and institutional structures. Her correspondence with her brother is a mature and socially important practice that she adopted out of the desire to participate in the network of support. Moje (2002) argued that educators must begin to view adolescents' out-of-school literacy practices, such as these that are negotiated across contexts and institutional barriers, as valuable tools for supporting literacy learning in school.

When Allesandra decides to continue the correspondence with her brother when all others in his support network stop, she exerts agency, identifying herself as a supportive family member and a sophisticated member of a mature network of social support. Likewise, as Carlee writes her family members to assure them that she is "staying off the streets," she positions herself as an adolescent who is in charge of her social situation. Carlee uses letter writing in order to take control of her world. Exchanging letters serves both a personally and socially supportive role, as well as a way of negotiating space within a community. Indeed, these are essential tools for each of the students' lives. As Carlee and Allessandra read and write texts as part of their relationships with their family members, they are actively negotiating their identities within these communities.

Another area in which the home/community allowed for literacy practices was with storybook reading. What became apparent was that this family practice led to adolescents reading to their younger siblings as well as being read to by their older siblings when growing up. This is a family practice (perhaps influenced by schooling) that offered many opportunities for the adolescents to share in literacy practices within the family. The idea that these students assume responsibilities for reading with their younger siblings must be explored as to how it facilitates literacy development over time, and how they become apprenticed into the practice. Exploring how to connect this literacy practice with academic practices taught in school might be beneficial for these students who are seen as deficient with reading. As argued by Barton and Hamilton (1998), studies of family literacy can give us the opportunity to rethink the home—school literacy connections, and lead to a more dynamic understanding of literacy across these domains.

LITERACY IN YOUTH CULTURE

The second social sphere in which literacy was important was in the students' experiences and identities as teenagers, and consumers and producers of youth culture. *Youth culture* is defined here as the social sphere that constitutes what it means to be an adolescent living in an urban area and to be a youth in the popular cultural world (i.e., the music they listen to, the films they watch, the signs and symbols they use to identify themselves as part of the group). Like all cultures, this space is in no way static. It is constantly metamorphosing as students negotiate the space. Studies of literacy in youth culture reveal how students navigate a variety of texts, and through these interactions, "make sense of and take power of their worlds" (Moje, 2002, p. 217). All four of these students engaged in reading and writing in authentic ways as they mediated the various texts saturating their everyday lives.

Listening to hip-hop was a major theme that ran through all four students' interviews. All were active listeners of hip-hop, and mentioned that they read the song titles on the CD cases and the lyrics downloaded from the Internet. Lashon bought *Word-Up!* and *Jet* (popular culture magazines) to learn of news of her favorite artists (e.g., B2K, Chingy, Nelly, Snoop Dogg). She said that she reads these magazines in order to "catch-up," revealing the importance of being up-to-date when locating and identifying oneself in the youth culture space.

Lashon spoke highly of her computer skills for finding lyrics on the Internet for her favorite artists, prompting her classmates to ask her to help them to do the same. Lashon quite often would share magazines and lyrics with her cousin who was also "crazy" about B2K. Alvermann and Hagood (2000) argued that it makes good sense to understand adolescents' loyalties with particular music artists and other fandoms as similar to our tastes and passions for particular objects. According to Alvermann and Hagood (2000), adolescent fandoms for things like particular music tastes and fashion styles (as was the case for Allessandra) should be seen as no different than our own passions for particular literature or films. Therefore, understanding these adolescents' fandom for hip-hop as a taste and preference, it makes sense for educators to then view these as resources and pathways into the passionate literacy lives of adolescent youth.

One particular passion that consumes the time and attention of many youth are video games. Marshon was an avid video game enthusiast, and spent a great deal of his time looking at a variety of Web sites related to video game "cheat" codes. These codes would enable him to experience parts of the game or become characters in the game that he would not otherwise experience without the codes (www.miniclip.com; www.cheatplanet.com). Within the actual video games, themselves, there are a wide variety of written texts that comprise the video gaming experience, such as the texts that are embedded in the game that determine the player's decisions and actions. There are also video game booklets that the game manufacturers produce that Marshon reads "when I get stuck." Marshon told me that he does not read the manual unless he runs into a problem, a problem situated in the activity of the game. Video games have increasingly been viewed as a technology that may have a great deal to teach us about literacy and how students learn and understand literacy learning (Gee, 2003). Easily dismissed as purely fun and entertainment, video games require and promote active reading and navigating practices within situated activities that are completed for pleasure and entertainment by youth.

Part of the literacy engagement of the youth culture has to do with the vernacular literacy texts that are produced by these students. Camitta (1993) defined vernacular text as: "that which is closely associated with culture which is neither elite nor institutional, which is traditional and indigenous to the diverse cultural processes of communities as distinguished from the uniform, inflexible standards of institutions" (pp. 228–229). Vernacular texts for these youth are those texts that are created within the space allowed by their social lives and cultures.

When Carlee first heard that I was interested in students' literacies in and out of school, she immediately responded, "I write my own poems." I first was thrilled that she would be eager to tell me this, considering she had been so resistant in class prior to this. After thinking about her comment a bit longer, I realized that she may also have been using literacy to position herself in the class and in her world. Carlee's comment, along with my discussions with her, revealed that her poems allowed her to "express her emotions," and produce texts that were embedded in the noninstitutional, unofficial sphere. Through my discussions with her, I began to see the role that her poems played in her life. She informed me that she often uses codes in the poems, as a way for only her to understand them. She would only share these poems with someone very close to her because she has written about personal topics, such as her father's disapproval toward her and her boyfriend's interracial relationship. Carlee's vernacular writing became a tool for her to take control and manipulate the realities of her own social and cultural world.

LITERACY IN THE OFFICIAL SCHOOL SPHERE

The third sphere in which literacy played a part of the students' lives was within the official/school world. The practices in this sphere are what most educators refer to as school literacy practices (e.g., formal written essays, worksheets, cannonical texts, textbooks, and traditional dialogues about texts). Not surprisingly, students reported these same literacy practices for their in-school literacy texts and practices. In this one classroom alone, the students were asked to engage in the following literacy practices: (a) formal, five-paragraph essay writing; (b) creating paragraphs that interconnect the week's vocabulary words; (c) writing names on the classroom attendance sheet; (d) copying definitions out of the dictionary; (e) reading traditional short stories from the course textbook; and (f) reading short stories of mythological texts. Topics for the five-paragraph essays included: an essay (biography) about the teacher; an autobiography, goals/dreams/school, fear, film review, music (song and lyrics), one's major life transitions, favorite quote, and argumentative essay; students were free to choose the topic.

The students were asked to complete an essay each week, and the teacher would spend time modeling what he might write for the topic, and then allow the class time to write in class. The teacher spent at least one to two periods a week introducing and working with the week's vocabulary words that were taken from the districtwide pacing guide. (It was important to the teacher for the students to be experiencing similar curriculum as the students in the other high schools in the district, in order for his students to be on-track with them the next year). At the end of the week, the teacher would quiz the students on the various vocabulary words that were discussed during the week.

In other classes, these students experienced similar types of literacy texts and practices. All the students mentioned the textbooks that were used in their math, science, and social studies classes. In her social studies class, Carlee had to read the newspaper for particular assignments. The students mentioned that they had journals in some of their other classes, used primarily to write notes from the board. The texts that students were being asked to read and write were clearly part of a different sphere than the texts and purposes for literacy in the other two social spheres.

BORDERLAND LITERACY PRACTICES

The three spheres just mentioned reveal the social networks in which literacy practices are embedded in the lives of these adolescents. Unlike classic views of culture, these sociocultural spheres are without rigid boundaries. The fluidity of these spheres allows for literacy practices to be simultaneously connected to more than one sphere. These literacy practices find themselves on the border of these social networks, as in the case of Allessandra looking up the cinema times in the newspaper in order for her to go to the movies with her mother and friend. Shopping at the nearby mall and going to the movies for Allessandra was on the boundary of the peer and home/community sphere. Often the literacy practices of these students revealed texts and purposes for literacy on the boundary between social networks.

The fluidity of the spheres also provides the means for literacy practices to cross borders, and be exported from one sphere to another. The dynamic nature of these spheres of social practice present an interconnected web of social networks across spheres that are shifting and evolving. Many of the literacy practices that were in the home were facilitated by the students' abilities to read and write, skills learned through formal schooling. In addition, some of the practices that were involved in the home/community sphere involved the influence of school literacy practices. For example, when Marshon was required to read a self-selected book in Grade 7, he chose *A Child Called "It": One Child's Courage to Survive,* by Dave Pelzer (1995), which his mother had read and recommended. While reading the book, he discussed it with his mother, as well as wrote a book report for class. The literacy practice of reading books and textbooks entered the household on a number of occasions, sometimes interacting with home/community spheres, other times remaining in the official school sphere.

More often than school texts and purposes entering the home sphere, peer and home/community texts and purposes entered the school hallways and the classroom. There were a few peer and home/community practices that were imported to the classroom. The essay topics that the students were required to write were often intended to tap into the students' peer and home/community spheres. Their autobiography, film review, and essay about their favorite song invited the students to write about some of the things that are affiliated with their nonschool experiences. In this way, the teacher was trying to incorporate the students' interests and experiences from outside the classroom in order to motivate them to write about what they know well—their favorite music and movies. Although recommended by many, this pedagogical attempt at building on what the students bring to class did not manage to provide meaningful authentic purposes for the students. These students still approached the essay as a five-paragraph essay for the teacher, and, although the essays were seeking to include out-of-school experiences, the purposes for literacy were not imported from the peer and/or home/community sphere.

Imports of peer and home/community texts and purposes into the school sphere did occur, though. Lashon's experience with newspapers (she reported reading a variety of sections of the newspaper), along with her enthusiasm and passion for participating in the production of a newspaper made reading and writing for the school newspaper an important, authentic practice for her. In her middle school, Lashon was on the school newspaper staff and she was waiting for her current school to start their newspaper. This overlap between Lashon's reading the newspaper in the home/community sphere and her participating in the writing of the school newspaper reveals a successful literacy import.

The students in the class were quite adept at finding space within the halls and in the classroom to engage in their "unofficial" literacies, especially when the teacher was involved in teaching a reading or writing lesson as part of the official curriculum. These literacy practices took many forms. The students brought in their own literature to read (i.e., J. K. Rowling's *Harry Potter*, comic books, and various magazines), passed notes in class, and wrote graffiti on the desks and blackboard. For the first 10 minutes of one class period, I saw one student reading a comic book, while she was quietly chatting with the student next to her who was flipping through two different *Paintball* magazines. In another class period, one student brought his own newspaper into the classroom, and for 15 minutes (while the teacher was reviewing the vocabulary words for the week), he searched for his name in the local newspaper as a result of a recent indictment. These literacy practices on the boundary of the peer and official school sphere were unsanctioned literacy practices, unrecognized by the official school institution.

It was apparent that these students engaged in literacy activities for purposeful and important reasons in ways that had very little to do with the official curriculum the teacher set forth (Dyson, 1993; Gutierrez & Stone, 2000). These borderland literacies often become hybrid literacy practices, the creation of a new practice in the interaction of the different spheres.

One of the most popular literacy practices in the borderlands of peer and the official/school sphere was the abundant note passing in class. Lashon described her experience passing notes in class: "We write notes everyday … I just wrote a note to a guy, but he didn't write me back … [My friends and I] [write] about what we're doing over the weekend." Passing notes was not a usual practice for these students outside of the classroom; therefore, through the interaction of these two spheres (peer and school/official) a new, hybrid literacy was formed.

In one instance, Carlee and another student were discussing an incident at a party they had been to the night before. They were engaged in a lively discussion and were asked a few times by the teacher to stop talking. It was then that the student who was talking with Carlee said, "I need to write this down," and produced about a half page of text, and gave it to Carlee to read. This literacy act was a result of the students using literacy to claim space in the classroom for an authentic purpose—sharing information and feelings in the service of maintaining social bonds.

Understanding the literacies in the classroom as hybrid literacies may be helpful for understanding the negotiation between the teacher and students. Rosaldo refers to two different notions of hybridity:

> Hybridity can imply a space betwixt and between two zones of purity ... On the other hand, hybridity can be understood as the ongoing condition of all human cultures, which contain no zones of purity because they undergo continuous processes of transculturation (two-way borrowing and lending between cultures). (cited in Cazden, 2000, p. 257)

In Rosaldo's second view of hybridity, the notion of transculturation speaks to the transactional nature of the literacies when involved in the borderlands, not one building off another, but a borrowing of each in the creation of new hybrid literacies. The transactional nature of these spaces, along with the fluid notion of zones, provides a look at a literacy practice that is created while on the boundaries. The hybrid texts and literacy practices that are created in the borderlands between spheres reveal how students negotiate diverse contexts with their appropriate resources. Further study of how students negotiate these spaces (i.e., borderlands between social and cultural spheres) can further our understanding of the creativity of these literacy practices, and the amphibious nature of the negotiation of different contexts (Moje, 2002).

TOWARD A RECONCEPTUALIZATION OF ADOLESCENTS' LITERACY PRACTICES

Apparent in each of the student's lives was a passionate engagement in the literacy practices that were culture-specific to three fluid social spaces: home/community, youth culture, and the official space of the classroom. Literacy mediated their participation in each of these spaces, as well as across them. Within and across these spheres, the students used literacy for a variety of purposes: (a) as a means to an end (e.g., Lashon reading the recipe off the television and then writing it down so she could make her cheesecake); (b) as ways of participating in the network of their sociocultural worlds (e.g., Allessandra writing to her brother in jail); and (c) as ways of understanding one's place in the world and exerting some power on that world (e.g., Carlee's poetry about her father's attitudes toward her interracial relationship).

My time in the school and in the classroom offered many insights into the literate lives of these adolescents that were not recognized as useful resources by the school or classroom teacher. Failing to acknowledge students' variety of literacy practices may have serious outcomes for students and for schools. One obvious outcome is that students will likely be seen inaccurately by themselves and by others as deficient of literacy, as not holding the requisite literacy behaviors needed for competence. Lashon, when asked what reading and writing meant to her, responded, "Something that is successful, something that I'm going to need for the rest of my life ... even though I hate it ... but I got to do it though in order to get credit to pass." Although she had just listed the variety of things that she reads and writes in her everyday life (e.g., in cooking, reading hip-hop lyrics), she still believes that she needs to get "credit" for it to be literacy, that literacy is intertwined with her achievement in school, and she "hates it."

Another effect of not recognizing students' multiple literacies may be that educators and students themselves may attribute the lack of success to ability, effort, or particular learning strategies without a strong consideration of the social, cultural, and political influences that shape literacy practice (Gee, 1996, 2001; Street, 2001). Educators with this view are likely to adopt a simplistic view of how to improve the students' skills (as separated from the sociocultural and political influences of literacy). In addition, by not recognizing the multiple literacies and the social, cultural, and political links with literacy, educators will miss many valuable literacy resources that could help shape academic literacy practices (Dyson, 2003; Moje, 2002). And finally, when students' literacy practices are unacknowledged in schools, they will miss opportunities for developing even further these rich literacies that are marginalized from dominant Discourses (Gee, 1996).

It is for these reasons that researchers and educators must take seriously adolescents' literacy practices in their culture-specific, fluid communities. It is through this approach that we will more fully understand adolescents' literacies in their everyday lives, as it is embedded in the variety of communities in which they participate. Understanding "at-risk" youth as active participants in a variety of fluid communities, we will develop a richer understanding of the resources that they bring with them to the classroom, and how they make sense of and adopt particular literacy practices.

REFERENCES

Alvermann, D., & Hagood, M. (2000). Fandom and critical media literacy. *Journal of Adolescent Literacy, 43*(5), 436–446.

Alvermann, D., Hinchman, K., Moore, D., Phelps, S., & Waff, D. (Eds.). (1998). *Reconceptualizing the literacies in adolescents' lives*. Mahwah, NJ: Lawrence Erlbaum Associates.

Barton, D., & Hamilton, M. (1998). *Local literacies: Reading and writing in one community*. London: Routledge.

Camitta, M. (1993). Vernacular writing. In B. Street (Ed.), *Cross-cultural approaches to literacy* (pp. 228–246). Cambridge, England: Cambridge University Press.

Cazden, C. (2000). Taking cultural differences into account. In B. Cope & M. Kalantzis (Eds.), *Multiliteracies: Literacy learning and the designing of social futures*. London & New York: Routledge.

Dyson, A. (1993). *The social worlds of children learning to write*. New York: Teacher's College Press.

Dyson, A. H. (2003). "Welcome to jam": Popular culture, school literacy, and the making of childhoods. *Harvard Educational Review, 73*(3), 328–361.

Gee, J. P. (1996). *Social linguistics and literacies: Ideologies in discourses* (2nd ed.). Philadelphia: Routledge/Falmer.

Gee, J. P. (2001). The new literacy studies: From 'socially situated' to the work of the social. In D. Barton, M. Hamilton, & R. Ivanic (Eds.), *Situated literacies: Reading and writing in context*. New York: Routledge.

Gee, J. P. (2003). *What video games have to teach us about learning and literacy*. New York: Palgrave Macmillian.

Gutierrez, K., & Stone, L. D. (2000). Synchronic and diachronic dimensions of social practice: An emerging methodology for cultural-historical perspectives on literacy learning. In C. Lee & P. Smagorinsky (Eds.), *Vygotskian perspectives on literacy research: Constructing meaning through collaborative inquiry* (pp. 150–164). Cambridge, England: Cambridge University Press.

Jet magazine. Chicago: Johnson.

Katz, K. (Executive Producer). (2003). *Emeril Live* [Television series]. New York: Television Food Network, G. P.

Luke, A. (2003). Literacy and the other: A sociological approach to literacy research and policy in multilingual societies. *Reading Research Quarterly, 38*(1), 132–141.

Moje, E. (2002). Re-framing adolescent literacy research for the new times: Studying youth as a resource. *Reading Research and Instruction, 41*(3), 211–228.

Paintball magazine. New York: CFW Enterprises.

Pelzer, D. (1995). *A child called "It": One child's courage to survive*. Deerfield, FL: Health Communications.

Rowling, J. K. *Harry Potter series*. New York: Arthur A. Levine Books.

Street, B. (2001). Introduction. In B. Street (Ed.), *Literacy and development: Ethnographic perspectives*. London: Routledge.

Word Up! New York: WU Magazine.

Chapter 10

School and Home: Contexts
for Conflict and Agency

Chad O'Neil
Michigan State University

Three young children sit, small hands and feet still in anticipation, with eyes focused. Their father moves the pen gently across a folded page; his eyes survey a familiar landscape. She is the first to break the silence. Youngest, and the only girl, Erin[1] shouts out " 'dollhouse'—5-across is 'dollhouse.' " Her father looks over; her brothers snicker at her excitement. After a quick smile he asks Erin how to spell "dollhouse" and together they see if 5-across is actually "dollhouse." Without correcting Erin's spelling, and ignoring his sons' suggestions, together they arrive at the correct spelling. A collective sigh of disappointment signals that 5-across has eluded them for the moment. Erin's smile is not extinguished, though, and she joins in laughter with her brothers. She laughs at the joy of being with her family and helping her father as he labors diligently doing the crossword puzzle in the evening newspaper.

At another time, and in another place, another family is together in their car. Will sits in the backseat as his mother begins a story. She tells him of a young boy, not unlike himself, who is taking a walk to the park. She describes the surroundings in detail as the boy walks to the park. As he clears the last hill he can see the park and breaks into a run. Will's mother describes how the park is laid out and all the different things in the park. Will sees the swings, slides, monkey bars, and teeter-totters. Just as the park grows closer, Will's mother stops narrating the story. Will, though, quickly

---

[1]All names are pseudonyms.

continues with the boy scrambling up a fence to get to the monkey bars without going around to the main park entrance. He tells of all the amazing tricks the boy does on the monkey bars. Then he stops; he and his mother laugh together. She quickly picks up the story; together they continue their turn-taking, fashioning an elaborate tale of a boy's day in the park. The trip goes quickly; Will smiles the whole way.

PARTICIPANTS AND CONNECTIONS

Will is a young Caucasian male, just under 6 feet tall. Will keeps his brown hair cut short, has a moderate amount of facial hair, and a slender build. Will quickly and easily relates to his fellow writing consultants. His casual disposition is reflected in his choice of clothing, even though he tends not to wear t-shirts. Will's parents both have college degrees; his father also has a master's degree. Will and Erin, the two participants in this case study, both grew up in Midwestern towns about an hour's drive from one another.

Erin is a young Caucasian woman, around 5½ feet tall. She has long curly blond hair and a slender build. She is quick to joke with her fellow consultants and tends to wear clothes that reflect the fashion of the day. Erin's mother has a master's degree and her father completed some college.

Erin and Will are undergraduate students at a Big Ten university in the Midwestern United States, and they both work at the university writing center as consultants. The writing center serves the entire university community from first year students to tenured faculty. I share the writing center space with Will and Erin where I work as a graduate writing consultant. All but one of our conversations about their literacy practices took place in the writing center after hours.

Positionality of Researcher

During the data collection period of this study, my duties as a graduate writing consultant included working with writers and supervising and developing undergraduate writing consultants. Typical supervisory tasks included signing off on hours worked by undergraduate writing consultants and assigning and working with them on other writing center activities such as housekeeping, filing, and other tasks assigned by full time staff and faculty. Developmental activities included time spent with undergraduate writing consultants, working on areas they are interested in or on graduate writing consultant concerns. I also helped consultants develop professional/academic goals and assisted them in reaching those goals. For Erin and Will, these activities ranged from conversations about resumes to advice about graduate school applications. Additionally, as a graduate consultant, I frequently coordinate the work of other consultants on large tasks such as preparing for upcoming conferences or presentations that will use the writing center space. The writing center at this university assists all consultants through weekly meetings and optional trips to various writing center conferences that take place throughout the year. While in the center, consultants can continue their development by working with each other and full-time faculty on both academic and professional writing.

Working Relationship

Although I worked with both Will and Erin on a weekly basis, I also shared responsibilities and experiences with other graduate and undergraduate writing consultants. Most of my interactions with Will fell into supervisory activities such as signing off on his hours and casual conversations before he showed interest in sharing his experiences with me regarding literacy in his life. On the other hand, I had a chance to work with Erin on one important piece of writing as a part of professional development before our conversations about her literacy practices began. The following is what I learned from my conversations with the both of them about their literacy practices. Their examples of multimodal text(s) (New London Group, 1996), misrecognized resources, and blended domains (Luke, 2003) together offer new ways "to imagine a range of possible relationships between school and non-school contexts" (Hull & Schultz, 2002, p. 2).

Erin and Will's views of their literacy practices seemed to reflect the influences of two different sociotextual domains and two different discourses (Gee, 1989). Both family and school shaped their feelings and understandings of their literacy practices. Family provided Will and Erin with their first literacy practices. School either "recognized[,] misrecognized, remediated [or] converted" (Luke, 2003, p. 140) these primary practices and discourses. Erin and Will's experiences of their literacy practices were both positively and negatively shaped by this. Analysis of the data revealed the themes of conflict and agency as this process took place, resulting in their current stances in relation to their own literacies.

LITERACY ROOTED IN HOME PRACTICES

My conversations around literacy and literacy practice with Erin and Will led to memories and insights for all of us, particularly related to the ways that current literacy practices have their roots in past, home-based practices, experiences, and values. As they answered questions about the literacy practices of their families when they were children, they both reached new insights regarding the crucial roles played by their families in how they each understand literacy in their lives.

For Erin and Will, the home-based literacy practices did not exist as isolated from other domains. Rather, each experienced an agency that was born through home-based literacy practices and that was further shaped through experienced conflict between those practices and literacy as practiced in school. This agency is now apparent—can be recognized—in the multimodal literacy practices that permeate their lives as young adults.

Erin and Will shared with me a range of literacy practices. Describing their lives as students, they both noted different types of texts and purposes for reading and writing that they engage in as a part of their academic studies. Although important to their success as students, these school literacy practices did not engage them as much in their conversations with me as did their "preferred" literacy practices. These were literacy practices that did not, in their minds, relate to school. Interestingly, although they also responded to my questions with descriptions of literacy practices within the writing center, neither chose to spend much time discussing the reading and writing they do as consultants. When they did speak about the writing center, it was always briefly, with the understanding that I, as a member of their working community, understood what they were talking about.

It was the out-of-school, or home literacy events that seemed to most engage Will and Erin. Even their recalled practices of school-based literacy was related as it integrated into, and transformed, their personal, home-based literacies.

The earliest literacy events that both Will and Erin recalled were bedtime story rituals (Heath, 1984). They each mentioned these only briefly, in part because they both, in Will's words, saw these practices as "fairly standard reading." Other home practices, though, such as those highlighted in the opening narratives—crossword puzzles and storytelling—connected in interesting ways to their current multimodal practices.

Bringing School Literacies Into the Home and Community

Erin shared such an instance as she related how her mother's need for child care resulted in the introduction of academic literacy practices into her young life. Erin's mother returned to college when Erin was 6 years old to pursue a teaching certificate. There were times when a babysitter could not be found so that Erin's mother could attend the required classes. At those times, Erin and her siblings would find themselves sitting in a college class where "we would absorb a lecture and/or class reading."

As Erin's mother began bringing assignments home with her, many of which involved designing school lesson plans, the literacy activities in the home were transformed and expanded to include these school-based practices. The reading and composing of storybooks was one textual practice experienced by Erin as the result of this life process. Erin's mother would make storybooks for after-school programs and for Head Start preschool programs. She would do much of this work at home, enlisting the help and participation of Erin and her brothers.

Will shared another way in which school-based literacy was imported into the home literacy context, influencing the ways in which he continues to relate to a particular genre of writing even today. This is the genre of poetry, and Will's teacher in elementary school spent considerable time with his class on reading and writing it. Poetry was assigned and poems were written by the children, including Will. Will's poems were sometimes selected by his teacher and sent to the local newspaper for publication in a section of the paper that highlighted local student writing. Thus, a school-based literacy practice was exported to a community-based one. When Will's poems were published, his grandmother cut them out and posted them on the refrigerator, thus bringing these school-initiated texts into the home for reading and consideration as public texts authored by a family member.

Will recalls these events with relish. He recalls, "... writing because that was the assignment, and if it got in [the newspaper], Grandma would put [it] on her fridge and that was great!" Despite this apparently seamless importation of school literacy practice into out-of-school practice, conflicts between the influences of the domains of school and home on literacy practice soon arose as a theme in the literacy stories told by both Will and Erin.

Conflict Between Home and School Literacies

Erin and Will's accounts of conflict differ. For Erin, the conflict began with the kind of literacy she had access to at home and that of school. At home, Erin enjoyed access to wide array of interesting books, provided by different family members. One recalled instance of this involved "a collection of history books with cartoons on different eras." These were very different, and much more engaging, than the books available to her at school—a fact that still remains very strong among Erin's memories of her childhood.

Erin also recalled with relish her addiction to such series as *The Little House on the Prairie* (Wilder) and *The Babysitters' Club* (Martin). She has fond memories of reading these books during her out-of-school time. *The Babysitters' Club* books served a very specific purpose for Erin: "While when I was younger there were connections in terms of friendship and being on the brink of having any form of responsibility just, you know, being a girl who lives wherever and has friends. I identified with the people in the book whether babysitters or being babysat."

While Erin was engaged with reading texts not sponsored by her school or its teachers, Will was experiencing a disaffection with reading, overall. For him, peer pressure was telling him that "reading wasn't cool," and he did not engage in reading or writing outside of school for a long period of time—from early elementary school until 9th or 10th grade. Erin and Will, though, both reached a point in their lives where they felt the act and meaning of reading changing for them.

Personal Interest in Reading

Will recalls this change taking place during 9th or 10th grade. He recalls reading some of Hemingway's short stories "here and there in a car ride or something, but not actively." Will's narrative of this change in his perspective on the value and role of reading continues:

> And then it was *Breakfast of Champions* by Kurt Vonnegut [1973]—I think the cover was bright orange caught my attention—lying around the house. That was the first book I enjoyed, (although) there had been books I read for school that I secretly enjoyed. That was the first one (though) where I said, "This isn't dorky; it's fun."

For Will, it is this change in his attitude toward reading that exposed the conflict between the school sociotextual domain and the new personal literacy practice of reading. Outside of school, reading is now seen as a pleasurable and rewarding activity.

Erin, on the other hand, did not so much change her attitude toward reading, as expand the types of reading in which she engaged. At this point in her literacy practice development, Erin recalled, she began to be influenced in her reading habits by those of her older brothers. Erin remembered specific authors—"Kurt Vonnegut, Tom Robbins, Philip Roth, and more contemporary authors"—that her brothers exposed her too. Erin recalled that if Tom, one of her brothers, "was reading something and sat it aside (he has pretty good taste) I would usually pick it up and read it too." By reading books that her brothers read, Erin not only felt she would be more likely to enjoy the reading, but was also able to bond with her older brothers. Thus the practice of recreational reading mediated the family domain and helped to accomplish important social functions among family members.

Prior to these experiences Erin's main resource for books had been her local library. The library served Erin both as a place from which to get books and a different system for picking from all the books she had available to read:

> Our library in our town was not that great—if a book had ever been censored our library wouldn't carry it. It had a lot of Hemingway, Dickens, Jane Austen and things like that. When I was younger—in middle school—I would just go through an author so that got me away from *The Babysitters' Club* and *Little House on the Prairie* into actual literature.

Although Will did not mention a significant location for motivating reading of particular authors, he did mention influences of his siblings in his values toward reading and literacy practice. He recalled his older brother doing very little reading, although his older sister did read, from what he could remember. Will, however, was not interested in the things his sister read before he entered high school; his changing attitude toward reading affected this stance, though:

> My sister, I don't know, it all kind of changed for me when I got into high school. Before that, I thought my sister [was] a nerd, so I made it pretty clear I wasn't interested in what she was going to suggest. Once I started getting interested, she'll occasionally give me books or tell me about books to read—I usually don't because I hate being told what to read. Sometimes, yeah, [I do read what she suggests].

For both Will and Erin, family remains an influential context for their reading practices. Although their attitudes toward reading differed during their tumultuous teenage years, Will and Erin still shared an awareness of this familial influence.

Agency

The interviews with Will and Erin revealed another important thread relevant to their developing literacy lives—that of *agency*. Through their narratives, one can see the development of agency on both their parts as they sorted out their likes and dislikes and as they responded to the various types of textual practices experienced within the different social domains in their lives.

The powerful role of home literacy worked its way into the types of literacy events Erin prefers and the ways in which she engages with them. As the youngest of three children, reading and writing had become an important bonding activity for her. Bonding could be seen both in the opening narrative, in the way Erin and her brothers gathered around their father, and in the literacy activities orchestrated by her mother from within the domain of school. There was, however, a point at which Erin began to initiate these textual practices on her own. Erin began to pursue these connections through the simple action of reading the books her brothers read, but she continued it in her own way with crossword puzzles.

For Erin, crossword puzzles were a marker of literacy in the home second only to bedtime stories. Unlike bedtime stories, though, the crossword puzzles done by her father began as an activity in which Erin could participate. Her father did not discourage Erin and her brothers, she recalls, as they "tried to help when we were six, but we could not spell yet." Although its nature changed, such interaction over crossword puzzles with Erin's father continued throughout her youth: "He still did the crossword puzzle in the Sunday paper, but our involvement lessened around the time we learned how to read, got a Nintendo™, etc. Basically, when we could adequately amuse ourselves, we stopped bugging him. But I still tried to help occasionally."

As school literacy practices entered Erin's life, she grew less involved with the crossword puzzle activity at home. They were still everpresent, however, until her father's death from cancer when she was 13, at which point crossword puzzles where no longer visible in her home. Erin, though, still remembered crossword puzzles as significant. It was not until the beginning of her junior year in college, however, that Erin began doing crossword puzzles again. For Erin, the first thing she thought of when considering crossword puzzles was how "[o]n some shallow level they make me feel smart." She continued her narrative by almost immediately, mentioning her brothers:

> Because there is a phrase with a blank there and what is going to be there? And [it provides] a sense of being smart and taking on the crossword puzzle. Plus I have older brothers who are incredibly smart—they both do crossword puzzles—Tom does them—Kevin is horrible at them and I'm better than him at them and I feel smart.

The importance of crossword puzzles for Erin and her brothers does not end with competition. It is still also used as a way of bonding. "When my brother is home we do crosswords puzzles together." Erin also uses crossword puzzles for social interaction outside of her family. For example, she often completes puzzles with another undergraduate student, George, with whom she has worked in the writing center.

> I knew [George] all last year, but he never talked. And this year I have a little more down time so I would just ask him, "So what's another word for whatever?" And pull him in. I do that all the time with other people. Use it as a way to start a conversation or get people to talk. Randomly. That interests people and they really start to think about it and then they want to know if [there is] something else then they'll try and get something else.

Crosswords are a way for Erin to involve others in her literacy; they are, however, not the only way she uses literacy for interaction. Most of these other nonschool interactions are restricted to her family, however. One example she mentions is of how she and her brothers send book reviews back and fourth via e-mail. In this way she is able to continue the mutual reading that began in her youth.

Although Will does not express the same interest in crossword puzzles as Erin, he does talk about what types of reading and writing—especially personal writing—are important to him. Will describes the writing he does the most outside of school, as poetry and autobiographical writing: "I dabble in the poetry a little bit, but not seriously or anything. I guess a lot of the stuff I write is kind of almost autobiography stuff—creative nonfiction. Putting a little twist on what happened—making it more important than it was." He connects his writing to the things he is reading by talking about "a natural urge to emulate it a little bit. Not seriously, but more seriously than before." The seriousness of writing came up throughout our conversation about both his writing and that of his mother: "I know that my mom is a fairly good writer because of the letters and e-mails. I can tell she has some experience, but I don't know where that comes from—she hasn't said here is a story I wrote." The importance of authorship in writing as it relates to agency further surfaces as Will talks about his writing as it changed from youth, influenced by school practices, to that of a young adult:

> I would write silly limericks or whatever we were asked to write. I wanted it to be good as I could—as much as a fourth grader can want that. There was no implication of getting better, I guess—improving my writing—I was writing because that was the assignment, and if it got [in the newspaper], Grandma would put [it] on her fridge and that was great. In high school, I don't know if I seriously considered writing as a profession, but it has been in the back of my mind since I started reading. When you are pushed to practice or get better by whatever, then you have some eye on the future, which implies a goal—then it becomes serious because of a focus on improvement.

Will clearly connects reading, writing, and published works within notions of a profession or a public life for himself. Agency thus surfaces within different dimensions for him than it did for Erin as evidenced in her continued engagement with crossword puzzles.

Family, School, and Work

For Erin, the crossword puzzle practice is a personal pleasure, one that is easy and that seamlessly emanates from the culture of her home and family:

> You could be really deep about it and be like [thinking that] doing crossword puzzles is a way to reconnect with my dead father. It's not that deep. I didn't start doing crossword puzzles until like a year ago because I had a class that was extremely boring and I like picked up a paper on the way to class to do something that was subtle. It's nice I can do something my father did—it's nice my grandmother can be like aw [your father did crossword puzzles, but] it's not like that deep. It's not like I do them because I have a heritage of crossword puzzles or because I grew up with them around.

Clearly, Erin is asserting an agency with this anecdote. Yes, the family literacy practice did make the doing of crossword puzzles seem natural and normal. Erin takes this practice, though, outside of the home domain and imports it into her school domain as a way of reading and writing that is engaging and enjoyable for her.

INSIGHTS

Erin and Will's views of their practices come through two important domains, discourses (Gee, 1989), for them. Both family and school shaped their views and understandings of literacy and literacy practices. Family, however, provided Will and Erin with their first literacy events. School either "recognized[,] misrecognised, remediated [or] converted" (Luke, 2003, p. 140) these primary practices (discourses; Gee, 1989). The primary and, ultimately, influential role played by literacy practices that were begun and/or shaped in the home becomes apparent, though, through Erin and Will's accounts of their developing agency as actors in their own literacy lives.

These accounts by two middle-class young people, growing up in the Midwestern part of the United States, offer compelling suggestions and evidence for expanding our view of literacy development. Rather than seeing the development of individuals as practitioners of literacy as primarily the function of schools, it seems more valid to expand our lens to view literacy development (defined as the development of literacy practitioners) as the function of both home literacy experiences and those of the school (Purcell-Gates, Jacobson, & Degener, in press).

REFERENCES

Gee, J. (1989). Literacy, discourse, and linguistics: Introduction and what is literacy? *Journal of Education, 171*(1), 5–25.

Heath, S. (1984). What no bedtime story means. In. B. B. Schieffelin & E. Ochs (Eds.), *Language socialization across cultures* (pp. 97–126). New York: Columbia University Press.

Hull, G., & Schultz, K. (Eds.). (2002). *School's out! Bridging out-of-school literacies with classroom practice*. New York: Columbia University Press.

Luke, A. (2003). Literacy and the other: A sociological approach to literacy research and policy in multilingual societies. *Reading Research Quarterly, 38*(1), 132–141.

Martin, A. M. *The Babysitters' Club series*. New York: Scholastic Books.

New London Group. (1996). A pedagogy of multiliteracies: Designing social futures. *Harvard Educational Review, 66*, 60–92.

Purcell-Gates, V., Jacobson, E., & Degener, S. (in press). *Print literacy development: Uniting cognitive and social practice theories*. Cambridge, MA: Harvard University Press.

Vonnegut, K. (1973). *Breakfast of champions*. New York: Delta Press.

Wilder, L. I. *The Little House on the Prairie series*. New York: HarperCollins.

New Pedagogies for New Literacies

Victoria Purcell-Gates

In chapter 1, I discussed the "Now what?" response to the work on literacies as multiple and social. This question raises the issue of real-world, classroom-situated, response to this new lens on literacy. In other words, now that we can see the ways that social practices pattern literacy practices, how can these new (in)sights shape new curricular responses. One noteworthy group of language and literacy scholars has been working on this since 1994. The New London Group (NLG), as they call themselves, began working in 1994 on such questions as "What constitutes appropriate literacy teaching in the context of the evermore critical factors of local diversity and global connectedness?" (Cope & Kalantzis, 2000, p. 3). The NLG counted among its members in 1994 Courtney Cazden, Bill Cope, Norman Fairclough, James Gee, Mary Kalantzis, Gunther Kress, Allan Luke, Carmen Luke, Sarah Michaels, Martin Nakata, and Joseph Lo Bianco.

Although the work by the NLG does not flow perfectly from that of multiple and social literacies theorists such as Street and Barton, among others, it does reflect underlying presuppositions of literacy as multiple, social, contextualized, and shaped by history and power relationships. The NLG work has looked more specifically at issues of instruction and learning, focusing variously on issues of multiple languages, scripts, modalities, and so on. In their book, *Multiliteracies: Literacy Learning and the Design of Social Futures*, edited by Cope and Kalantzis (2000), the group, with the addition of some new contributors, provide a broad blueprint for a new pedagogy of multiliteracies. For the NLG, the construct of multiliteracies implicates multimodal meaning-making systems: linguistic, visual, audio, gestural, and spatial. Their pedagogy calls for situated practice, overt instruction, critical framing, and transformed practice.

Taking up this extension of the "Now what?," Doug Eyman, in the final case study (chap. 11), moves the discussion of literacy practice into the area of *technology*—literacy practices enacted in digital space. This new literacy is explored as it particularly offers a concrete instantiation of the NLG's pedagogy of multiliteracies. He explores a definition of *digital literacy* through several sources: the perspectives of his informants (students in a college-level course on writing and technology) and the published literature on the subject. A value-added dimension of Eyman's chapter is the clear and specific definition he provides for the construct of digital literacy, a definition that should prove useful to future work in this area.

Case studies of practice as instances of theory are particularly valuable in that they provide readers with a case of the concrete, of theory on the ground.

They provide us with a "See, this is what it can look like." One reflective presentation, of course, is not meant to serve as a blueprint or model. In that sense, the content of the actual class is not as significant as the ways in which theory is played out in practice. A case study of a class on technology is based around content that is, by definition, outdated by the time it is written. Eyman's chapter joins a few others (see Newfield and Stein, Bond, & Cazden, in Cope & Kalantzis, 2000) in offering a beginning look at what I hope will be evolving resolutions to the "Now what?" question regarding literacy instruction in the new literacies world.

REFERENCES

Cope, B., & Kalantzis, M. (Eds.). (2000). *Multiliteracies: Literacy learning and the design of social futures*. London: Routledge.

Chapter 11

Digital Literac(ies), Digital Discourses, and Communities of Practice: Literacy Practices in Virtual Environments

Douglas Eyman
Michigan State University

The first thing you notice about the classroom is its aural texture—not quite silent, but very quiet—just a staccato, percussive clicking of fingers on keyboards rapidly typing, then pausing in a cyclic rhythm, repeated around the room; the quiet hum of the computer fans complements the buzz of the fluorescent lights. Here and there a sigh, or a gasp, or a giggle escapes from the otherwise intently typing students. Despite the quiet, a discussion is nonetheless taking place; it is, in fact, a virtual cacophony of voices all speaking at once—holding multiple conversations, firing questions at one another, dropping and picking up discussion threads as they weave the classroom discussion on-screen.

The students in question are taking part in an upper level writing course titled "Writing and Technology," taught at a midsized public university on the east coast of the United States. The class is primarily made up of White, middle-class women and men who are in their junior or senior year of their undergraduate careers; 90% of the 20 students are White, 20% are male. The class meets on Tuesday and Thursday mornings in the sole computer classroom in the department, in which the computers are arranged around the perimeter of the room, facing the walls. There are several tables in the center of the room that students can gather around when not working at their terminals. Because the course is project-based, much of the class time is devoted to working in groups with the technologies available in the classroom, rather than the more traditional lecture and discussion formats common in humanities courses.

The goals of this course, as stated in the syllabus, are equally concerned with practices of writing with new technologies and efforts to understand and critically reflect on how these new technologies transform writing:

This course is designed to teach students to:

- develop strategies for learning and using a variety of technologies to compose print and online texts;
- learn to analyze writing situations and select the best technologies for each project, audience, and subject;
- critically analyze the effects that various technologies have on our definitions and conceptions of writing;
- understand some of the theoretical commentary surrounding the intersections of writing and technologies in education, workplaces, and communities;
- work with others to improve your writing and produce texts and presentations;
- explore issues of technological literacy and examine how definitions of technological literacy affect you and others in your communities;
- understand the ethical considerations involved in selecting and changing technologies for producing and distributing texts.

My primary observations of this course focused on one of the class projects: the remediation of a traditional essay into a virtual exhibit in a MOO (a multiuser virtual environment). I was particularly interested in the way the MOO as a virtual space embodied the multimodal design model proposed by the New London Group in their seminal 1996 article, "A Pedagogy of Multiliteracies: Designing Social Futures." The virtual environment of the MOO incorporates all of the design modes identified by the New London Group: linguistic, visual, audio, gestural, and spatial; because of the interconnectedness of these modes, the MOO itself can be described as multimodal. Additionally, the MOO project itself also exemplified the four-element pedagogy espoused by the New London group, as students engaged in situated practice, overt instruction, critical framing, and transformed practice. In short, the course serves as an excellent model of a multiliteracies pedagogy, precisely because of the new media spaces made possible by new information and communication technologies.

These new technologies also served an important role in the methodology for this case study. Because my informants were working in a university setting far from my own, I had only a few opportunities for direct observation of the classroom; however, I had a great deal of access to the coursework produced by the students and I was able to observe their virtual class meetings and interact with them via both synchronous discussion (in the MOO) and asynchronous semistructured interviews (by e-mail).

In the past, I have taught in very similar locations and found myself struggling to effectively teach both writing and digital literacy practices. This struggle was, at the time, both curricular (as neither my pedagogy nor the technologies to support it were fully developed at that time) and political (as departmental administrators were then unconvinced that technology should be a part of any humanities-oriented course); I was excited to find a course that had clearly overcome both of these obstacles. And although digital literacy is a specifically stated goal of the course, the professor teaching the course did not develop it as a vehicle for literacy instruction (digital or otherwise); it was, instead, developed using common curricular models from the field of technical and professional communication.

I selected this course as a location for this case study not only because it directly addresses questions of changing literacy practices as they are impacted by the advent of new media technologies, but also because it provides a useful curricular model for developing digital literacy courses. The academy hasn't traditionally recognized digital literacy as a form of literacy that needs to be taught; it's assumed that individuals in a technological society will naturally acquire digital literacies—so there is no place in school specifically designated for teaching digital literacy. This writing and technology course, however, may serve as a model both for teaching digital literacy and for developing a curriculum that supports the pedagogical structure envisioned by the New London Group (1996). The literacies employed by the students in the course are certainly multimodal, and the course structure uses situated practice, overt instruction, and critical reflection to produce transformed practice in nearly all of the course projects (not just in the MOO project, although that is where it is most accessible). The course's focus on remediating texts also supports Kress's (2000) description of a "dynamic, constantly remade and re-organised set of semiotic resources" and the actions of individuals "as the remakers, the transformers, the re-shapers of the representational resources available to them" (p. 155).

In this chapter, I begin by working toward a working definition of digital literacy and proceed from there to marking the connections between the course work as both a vehicle for digital literacy and a model of the New London Group's mutlimodal/multiliteracies pedagogy. I finish by invoking Gee's notion of Discourse to develop the notion that digital literacy relies on the acquisition of a digital Discourse, which can be gained by immersion in communities of practice—the object of this case study being a specific example of a community of practice wherein one can work toward acquiring a digital Discourse, and ultimately, digital literacy.

DEFINING DIGITAL LITERACY

As my particular interests lie at the intersection of rhetoric, technology, and pedagogy, an examination of digital literacy, rather than traditional print literacy, seemed an appropriate problem space for me to encounter and observe. But early in the study I realized that there is currently no stable definition of digital literacy. Different theorists have spoken of computer literacy, media literacy, electronic literacy, or silicon literacy in attempts to identify communicative technology use as a valid domain for literacy instruction; however, other theorists have rejected the coupling of these modifiers with the term *literacy* as it serves to dilute our understanding of (print) literacy. In *Literacy in the New Media Age*, Kress (2003) argues:

> ... *literacy* is the term to use when we make messages using letters as the means of recording that message .... my approach leaves us with the problem of finding new terms for the uses of the different resources: not therefore "visual *literacy*" for the use of image; not "gestural *literacy*" for the use of gesture; and also not "musical *literacy*" or "soundtrack *literacy*" for the use of sound other than speech; and so on. (p. 23)

Kress very specifically differentiates literacy as specifically oriented to writing, although he acknowledges that computer technologies problematize this artificial distinction between modes. It appears that Kress seeks to make a distinction between resource (knowing how to write) and its use:

> *Literacy* remains the term which refers to (the knowledge of) the use of the resource of writing. The combination of knowledge of the resource with knowledge of production and perhaps with that of dissemination would have a different name. That separates, what to me is essential, the *sense of what the resource is* and what its potentials are, from associated questions such as those of its *uses*, and the issue of whatever skills are involved in using a resource in wider communicational frames. (p. 24)

Although this distinction may be useful for the construction of his social-semiotic theories of language use, it seems to me that separating the resource from the production (use) and dissemination is to decontextualize literacies by disembedding them from their social, historical, and cultural milieu; moreover, by limiting "literacy" to "writing with letters" (Kress, 2003, p. 61), one is forced to separate the written from the visual, despite the inherently visual nature of writing. If we agree that literacy is rooted in sociohistorical contexts (Street, 1984), it must encompass more than the particular sign system of writing with letters. And although literacy itself is multimodal, it is useful to differentiate the particular modes or uses of literacy when seeking to observe the effects of literacy practices; thus, rather than seeking a different name for meaning production that includes more than just writing, I would prefer to couple the concept of *literacy* as sociohistorically situated practice with a modifier that allows us to make a distinction between those practices that are culturally located within print media and those located within digital media.

I prefer the term *digital literacy* because I believe it captures the notion that the literacy practices referred to are enacted in digital spaces. I would contrast this sense of media, location, and context with terms such as *computer literacy*, which evokes a concept of mere tool use; *Internet literacy*, which is too specific both in locale and in historical moment; and *electronic literacy*, which is too broad in scope (as it can be seen as referencing any electronic device). *Technological literacy* or *technology literacy* is similarly too broad, as nearly all modes of communication are technologies—so there is no functional distinction between print-based literacy and digital literacy. Snyder (2002) suggested *silicon literacy* as the intersection of traditional and digital literacy practices:

> Now, for the first time in history, the written, oral and audiovisual modalities of communication are integrated into multimodal hypertext systems made accessible via the Internet and the World Wide Web. Silicon literacy practices represent the ways in which meanings are made within these new communication systems. (p. 3)

Even though her term does reference the materiality of the communication media (as silicon is currently a key element in the production of computer chips), it also carries connotations of a specific location (Silicon Valley) and a specific moment in time (as computer technologies in the very near future may no longer rely upon silicon as a major component).

What, then, is digital literacy? In order to articulate my definition of digital literacy, I chose to draw on two sources: the published literature in the field of literacy and technology studies and the definitions offered by the informants of this study.

Participants' Definitions of Digital Literacy

When I asked the students in the writing and technology class to define digital literacy, the responses focused either on effective, efficient uses of computer technologies in general, or more specifically, on applying print literacy practices of reading and writing to new media. I had expected the computer-use, literacy-as-skills response both because common articulations of literacy in American schooling have traditionally focused on teaching literacy as a simple set of skills that can be explicitly taught exclusive of context. Additionally, according to a survey taken by the instructor at the beginning of the course, students' stated goals for the course nearly all included gaining technological competencies and improving their knowledge and use of computer-facilitated communicative skills (the exceptions were those students who self-identified as highly skilled, or, as one student put it, "I've always been a computer 'geek' :-)").

The second form of response shows the strong connection that the students have to print-based literacy practices, as shown in this representative response by Kelly:

> I hear the term "computer illiterate" all of the time and that has nothing to do with the written word. I think that to be fully literate you have to be able to apply the ability to read to several types of mediums .... To be fully digitally literate you have to continuously learn new things as new things are presented.

Interestingly, none of the students made connections between the visual and the textual modes of representation that are afforded by the technologies; however, one student, Cassy, did implicitly reference the notion of digital media as representing virtual spaces; she identifies digital literacy as "… the ability to read and write through the use of computers, as well as the ability to navigate through electronic interfaces."

For these students, then, digital literacy is seen as a transference of traditional literacy practices (reading and writing), to new media, and this is a good starting point—digital literacy is ineluctably tied to text-based literacy practices. However, digital literacy also goes beyond the textual, and includes the effective use of symbolic systems, visual representations of language, and digital object manipulation. Snyder (2002) argues:

> in an electronically mediated world, being literate is [sic] to do with understanding how the different modalities are combined in complex ways to create meaning. People have to learn to make sense of the iconic systems evident in computer displays—with all the combinations of signs, symbols, pictures, words and sounds. (p. 3)

Luke (2000) frames her articulation of digital literacy practices via the notion of *multiliteracies*:

> The Multiliteracies of digital electronic "texts" are based on notions of hybridity and intertextuality. Meaning-making from the multiple linguistic, audio, and symbolic visual graphics of hypertext means that the cyberspace navigator must draw on a range of knowledges about traditional and newly blended genres or representational conventions, cultural and symbolic codes, as well as linguistically coded and software-driven meanings. (p. 73)

Digital literacy then is both tied to traditional notions of print literacy practices, but it changes and transforms those practices when they are enacted in new media spaces; digital literacy practices are multimodal and recombinative, constantly reconfiguring themselves from the available modes and resources of the digital medium. And even though the students in this study could not explicitly articulate a full definition of digital literacy, they were, through the course projects, engaging in digital-literacy practices. These practices were perhaps most evident in the MOO remediation project.

DIGITAL MULTIMODALITY

In 1996, the New London Group published *A Pedagogy of Multiliteracies*, in which they identify six major modes of meaning, "areas in which functional grammars, the metalanguages that describe and explain patterns of meaning, are required—Linguistic Design, Visual Design, Audio Design, Gestural Design, Spatial Design and Multimodal Design" (p. 76). They designate Multimodal Design as representing the patterns of interconnection between the other modes of design. The MOO remediation project incorporates all of the available design elements within its scope; I would therefore designate this activity as *multimodal*.

MOOs and MUDs

Just what is a MOO? First, let me assure you that it has no relation to cows or any other barnyard metaphor or activity: MOO stands for Multi-User Domain, Object Oriented. A MOO is a "computer program that allows multiple users to connect via the Internet to a shared textual world of rooms and other objects, and interact with each other and this virtual world in real time ... the MOO is a living, ever-changing textual environment" (Holmevik & Haynes, 2000, p. xv). Multi-User Domains (or MUDs) were initially developed as social arenas, primarily focused on role-playing games. As the technology matured, MUDs evolved from game-spaces to social communities; with the advent of Object-Oriented MUDs (i.e., MOOs), the spaces could be extended and produced by the users, rather than only by system administrators. Professional organizations, businesses, and educational institutions have been using MOOs for research and education for the past decade; despite their origins as online games, they now are primarily used as teaching spaces. Figure 11.1 represents the interface to *Connections*, a text-only MOO that is available for classroom use.

MOOs are particularly rich environments for the teaching of writing, as they "combine the power of the written word with the informality of the spoken context" (Holmevik & Haynes, 2000, p. xvi); Oren (1996) identifies

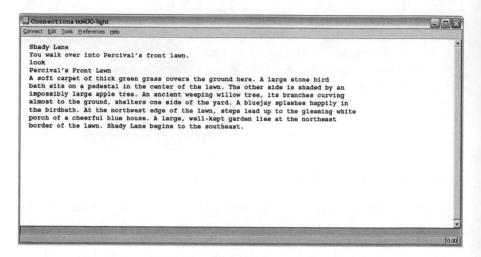

Figure 11.1.   Connections, a text-only MOO. Text by Tari Fanderclai. Reprinted
with permission.

several reasons why MOOs are ideal vehicles for teaching, including the notion that "significant learning is achieved if based on a construction process" engaged in by students who build spaces in the MOO, and "the belief
that some skills like mapping and linking are part of information literacy
that should be imparted to students" (http://english.ttu.edu/kairos/1.2/
binder2.html?coverweb/avigail.html). Another use of the MOO as an educational medium, is to allow "students to explore multiple subjectivities, to
explore and develop a character or characters that might differ in slight or
significant ways from that of their 'real' lives" (Sanchez, 1998, p. 102).

For the students in this study, the MOO served as a place in which they
could reconfigure traditional academic texts into multimodal new media
exhibits; the MOO that they worked in has a Web-enabled interface (see
Fig. 11.2), which allows them to incorporate graphical and multimedia elements into this text-based virtual reality.

Remediation Within the MOO

One of the primary texts in the writing and technology course is Bolter and
Grusin's (1999) *Remediation: Understanding New Media*, in which the authors
examine the practice of remediation—"the representation of one medium
in another, [which is] a defining characteristic of the new digital media" (p.
45). The first major project in the course asked students to engage in the
practice of remediation within the MOO:

For this project, you will remediate a paper that you have written for a previous class into a MOO exhibit. The exhibit you create should provide the information in the paper as well as present your argument or thesis using the MOO objects you create.

The MOO exhibit must provide instructions for visitors about how to read the room, use the objects, and best navigate your space. Additionally, the MOO exhibit should not contain large chunks of text copied and pasted right from your paper, but should employ the objects that the MOO contains to make the same or similar points as your original text.

The MOO exhibits created by the students utilized all of the design modalities identified by the New London Group: The texts of their projects drew on the mode of Linguistic Design, the graphics and icons they selected required the use of Visual Design, some students included multimedia sound files, thus engaging in Audio Design, they had to map out the location and architecture of their space in metaphors of rooms and exits, and were required to connect their projects back to the main room for the course (Spatial Design), and the objects they created, which could be manipulated by any visitor to their space, I would designate as involving Gestural Design (one student programmed an interactive virtual robot who could explain to visitors how to navigate and use his exhibit; this too, I would designate as gestural).

When the students had completed their MOO exhibits, they held an open house for visitors; as part of the final product, they also wrote reflec-

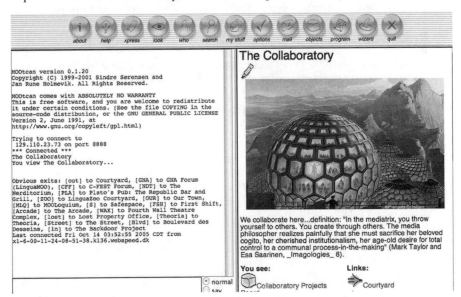

Figure 11.2.   LinguaMOO, a MOO with a graphical Web interface. LinguaMOO, copyright © by C. Haynes and J. R. Holmevik, artwork by F. Schuiten and A. Nandi (www.urbicande.be). Reprinted with permission.

tive essays about the process of creating the exhibits and why they designed them as they did. One of the students, Gary, explained that his MOO exhibit was "remediating a paper I wrote on Bertolt Brecht's (1949/1991) *Mother Courage and Her Children*":

> The first part of the page is a note, entitled "INSTRUCTIONS." This note gives a rundown of what everything on the page is for. It mentions the bookshelf, the Web projector, the message board, the boombox, the projector and the three Web pages (Brecht Time, MC Characters, and Play Overview). It succinctly explains the functions of the room's objects.

Gary's creation and use of objects to support reading and writing within this virtual context constitute an example of digital literacy practices; traditional print-based literacies have been remediated and transformed within the digital medium. In order to negotiate this "text," readers must not only be able to read, they must also be able to manipulate the digital–textual objects in this space. Additionally, the exhibit space created by Gary is multimodal because it uses a rich combination of graphical representations (logo, icons), visual elements (color scheme, font selection), text, sound, and interactivity (through the creation of the "Brecht Bot 3000XL"). The interactivity provided by the Brecht Bot represents an extension of the author of the exhibit, thus occupying the gestural mode defined by the New London Group (1996):

> Brecht Bot 3000XL says, "You should check out the play overview, or the slide proj."
>
> First_Guest says, "slide proj?"
>
> Brecht Bot 3000XL [to First_Guest]: You should check out the projector for info on Mother Courage

Another student, Patty, presents an argument that her MOO exhibit (Fig. 11.3) is successful:

> The reasons I think my MOO exhibit is successful are: 1) the text is chunked and shown in an easy-to-use slide projector; 2) the directions I provide are brief but thorough and detailed; 3) the objects I created are entertaining but add to a sense of physical space and appealing knowledge about various topics; 4) my room is consistent but attractive so that players can focus on the text and other components without feeling overwhelmed; and 5) the exhibit is easily navigable and contents are located in appropriate places.

Patty addresses her linguistic, visual, and spatial design choices directly, rather than enumerating the objects she has created and their use. Here, the digital literacy practices are more explicit in the student's reflection.

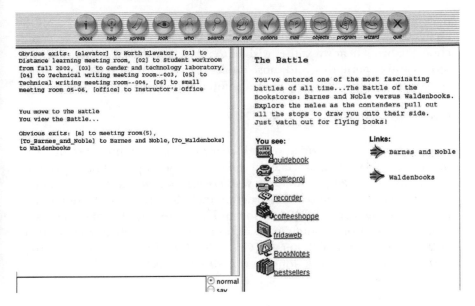

Figure 11.3.   Student MOO project.

TEACHING DIGITAL LITERACY

As I observed the writing and technology course for this study, it became clear to me that it represented an instance of the specific pedagogical practices proposed by the New London Group (1996) in "A Pedagogy of Multiliteracies." And although the course seemed almost directly informed by the work of the New London Group, the instructor had not read it. Her course engaged students in situated practice, overt instruction, critical reflection, and transformed practice. This pedagogical model was most visible in the MOO exhibit project, but it also appeared in the other projects in the course.

Situated Practice

The MOO itself is a kind of instantiation of situated practice as a "simulation of the relationships to be found in workplace and public spaces" (New London Group, 1996, p. 84). Indeed, the MOO is an actual public space, so it is both a simulation of the social arena (and the classroom), but it is also a real location that nonclass members can visit and explore. The New London Group's definition of situated practice also included the notion of "immersion in experience and the utilisation of available Designs of meaning, including those from the students' lifeworlds" (p. 88). Not only is the MOO an immersive experience, but for the MOO exhibit project, students could choose to bring in any text they wished to remediate, based on their own interests and experiences, and those choices ranged from essays created for courses in scientific disciplines to traditional academic argument to fiction.

Overt Instruction

The professor also provided overt instruction through modeling, in-class discussions of building practices in the MOO, and by providing written instructions such as a handout on how to create space in the MOO using the "@dig" command; this overt instruction included "the introduction of explicit metalanguages, which describe and interpret the Design elements of different modes of meaning" (New London Group, 1996, p. 84), particularly through the use of Bolter and Grusin's (1999) *Remediation* text as a theoretical base for the work done on the MOO project.

Critical Reflection

Critical reflection in the course was achieved both through the postproduction reflections and through the continuing online and face-to-face discussions of their projects in terms of *immediacy* (the attempt to remove the technological interface from the user experience) and *hypermediacy* (a positioning of the technology such that it is not hidden, but overly obvious; Bolter & Grusin, 1999). Critical reflection was also supported by the use of outside reviewers in the course, both of the MOO exhibit project and the instructional digital video project—the incorporation of real audiences helps the students to gain the distance needed to perform critical reflection on their own work.

Because of the nature of the course, the students also discussed issues of accessibility and of the effects of technology on identity formation and on sociocultural norms and practices (e.g., at one point the class viewed and discussed a Web site that featured a Web cam at a laundromat in Paris, which highlighted issues of possible privacy invasion as well as considerations of technology-mediated public display). It was clear from the discussions in the class that the professor sought to invest her students with a critical understanding of the technologies they use and the issues of power and cultural capital that are tied to those technologies. As Lankshear and Snyder (2000) point out:

> To participate effectively and productively in any literate practice, people must be socialized into it. But if individuals are socialized into a literacy without realizing that it is socially constructed and selective, and also that it can

be acted on and transformed, they cannot play an active role in changing it. (p. 31)

Transformed Practice

Transformed practice was most visible in the MOO exhibit project, as students used critical reflection and overt instruction within the realm of situated practice to build their exhibits; the act of remediation (transforming meaning by placing media within new media contexts) is a kind of transformed practice, in that it performs a "transfer in meaning-making practice, which puts the transformed meaning (the Redesigned) to work in other contexts or cultural sites" (New London Group, 1996, p. 84).

DIGITAL DISCOURSE AND COMMUNITIES OF PRACTICE

The focus in the writing and technology course on critical reflection also provides a bridge to Gee's (1989) distinction between discourses and Discourses; digitally mediated spaces, such as the MOO, the Web, or Instant Messaging, each have their own rhetoric, that is, their own forms of discourse within particular contexts, but it also is possible to view digital literacy as an acquisition of a technology Discourse. In "Literacy, Discourse, and Linguistics," Gee (1989) identifies Discourse with a capital D as a "sort of 'identity kit' which comes complete with the appropriate costume and instructions on how to act, talk, and often write, so as to take on a particular role that others will recognize"; capital D Discourses are combinations of "*saying (writing)-doing-being-valuing-believing*" (p. 526). According to Gee (1989), "Discourses are not mastered by overt instruction ... but by enculturation ('apprenticeship') into social practices through scaffolded and supported interaction with people who have already mastered the Discourse .... You cannot overtly teach anyone a Discourse, in a classroom or anywhere else" (p. 527). Thus an experiential pedagogy, such as that enacted in the writing and technology course—a pedagogy of situated practice, overt instruction, critical reflection, and transformed practice—provides a valuable space for students to engage in the acquisition of a technology Discourse. Additionally, Gee (1989) argues that in order to acquire new Discourses, one has to be in a position to critique that Discourse, using metaknowledge. My observations of the writing and technology course revealed students actively engaging in the development of metaknowledge through the practice of remediating and reflecting on the activities of remediation; the students are not only immersed in the technology Discourse, they are also aware of it and simultaneously engaged in a critical study of it.

Discourses, as Gee (1989) articulates them, are clearly socially constructed; to engage in a Discourse is thus an indication of belonging to a
particular social network. These social networks can be developed both in
school and outside of it. Eckert (2000) identifies the kind of social networks
inscribed by Discourses as "communities of practice" (p. 39)—groups of
people who work together toward a particular enterprise; these communities of practice are the interactional sites where social meaning is most
clearly indexed by language, and where language variation and social
meaning are co-constructed. Through my observations of the writing and
technology class, I came to view them as a community of practice, engaged
in the project of socially constructing an understanding of digital literacy as
a technological Discourse.

Intersection of School and Community

The students' use of (and construction of) the MOO entails the most visible
aspects of their community of practice at work, and it serves as an interesting space—an intersection between school and community. Luke (2003)
argues:

> literate practice is situated, constructed, and intrapsychologically negotiated
> through an (artificial) social field called school, with rules of exchange de-
> noted in scaffolded social activities around particular selected texts. But any
> acquired skills, whether basic or higher order, are reconstituted and
> remediated in relation to variable fields of power and practice in the larger
> community. (p. 140)

The MOO is both a part of the artificial social field of school and apart from
it; it is virtual, yet it is essentially a less artificial construction than is the
classroom. The MOO privileges interactivity, provides access to a real-
world audience, supports community development, and within the context
of the class in this study, it serves as a location that fosters critical reflection
of technology use.

CONCLUSION: DIGITAL LITERACY INSTRUCTION

In this chapter, I have examined the curricular and pedagogical work of a
course in writing and technology that appears to support a useful framework for helping students to acquire a technology Discourse and to engage
in critical reflection of their digital literacy practices. This framework follows the pedagogical practices suggested by the New London Group (situated practice, overt instruction, critical reflection, and transformed
practice), enacting them in a project-based, multimodal curriculum. A
unique aspect of the course is the incorporation of the multiuser tex-

tual/graphical virtual environment of the MOO, which provides a space that bridges the artificiality of classroom instruction and real-world community development. The combination of the pedagogical framework and the virtual environment-as-context supports both digital literacy instruction and the development of communities of practice: two key activities required of a curriculum that seeks to both prepare and empower students who are likely to be engaged in information-based "text work" (Luke, 2003, p. 137).

REFERENCES

Bolter, J. D., & Grusin, R. (1999). *Remediation: Understanding new media*. Cambridge, MA: MIT Press.

Brecht, B. (1991). *Mother courage and her children*. New York: Grove Press. (Original work published 1949)

Cope, B., & Kalantzis, M. (Eds.). (2000). *Multiliteracies: Literacy learning and the design of social futures*. London: Routledge.

Eckert, P. (2000). *Linguistic variation as social practice*. Oxford: Blackwell.

Gee, J. P. (1989). Literacy, discourse, and linguistics: Introduction and what is literacy? *Journal of Education, 171*(1), 5–25.

Holmevik, J. R., & Haynes, C. (2000). *MOOniversity: A student's guide to online learning environments*. Boston: Allyn & Bacon.

Kress, G. (2000). Design and transformation: New theories of meaning. In B. Cope & M. Kalantzis (Eds.), *Multiliteracies: Literacy learning and the design of social futures* (pp. 153–161). London: Routledge.

Kress, G. (2003). *Literacy in the new media age*. London: Routledge.

Lankshear, C., & Snyder, I. (with Green, B.). (2000). *Teachers and technoliteracy: Managing literacy, technology, and learning in schools*. Crows Nest, Australia: Allen & Unwin.

Luke, A. (2003). Literacy and the other: A sociological approach to literacy research and policy in multilingual societies. *Reading Research Quarterly, 38*(1), 132–141.

Luke, C. (2000). Cyber-schooling and technological change: Multiliteracies for new times. In B. Cope & M. Kalantzis (Eds.), *Multiliteracies: Literacy learning and the design of social futures* (pp. 69–91). London: Routledge.

New London Group. (1996). A pedagogy of multiliteracies: Designing social futures. *Harvard Educational Review, 66*, 60–92.

Oren, A. (1996). MOOing is more than writing. *Kairos: A Journal of Rhetoric, Technology and Pedagogy, 1*(2). Retrieved April 20, 2004, from http://english.ttu.edu/kairos/1.2/binder2.html?coverweb/avigail.html

Sanchez, R. (1998). Our bodies? Our selves? Questions about teaching in the MUD. In T. Taylor & I. Ward (Eds.), *Literacy theory in the age of the Internet* (pp. 93–106). New York: Columbia University Press.

Snyder, I. (Ed.). (2002). *Silicon literacies: Communication, innovation, and education in the electronic age*. London: Routledge.

Street, B. (1984). *Literacy in theory and practice*. Cambridge: Cambridge University Press.

Chapter 12

Comprehending Complexity

Victoria Purcell-Gates
University of British Columbia

The case studies presented in this edited volume cover a range of contexts and explore a number of relevant dimensions in the evolving picture of literacy as situated, multiple, and social. Across the studies, we move through issues of postcolonization, English and Arabic linguistic hegemony, immigration, literacy in and out of official and unofficial school and social spheres, and into the world of digital literacy. The actors' ages in these case studies range from 8 to 88. Some are speakers of multiple languages and readers/ writers of multilingual texts. Others are monolingual and read/ write only English. All of them provide accounts of reading and writing many and varied textual genres as they engage in shifting social spheres and sociotextual domains. Taken as a whole, the case studies in this volume provide a rich, nuanced, and textured portrait of lived literacy.

This collection is noteworthy not only for this range and variety but also for the insights provided by informants on relationships between literacy as it occurs in official school contexts and as it is taken up and practiced in out-of-school contexts. The Cultural Practices of Literacy Study (CPLS), of course, intentionally focuses on this question so that, within the individual studies, this information emerged along with the different themes and interpretations. Researchers observed children directly in and out of school, and adults were probed for recall and reflections regarding their schooling, literacy, and literacy practices in their lives.

With this concluding chapter, I will focus on some common themes and insights that are apparent to me across different sets of studies. I attempt to set each of these in larger theoretical and material contexts, and I focus this analysis around the general and specific goals of the CPLS study. Within this, I further specify and theorize some of the developing constructs that we are working on within CPLS. In particular, I focus on the construct of *sociotextual domain* and the continuing search for insights into the in- and out-of-school practice(s) of literacy—insights that both contribute to theories of literacy and literacy development but also promise real change in educational policy that will disrupt the almost perfect correlation between marginality status and academic underachievement in literacy.

CPLS EVOLVING DATA BASE

Beginning with the studies presented in this book, we began building a database of literacy in practice to allow for and to facilitate ongoing cross-case analyses. First, we created a metamatrix (Miles & Huberman, 1994) for the purpose of aggregating basic descriptive data on literacy events and texts read and written.[1] Included in the metamatrix are data (i.e., column headings) for the following: researcher; participant's pseudonym; participant's age, gender, and ethnicity; participant's country of birth; participant's native language, language spoken at home, and other languages; participant's citizenship; participant's student status, level of schooling completed; (if participant is a child) mother's and father's schooling and occupations; participant's urban, rural, suburban status; texts, read, written, or oral; language of text; and sociotextual domain(s) within which a particular text is used by the participant.

In addition to ongoing additions to the basic metamatrix, we are also collecting the following data sources for each case study: transcribed interviews, photographs, field notes, and final write-ups in which the researcher interprets and presents the findings from the situated case. For cross-case analyses, we use all of these sources in attempts to preserve the contexts and situated natures of each case as we, at the same time, look across cases for similar themes and supporting data (LeCompte & Schensul, 1999).

My discussion of common themes and insights now presented is based on these data sources. Some of these are simply emerging themes, worthy of discussion but without the status of a systematic cross-case analysis, with the exception of the discussion of power and agency, which has been presented to an academic audience and published.

HOME/SCHOOL CONNECTIONS

As noted in chapter 1, a primary goal of the CPLS study is to explore and begin to theorize the relationships between situated literacy practice and liter-

---

[1]Kristen Perry was instrumental in this process and deserves much of the credit for the actual creation of the metamatrix.

acy as it is learned within formal school contexts. Chapters 7, 8, 9, and 10 in this volume provide particularly rich fields for us to mine for insights into this relationship. First, though, let me provide you with more background regarding this interest in exploring the in- and out-of-school literacy connections, particularly the, perhaps, newer interest in how experiences with school literacy relates to how literacy is practiced by different individuals in situated sociocultural contexts. I begin with a theoretical and analytical clarification of a construct that is central to work in this area of literacy as situated and multiple.

Sociotextual Domain and Genre Theory

My work in this area of literacy practice differs, perhaps, from that of researchers like Street, Barton, and others who have been so instrumental in documenting the ways in which people use reading and writing in their lives. This body of work demonstrates how acts of reading and writing mediate the social lives of people and cannot be considered to exist separately, autonomously, from social activity. As such, many researchers within this tradition conduct various types of analyses involving the identification of specific literacy acts, or practices, with domains of social activity. With this, we can more clearly see the influence of the discipline of sociology on this area of research.

My analytical method follows this tradition with a slightly altered focus. I, like others within this tradition, very much see literacy acts as situated, and essentially part of, social activity. Thus, I also attempt to document and consider literacy practices within social domains. I differ, however, in that I foreground text(s) in this process, against the background(s) of social domain(s), reflecting my long-time interest in textual analysis and the acts of reading and writing different texts for different purposes within variable and shifting social contexts.[2]

Texts and Genre Theory. My focus on the texts involved in different literacy events within different literacy practices is theoretically framed by North American genre theory.[3] Halliday and Hasan's (1985) theory of social semiotics, with its focus on the social functionality of language, is the basis of this view of genre. Genres, in the instance of written language, are differentiated and identifiable written text types. The social semiotic view of language considers genres as socially constructed language practices, reflecting com-

---

[2]See the following as exemplars of this interest: Duke and Purcell-Gates, 2003; Purcell-Gates, 1988, 1996; Purcell-Gates and Duke, 2004.

[3]See A. Luke's (1994) discussion of North American genre theory as contrasted with the Sidney School application of genre to education.

munity norms and expectations. These norms are not static but change to reflect changing sociocultural needs and contexts (Berkenkotter & Huckin, 1995; Martin, Christie, & Rothery, 1987). Thus, *genres* are identifiable linguistic forms that are dynamic, fluid, and constructed by members of fluid and dynamic communities to serve social purposes that are situated within sociocultural contexts.

Within this frame, I see written genres as written language text types, or forms, that are socioculturally constructed, or formed, to serve social functions. Written language forms serve functions that require written, rather than oral, purposes. The forms, themselves, reflect these purposes.[4] In this way, written genre function always drives written genre form.[5]

I have used this functional, social semiotic frame for several research studies of written texts in use both in and out of school.[6] It is the basis of the construct of *authentic reading and writing activity*, discussed now.

For the CPLS study, I enlist the analytical technique of sorting reported reading and writing events and their texts into categories of *social activity*. To do this, I focus initially on the text involved in the literacy event and ask the question, "Within this context (reported by the informant), what social activity function is served by this text?" In this way, I enlist both dimensions of text type and social domain, invoking the construct of *sociotextual* domain. For example, the genres of phone messages, calendars, and driving directions appear within the sociotextual domain of *memory/record keeping* when they serve this purpose. Similarly, the genres of bathroom signs and personal function journals are categorized within the sociotextual domain of *personal care* when they serve that purpose. One can see how specific textual genres can be grouped within more than one sociotextual domain, depending on the social activity within which they function, for example, forms (read or written) appear within the sociotextual domains of both *work* and *bureaucracy*. The CPLS's sociotextual domains arise from the data on literacy textual practices reported by informants and are, thus, subject to reformulation and growth with additional data from new case studies.

Authenticity and Literacy Instruction

I described in chapter 1 some of the theorizing that resulted from the Literacy Practices of Adult Learners study (Purcell-Gates, Jacobson, & Degener,

---

[4]See Chafe and Danielewicz, 1986, for a description of pregenre-theory research findings on oral/written language differences.

[5]I certainly do not view written genres as the only language genres; genre theory is a theory of language genres and so assumes that oral as well as written genres are socioculturally based forms driven by social purpose. My focus on written genres reflects my specific interests and history as a teacher (of reading and writing) and as a researcher.

[6]See Purcell-Gates (1995, 1996), Purcell-Gates, Degener, Jacobson, and Soler (2002), and Purcell-Gates and Duke (2004).

2004) that motivated the CPLS work. The study, itself, focused on adult literacy instruction and relationships between elements of that instruction and *change* in the literacy practices of the students in their lives outside of schooling. We documented the literacy instruction for 79 different adult classes across the mainland United States and conducted interviews with 180 students in their homes every 3 months for 1 year, asking about all possible types of reading and writing events and texts, frequencies of these textual practices, and information about when they either began or stopped engaging with them. For our analysis, we controlled for student factors as well as classroom factors. We found that the degree to which teachers involved students in authentic literacy events had a significant impact on the degree to which the students reported change in their literacy practices. In other words, the higher the degree of authenticity in the literacy events during literacy instruction, the more the students read and wrote with greater frequency in their lives and the more new textual practices they began, most of which involved more linguistically complex texts than previously read and written.

It is important to apprehend our specific definition for this construct of *authenticity*, as we apply it in the context of literacy instruction. The term is not to be confused with a generalized meaning of *real*. Rather, our use of this term relates specifically to the nature of the reading and writing acts, or events, in which students engage while participating in the activity of schooling, an activity primarily designed to promote the learning of skills, content, attitudes, and values. For our purposes, which focus specifically on the acts of reading and writing, we further specify *schooling* as learning or developing reading and writing skills, strategies, values, and attitudes under the direction or guidance of intentional instruction.

Within this context of literacy instruction, we define *authentic* literacy activity as (a) reading and writing the textual types, or genres, that occur in the worlds of the students *outside* of the activity of literacy instruction; and (b) reading and writing those texts for the purposes for which they are read or written in the outside-of-literacy instruction world. These authentic *texts and purposes* are contrasted, within our frame, to those texts written primarily to teach reading and writing skills for the purposes of learning to read and write or to develop literacy skills, strategies, values, and attitudes—literacy activity we term *school-only*.[7]

According to this definition, prototypical authentic texts would include such real-life genres as novels, news articles, flyers, memos, health procedures, greeting cards, and so on—all of the text types read and written by

---

[7]See Purcell-Gates et al. (2002), Purcell-Gates, Jacobson, and Degener (2004), and Purcell-Gates and Duke (2004) for a fuller treatment of the construct of authentic literacy within literacy instruction.

people as part of their social and cultural lives. Authentic purposes for reading these different texts would include reading a novel for relaxation, escape, entertainment, and so forth, reading news articles for the latest news about an event of interest, reading flyers to see which music group is appearing in town, reading health procedures to manage one's health, and so on. Authentic purposes for writing such texts would include writing a newspaper article to inform a reader about the latest news of an event, composing a health brochure to help a reader follow appropriate procedures for managing a disease, composing a greeting card (or writing on one) to facilitate social bonding, and so on.

Prototypical school-only texts are genres such as worksheets, spelling lists, short passages with comprehension questions, flash cards, lists of sentences to be punctuated, and so on. School-only purposes for reading these texts are to learn or improve reading and writing skills. School-only purposes for writing these texts would be to assist in the teaching and learning of literacy skills.

Authentic texts can be read or written with school-only purposes, rendering the literacy activity less authentic (i.e., more school-only) because our determination of the degree to which literacy activity within instructional contexts is authentic is based on both text type and purpose for reading/writing specific texts For example, novels can be read in preparation for an exam on one's comprehension and interpretive skills, news articles can be read for purposes of identifying new vocabulary words, or flyers can be composed for purposes of completing a history unit with an innovative assignment designed to link to art and language arts—in this case, the flyers might be posted on the bulletin board as decoration and display of learning.

Again, the statistically significant impact on adult learners' literacy practices of authentic reading and writing within instructional contexts is highly suggestive of the power of bringing real-life texts and purposes into the classroom. Whereas the Literacy Practices of Adult Students focused on adult learners, a later study with second and third graders found a similar effect of authentic reading and writing activity within literacy instruction, this time on rate of growth in comprehension and composition (Purcell-Gates & Duke, 2004).

"Simply" Learning to Read and Write

However, another significant relationship with literacy practice change also surfaced in the analysis of the adult study data. The variable showing the highest effect size (of impact on changes in literacy practice) was for that of students' literacy levels at the beginning of their attendance in their literacy class. The lower the level of literacy ability at the start of the class, the more the students reported increased frequency and textual complexity of literacy practices in their out-of-school lives, irrespective of the degree of authenticity of the literacy in those classes.[8]

This suggests that school literacy instruction is basic to out-of-school literacy practice—to the ways students make literacy theirs and functional in their lives. It was this empirical link between formalized literacy instruction and multiple, situated literacy practice that motivated me to begin exploring this relationship with the CPLS research.

An obvious link between learning to read in school and using literacy in one's life is that of skill acquisition. It seems ridiculously clear that simply learning to read and write (a process that in the majority of cases requires some type of focused instruction) is a prerequisite to, and enabler of, reading and writing for different purposes outside of instruction. However, the additional impact of authentic literacy activity within instruction suggests that it is not so simple.

I have chosen to view the two major results of the adult literacy practices study as strong indications that a transaction exists between school-based (even, dare we say, academic/autonomous) literacy instruction and out-of-school situated multiple literacy practice. The influence of authentic textual practices on in-school literacy achievement, or development, transacts in yet-to-be fully understood ways with in-school, technical skill-focused, and autonomously administered literacy instruction to enable situated multiple literacy practice.

With this empirical and theoretical justification for exploring the influence of school-based literacy on out-of-school practice, I now present some of the initial insights into this transaction that arise within several of the case studies within this volume.

Influence of School Literacy Practice on Home/Community Practice

My search for influences of school-based literacy instruction on out-of-school practice is primarily for factors that went beyond the initial levels of acquiring the technical skills needed to decode and encode print. However, looking at the data in these cases that were collected with the protocol designed to begin to reveal these influences, I must conclude that these data suggest for the most part that it is apparently only when teachers make literacy instruction authentic (in the sense already discussed) that many students report a connection between literacy as taught in school and literacy as they practice it in their lives.

---

[8]Of course, the significant effect of degree of authenticity activity during instruction held irrespective of students' literacy levels at start of instruction. The Literacy Practices of Adult Learners data was analyzed using HLM techniques, which allowed us to control for a number of student-level and class-level factors.

O'Neil's case (chap. 10, this volume) of the two university students provides a good example of this. When asked how he thought literacy as practiced in his schooling is related to, or has influenced, how he practices it now, Will recalls his introduction to poetry. According to Will, he was first introduced to poetry as a textual and literacy practice by his elementary school teacher, who spent a great deal of classroom time involving her students in reading and writing poetry. Many teachers do the same. However, this teacher apparently moved the writing of poetry into the authentic realm when she sent several of Will's poems to the newspaper to be published. This rendered the act of writing poetry in school an authentic literacy event for Will; he wrote an authentic genre (poetry) for another authentic text type (the newspaper) for an authentic audience (the newspaper readers). His school texts became public texts and brought into the home to be considered as such, according to O'Neil. To this day, Will reports poetry—the reading and writing of it—as a significant literacy practice in his life.

Kersten (chap. 8, this volume) and Gallagher (chap. 10, this volume) provide additional support for the notion that the school-to-home influence is primarily that of technical skill acquisition unless instruction includes authentic literacy activity. Responding to the same CPLS interview protocol, Nakita, Kristen, and Jessica in Kersten's study agree that school literacy is important—to learn to read and write. Kristen and Jessica do not mention any actual genre-based practice that they first encountered in school and then used in their out-of-school lives. Nakita does see a connection between the literacy needed to count and use money to buy things with—an authentic practice apparently taught in her school and for which she recognized its value in her life. Ranicia, though, again reveals her perception of school as the source of technical skill when responding to the query about how writing in school is like writing outside of school. She focuses on technical form when she asserts that she can now write in cursive (for her out-of-school writing activities) because they had been practicing it in school.

Differentiating herself from the others, Katie, in Kersten's study, sees no relationship between literacy as practiced in school and literacy as practiced in her home and community. Kersten points out that Katie experiences multiple literacy practices in her home and community, such as reading chapter books, writing poetry, reading and writing as part of participating in Sunday school, and so on. The fact that she sees no connection between those practices and the literacy practices she associates with school may suggest that even the chapter book reading she does in school is 'taught' in such a way as to render it school-only. At the very least, this young student perceives it as such.

Such was the case with Gallagher's (chap. 10, this volume) at-risk adolescents. Although they each reported multiple literacy practices as embedded within their out-of-school lives, they did not perceive the literacy embedded in their instruction as related. Gallagher concludes that their teacher's attempt to bring in authentic texts in order to motivate them (to engage in the assigned work) failed to have the desired effect because the purposes for which he had them read and write them were patently school-only, as recognized by the students.

Throughout these case studies, we see, when looking for influences of school literacy practice on out-of-school practice, similar indications: Children and adults, retrospectively, recognize that school-based instruction gave them the technical skill to read and write, but, unless that instruction involved them in authentic literacy activities, the literacy as learned in school ended there, at the school door. This line of work deserves much more research and thought. If literacy is situated, then literacy practices are developed in response to specific life and social situations. The influence of schooling does not, by itself, extend to life situations, at least as far as literacy practice is concerned. What apparently (at least as far as these data and those of a few other studies indicate) is needed is for schooling to incorporate situated literacy practices into instruction before students will incorporate them into their own lives and social situations outside of school.

Children at U.S. Chinese Schools: A Case of Disconfirming Evidence. Complicating this picture, however, is disconfirming evidence to this hypothesis of the necessity of authentic literacy activity within instructional contexts to out-of-school literacy practice. Zhang (chap. 5, this volume) describes how Cindy first learned poetry in English and in school. Cindy's description of this school activity gives no suggestion of authentic purpose beyond the school-only one. "She was required to read a number of poems, and summarize them to enhance her comprehension of the poems. Then, she was instructed to write several poems as homework assignment" (p. 93).

Cindy tells Zhang that it was while writing the poems for homework that she found that she truly enjoyed this textual practice and took up writing poetry in both English and Chinese for her own purposes, this time writing for authentic audiences like herself and her parents. Zhang reports a similar importation of school literacy practice when she describes Cindy's love of making polyhedrons, something she learned about in school. Again, she took what was apparently a school-only practice and transformed it into an authentic one when she began making the decorative objects for her own enjoyment and room decor.

Cindy's importation of school literacy practices into the sociotextual domains of her out-of-school life reflects similar findings from the Literacy Practices of Adult Learners Study (Purcell-Gates, Degener, Jacobson, & Soler, 2002). Some of the participants for that study also reported that they had been introduced to new text types within their instruction that, previously, they had not engaged with, and in many cases had not encountered in their lives. There was the strong suggestion that if these texts had not been assigned, these adult students would not have read or written them at all. Some of the students reported that they did not continue reading or writing those new genres—most of which were more complex school-like texts like novels, poetry, journals, and essays—in their out-of-school lives. However, several others said that they, like Cindy, had discovered authentic reasons for continuing one or more of these practices.

Features of the qualitative analysis that revealed these findings rendered it not possible to ascertain whether or not these adult students encountered these imported textual practices within the context of authentic literacy activity in their classrooms. However, the existence of this data, along with Zhang's findings, provides the rationale and motivation for more systematic study of this issue.

Why is this important to us, as literacy theorists and researchers, and to schools and society? To answer this, we need is to consider the very role of schooling itself. The answer to this question must include political, social, cultural, ethical, and economic contexts and concerns. The question is much too broad and extensive for due exploration here. However, the role of schooling, and of literacy acquisition and development within schools, is essentially related to concerns raised in chapter 1 as to the very definition(s) of literacy and measurements of literacy ability/levels that consume so much political attention by national and world political bodies. For me, this question is intimately related to the critical heuristic driving the CPLS project: While I am convinced that most people learn to read and write within school-like contexts, what do they actually do with this literacy? And, does what they do with literacy reflect, or relate to, their literacy schooling?

The role of schooling is also related to another of the emerging patterns visible when looking across the cases contained in this volume. This is the role of schooling that is often cited but rarely fully acknowledged—that of credentialing.

Literacy as Credentialing

The question as to what do people do with the literacy learned in school is presupposed by the notion that schooling is, in some sense, a training ground for social activity—that one learns how to do something in school that one plans to do when schooling is finished. However, both implicitly and explicitly, the participants in several of these case studies expressed the belief that the primary value of school and literacy-as-practiced-in-school beyond the decoding/encoding stage was to provide one with credentials that will allow access to the goodies of modern life—a good job, a high salary, prestige, and so on. Penny (in Collins, chap. 7, this volume) values school only for credentialing purposes—to be like Steph, who she sees as educated and financially successful. Granted, Collins admits to stressing this role of schooling with Penny while trying to convince her of at least one reason to apply herself to her studies. However, Collins laments that Penny took on this externally based value without a full understanding. "For Penny, 'education' and in-school reading and writing function as tools devoid of instructions" (p. 130)." Going through the motions suffices for Penny who holds this credentialing model of education literally but superficially.

> Penny truly believes that in pretending to read her social studies textbook she meets the literacy demands before her and, furthermore, truly believes that such an approach to school literacies will gain her the credentialing that I and others have sold to her—sold to her but not adequately explained to her; Penny means it but does not "get it" when she says she reads and writes in school to "to get good grades, get an education, be like you." (Collins, p. 130)

Perry, in chapter 4, concluded that certification and credentialing are of high importance to the southern Sudanese refugees and emanate from schooling. The literacy practices they must struggle with as part of their community college courses in the United States (decontextualized English as a second language [ESL] worksheets, problems sets, and so on) is seen as a necessary process they must go through in order to achieve the credentials they need. The rich and varied literacy practices with which they engage outside of their classes are not seen by them as part of, or the result of, this schooling.

English, as a language of power, is viewed similarly in the case studies of Puerto Rico (Mazak, chap. 2, this volume) and Botswana (Molosiwa, chap. 3, this volume). In many ways, the participants in Mazak's case study—a Puerto Rican farming family—suggest the high credentialing value that formal schooling, and schooling in English, hold. Mazak concludes:

> English is seen as the key to financial success, to scientific and technological advancement. For this reason it is taught in the schools, and the aspirations of even the procommonwealth government who declared Spanish the sole official language were to promote bilingualism with English, not because it was an official language but because it was necessary for participation in the global economy. (p. 27)

Similar values of accreditation and credentialing for English-language learning and formal schooling (at the higher levels, these two are virtually synonymous) is reported by Molosiwa's (chap. 3, this volume) participants for people of Botswana.

One of Mazak's points is that the ascribed value of credentialing for the English language does not translate to the practice of English speaking, reading, or writing outside of school. This is the point, I believe, that drives the rationale for probing this school-to-life relationship further. Although most of us can concur that the technical level of decoding and encoding is critical to later literacy learning, what happens to those academic, essayist literacy practices that are taught and assessed in later levels of education? This seems critical to ask, given the time and funds expended by students and the public for education that extends over years and years. Mazak's analysis raises issues of culture, power, and life contexts when describing how, when, why, and by whom certain school-based literacy practices valued for credentialing purposes become imported and transformed by people in their out-of-school lives. It is this kind of complexity that we need to bring to this issue. Until we can understand much more about this process of school-to-life literacy practice, at similar levels of complexity, we will continue to hold simplistic assumptions and expectations about the role of schooling in the literacy lives of people.

Agency and Power[9]

Complicating these questions regarding relationships between literacy-as-learned and practiced in school and out-of-school literacy practice, are those raised by A. Luke (2003) and presented in chapter 1, this volume. In a politically and economically globalized world, how are language and textual resources made accessible, to whom, and under which conditions? Learners who engage with formal literacy instruction bring complex sets of linguistic resources to the school setting: different languages with different economic capital, varied textual resources, and an array of multiliteracies embedded in culturally contextualized multiple literacy practices. Any discussion of authenticity of literacy practice within schools must consider such factors and dimensions: How does power relate to students' acknowledgment of linguistic and textual legitimacy and how does this affect perceptions of authenticity of literacy practice within schooling contexts?

As I noted in chapter 1, poststructuralist frames have allowed us to move beyond structuralist notions of linguistic hegemony wherein subjects are always subjugated by dominant, hegemonic discourses to a stance that recognizes the agency of different individuals and groups who move more fluidly between and among multiple sociocultural contexts. It is this frame that allows us to see evidence of linguistic agency within and across the CPLS case studies in this volume. I believe that such analysis contributes to the explor-

---

[9]I am indebted to Kristen Perry and Erik Jacobson for contributing to my thinking about this issue.

ations central to the CPLS project—explorations that presuppose complex relationships between and among issues of power, language, literacy practice, literacy learning, and schooling.

First of all, several of the chapters in this volume reveal, not only the fact of the impact of linguistic hegemony on literacy practice, but also some of the complexities that are often not thought of by those who decry the effects of English dominance in the world. Many of the chapters that deal with populations outside of the United States document the role of English hegemony on the literacy practices of the people. English has become the language of world markets in this era of increased globalization. Further, English continues to dominate as the language of colonization in much of the world. Finally, with the end of the cold war, English, as exported by the United States, has become the language of military dominance and oppression. Mazak (Puerto Rico, chap. 2, this volume), Molosiwa (Botswana, chap. 3, this volume), and Perry (Sudan, chap. 4, this volume) all provide compelling descriptions of the ways that English is levered into literacy practices through both official decrees and unofficial social and economic pressures.

These chapters also raise new and interesting variables to consider regarding linguistic hegemony. Mazak reports on how the Puerto Rican people have fought to maintain their Spanish language use and heritage and how a close reading of environmental print reveals the facade of English over the substance of Spanish. She also provides compelling detail for the ways that social class and English-language use transact in the lives of Puerto Ricans. This relationship between the use of English and social class is also apparent in Botswana, as described by Molosiwa. Perry documents the ways that power and language intersected the lives of the young Sudanese orphans fleeing the violence and repression resulting from the civil war in Sudan. In this case, the power–language relationship is brought into even sharper relief as we can see the hegemony of both English and Arabic in action. The ways in which the tribal languages of the people (primarily, in this case, Dinka) weave throughout the participants' language and literacy practices adds more texture and complexity to this report. Such complexity is also present in Molosiwa's account of Botswana, with tribal languages and English employed separately for different purposes as well as together, responding to such considerations as geography, social settings and domains, communicative participants, as well as social-class issues, discussed previously.

Other aspects of agency came up in several of the case studies—agency as the self-determined taking up of literacy practices within the contexts of power and hegemony. Mazak, and Molosawi, in particular, uncovered reports of this factor in their accounts of language and textual domination by English in Puerto Rico and Botswana, respectively. Perry notes similar accounts as related to English and Arabic hegemonic practices in the Sudan.

Lara, in the Rosolová chapter (chap. 6, this volume), is particularly adamant about her ability and will to pick and choose her language and text according to her own wishes and needs. This was true for her both in her native Cuba and in her life in the United States.

Within these reports, participants relate how they, as agents, choose English or native language, written or oral texts, depending on their needs, beliefs, and values as they move within and across different and specific contexts of culture and communication. This has a different feel from traditional accounts of English hegemony, which position people more as acted-upon rather than as actors. In fact, in these chapters, the taking up and putting aside of literacy practices and languages has more of an imported/exported feel rather than an imposed one.

Of course, this is a complex issue and one that must be considered within its totality. Agency is never available outside of a system of choices. This framework of choices is, at the same time, determined by the existing power structure(s). Available languages, discourses, and texts, from which one may exercise agency and choose to use for personal, communicative purposes, are constrained by frameworks of power. Thus, what appears to be an exercise of agency is contextualized by available resources and prevailing ideology. As E. Jacobson (personal communication, February 10, 2004) puts it:

> This, in fact, is the most powerful part of hegemonic power, getting people to "choose" their poison. Think about "Learning to Labor" in which the lads "reject" the schooling that mainstream society is forcing upon them, only to end up being exploited labor in factories .... Some agency is key, how much agency is the question. Even when importing, you have a choice to import some things and not others. And what you can import is limited by your financial capital. Does cultural capital determine what literacy practices you can import? Does the power structure export good things, or things it knows are? Some of my ESL students told me that they thought the ESL system in the U.S. was giving them bad English to keep them down ...

A significant contribution of these case studies to this discussion of agency and hegemony, I believe, is the self-report nature of the data. The accounts of literacy practice choice in this volume are provided from the participants' perspectives. These are the linguistic, discourse, and textual realities as lived and experienced by the actors. This adds powerful empirical data to the discussion, much of which has been constructed by researchers and theorists from the outside.[10] It complicates the notion of *linguistic hegemony* and that is good. If we are to ultimately understand the

---

[10]A notable exception to this is the research by Canaragarajah (1999), reported in *Resisting Linguistic Imperialism* in English Teaching.

construct, how it works in the process of literacy practice and literacy de-velopment, we must begin to recognize, name, and describe complexity in order to study it.

Influence of Home Literacy Practices on Literacy Learning

Adding another complexity to our consideration of literacy learning in school, authenticity within literacy instruction, and literacy-in-use outside of schooling contexts and purposes is that of how literacy practice in the homes and communities of learners appears to influence the effectiveness of early literacy learning in school. Having conducted my share of this re-search, I conceptualize this body of knowledge as a piece of the complex whole just described. Luke's call for systematic investigation of the linguistic capital and resources brought to school by actors whose life conditions re-flect multiplicity and fluidity across social, cultural, and linguistic domains can be seen as reflecting what I, and many others, believed we were doing when we engaged in what is now referred to as *emergent literacy research*. Granted this research was conducted within different theoretical frames. It has also been (in my opinion) misused by some who would forward a hege-monic agenda against nonmainstream, linguistic minorities. Although these factors render emergent literacy findings in need of reinterpretation, it does not render them void.

The significant ways in which literacy practices manifest in the home, out-of-school, lives of participants cut across political, geographic, and economic boundaries in the case studies. I have written of the different ways that literacy practice is engaged in homes and communities. The data in these reports document the tremendous variability of print liter-acy frequency and type of written textual practices found in different homes and communities. Further, analysis of this data has revealed the ways in which home literacy practices transact with and relate theoretically and empirically to in-school early literacy achievement (Purcell-Gates, 1995, 1996).

Although studies within this particular tradition have often been simplis-tically interpreted by policymakers and the public ("School underachieve-ment is the result of homes where people don't, or can't, read and write."), this should not lead us to reject the suggestion that variability in home liter-acy practice is related to school achievement, or, perhaps more signifi-cantly, to literacy development and ultimate literacy practice in life. In this collection of case studies, we see this influence of children's home literacy culture on their literacy lives as adolescents and adults self-reported by Batswana, Cubans, Puerto Ricans, and Americans. We see it reported by ur-ban children, immigrant adults, and Midwestern U.S. college students, some of whom are visiting foreign nationals to the United States.

   This aggregation of evidence of the influence of children's home literacy cultures on their adult practice(s) of literacy strongly argues for continued investigation along these lines. Moving forward, emergent literacy researchers, or their heirs, can significantly contribute to the developing picture of complex and synergistic relationships among home literacy practice and linguistic capital within contexts of power, language, hegemony, and textual resources and accessibility.

Experienced Literacy Practice by Children

An important piece of this pattern of complexity, and one that is uniquely provided by the CPLS data is the phenomenological perspective of school children—those very learners with whom we are concerned. Several of the case studies in this volume focus on how children use reading and writing in their lives. This goes beyond the typical focus on children's reading and writing as defined and shaped by schools. Rather, the researchers observed and explicitly questioned their young participants about texts and social practices in which these texts are embedded in their out-of-school lives. Thus, we get a glimpse of embodied literacy practice in the lives of those who are still very much involved in learning how to read and write in school, and this glimpse is through the perspectives of the children themselves.

   In addition to this direct look at current literacy practices of our informant children, we also elicited self-report retrospective accounts of literacy practice during childhood from our adult informants. Qualitatively, of course, this data is different in that retrospective accounts are filtered through memory and adult notions of literacy and literacy practice. However, it does provide us with suggestive insights into literacy practice in the worlds of children that can be added to the accounts from the child-focused studies (Collins, chap. 7, Kerstin, chap. 8, and Zhang chap. 5, all in this volume). What have we learned from these perspectives?

   Looking across the different studies, we see children using printed texts to participate in several sociotextual domains other than school. They read and write to maintain social cohesion with family and friends. They read and write for purposes of relaxation and entertainment.

   One unexpected purpose for reading and writing was reported by several children: helping, or apprenticing, with parents as they participate in their own overlapping social domains. Sometimes this was related to children who served as language brokers between their parents and the English-speaking world with which the parent engaged. Other times, though, this seemed to take the form of helping (in the true sense, not "playing work"). For example, Kersten reports that one of her young informants relayed how she helps her mother write lists of her students' names. Another child helps her mother with different writing tasks associated with her mother's different volunteer roles at church. Erin, in O'Neil's chapter 10, this volume, tells how she and her siblings would attend college courses with their mother due to the need for child care. During these events, the children would find themselves experiencing academic oral and written texts designed for adults. In addition, Erin would help her mother, who was training to be a teacher, design lessons and make storybooks for other children. These glimpses into the practice of literacy by children as they participate in the lives of their parents suggests an area in much need of more research by those attempting to describe and chronicle the development of print literacy skill and practice.

Digital Literacies

One dimension of children's developing literacy practice was explored as a small, initial, pilot of the possibilities of cross-case analysis of data such as that collected for CPLS case studies. This is the dimension of digital literacies. The New London Group (Cope & Kalantzis, 2000) constructed an elaborated theoretical framework for studying literacy and literacy pedagogy for the 21st century. Within the multiliteracies frame, they emphasize the need to recognize, describe, and develop instruction that addresses the different semiotic systems and modalities through which literacy is practiced today. One area of focus is the world of digital literacies. Kress (2000) and C. Luke (2000) are two prominent voices raising this area as significant for scholars of literacy studies.

Certainly, over the past 20 years, educators and the general public have expressed concern as well as excitement over the increased usage of computers, the Internet, and the World Wide Web. Some have fretted that computers are replacing books. Others have worried about the unfettered access to dubious information on the Web. Schools have struggled to provide experience with computer technology for all children with the belief that job markets consider such knowledge essential. Computer companies have eyed this potential market and have provided, sometimes free-of-charge, at least minimal technology to classrooms, at least in the United States.

No one really knows, however, how children are actually taking up digital literacies, the degree to which they are employing the computer technologies increasingly available to them, or the degree to which they are incorporating such literacies into their literacy lives. An analysis of the reported and observed literacy practices across the different case studies in this book provides an initial glimpse into some of the answers to these questions.[11]

As just discussed, children's literacy practices in many ways mirror and overlap those of the adults in their lives. So it is for digital literacies, at least in our total sample (recall that some of the data on children's literacy practices are retrospective). The total number of texts entered in the database were 1,361. Of the total number of texts ($N = 1,361$) reported as read or written by both children and adults, 14% were digital texts. Thus, at least with this sample, with its overreliance on participants contextualized by Internet literacy, it does not seem that computer literacies are replacing paper, pencil, or books. Rather, people seem to be incorporating digital literacies into already existing purposes and social domains that are mediated by reading and writing. Digital literacy looks like just another technology, albeit one with its own modalities, designs, and representational resources (Kress, 2000).

Examining the sociotextual domains that contextualize these digital literacies, we see the domains of children's lives and not those usually of adults'. Of the 22 different domains (see chap. 1, this volume), digital literacies were observed or reported within 13. Of these, digital literacies are most represented in the domains of self-motivated education, information/news, and interpersonal communication. The domains that did not show any involvement of digital texts for the children in our sample included: bureaucracy, clubs/organizations, community information, community organization, fashion, finances, health, parenting, politics, personal care, personal writing, religion, social cohesion, and work.

It appears that digital literacies mediated the lives of the adults in these case study samples more than the children. Digital literacies appeared in 12 domains for the adults, as opposed to only 9 domains for the children. In addition, digital-related texts appeared in various domains in higher percentages for adults than for kids. For example, the domains of entertainment, information/news, interpersonal communication, public writing, school, self-motivated education, and shopping contained digital literacies for both kids and adults. The adults used digital literacies more frequently

---

[11]Kristen Perry contributed jointly to this analysis and report. These data must be considered very temporary and initial, given the limitations of the larger sample from which they come. The participants across the different case studies should in no way be taken as representative. They were selected to suit the interests of the individual researchers and to provide access to information that would address the focus questions of the CPLS study, listed previously. Another factor to keep in mind when frequencies are reported now is that one of the studies (see Eyman, chap. 11, this volume) involved only those participants who were at the time involved in a class on creating an Internet space. The data reported come from a cross-case analysis of the different case studies. The analysis involved the following descriptive variables: 53 females and 33 males, ranging in age from 8 to 71+; 21 children from ages 8 to 18; half of the people entered into the metamatrix spoke English as their first language.

than the kids in the domains of interpersonal communication, public writing, school, and shopping. Adults and children used digital literacies at about the same frequency in the domains of entertainment and information/news, and self-motivated education.

These data are interesting in light of the discussions and debates swirling about the growth of digital literacy practices, at least in developed nations. They provide a more nuanced look at the roles that digital literacy is playing in people's lives, adding detail to a complex pattern of literacies and social activity. They also provide a sense of the possibilities of continued case study and cross-case analysis of literacy as situated and practiced when we consider issues such as schooling and curriculum for children of today.

COMPREHENDING THE COMPLEX FOR COMPREHENSIVE CHANGE

It is my belief that research such as that represented in this volume could lay the foundation for real and comprehensive change to the way we do literacy instruction in our schools. Please note that when I use the term *our schools*, I am thinking of any form of intentional literacy instruction in all types of settings in developed and developing countries. I am also assuming a definition of literacy that includes reading, writing, listening, speaking, and viewing.

How do we get from a collection of carefully documented and analyzed situated literacy practices to meaningful change in literacy instruction? We do this, I believe, by building a comprehensive understanding of how students actually understand, value, and practice literacy and, armed with those insights, construct curriculum that will, simply put, make sense to them and be seen by them as providing them with the literacy skills and abilities they currently need and will need in the future.

To reach the point where we can begin to feel knowledgeable about students' literacy lives, though, we must continue to collect focused data about literacy practices, their texts, events, participants, and sociotextual domains. At the same time, and as part of this process, we will begin to really see, sometimes for the first time, the instantiations of literacy in the lives of our students. As this occurs, the lives and realities of students will appear with greater clarity. This, I believe, can lead to the development and delivery of literacy instruction that is taken up and actualized by students.

REFERENCES

Berkenkotter, C., & Huckin, T. N. (Eds.). (1995). *Genre knowledge and disciplinary communication: Cognition/culture/power* (pp. 1–25). Hillsdale, NJ: Lawrence Erlbaum Associates.

Canaragarajah, A. S. (1999). *Resisting linguistic imperialism in English teaching*. Oxford, U.K.: Oxford University Press.

Chafe, W., & Danielewicz, J. (1986). Properties of spoken and written language. In R. Horowitz & S. J. Samuels (Eds.), *Comprehending oral and written language* (pp. 83–113). New York: Academic.

Cope, B., & Kalantzis, M. (Eds.). (2000). *Multiliteracies: Literacy learning and the design of social futures*. London, England: Routledge.

Duke, N. K., & Purcell-Gates, V. (2003). Genres at home and at school: Bridging the known to the new. *Reading Teacher, 57*, 30–37.

Halliday, M. A. K., & Hasan, R. (1985). *Language, context and text: A social semiotic*. Geelong, Australia: Deakin University Press.

Kress, G. (2000). Multimodality. In B. Cope & M. Kalantzis (Eds.), *Multiliteracies: Literacy learning and the design of social futures* (pp. 153–161). London: Routledge.

LeCompte, M. D., & Schensul, J. J. (1999). *Designing and conducting ethnographic research*. Walnut Creek, CA: AltaMira Press.

Luke, A. (1994). Locating genre studies. In A. Freedman & P. Medway (Eds.). *Genre and the new rhetoric* (pp. 1–22). London: Taylor & Francis.

Luke, A. (2003). Literacy and the other: A sociological approach to literacy research and policy in multilingual societies. *Reading Research Quarterly, 38*, 132–141.

Luke, C. (2000). Cyber-schooling and technological change: Multiliteracies for new times. In B. Cope & M. Kalantzis (Eds.), *Multiliteracies: Literacy learning and the design of social futures* (pp. 69–91). London: Routledge.

Martin, J. R., Christie, F., & Rothery, J. (1987). Social processes in education: A reply to Sawyer and Watson (and others). In I. Reid (Ed.), *The place of genre in learning: Current debates* (pp. 58–82). Melbourne, Australia: Deakin University, Centre for Studies in Literacy Education.

Miles, M., & Huberman, M. (1994). *Qualitative data analysis: An expanded sourcebook* (2nd ed). London: Sage.

Purcell-Gates, V. (1988). Lexical and syntactic knowledge of written narrative held by well-read-to kindergartners and second graders. *Research in the Teaching of English, 22*, 128–160.

Purcell-Gates, V. (1995). *Other people's words: The cycle of low literacy*. Cambridge, MA: Harvard University Press.

Purcell-Gates, V. (1996). Stories, coupons, & the *TV Guide*: Relationships between home literacy experiences and emergent literacy knowledge. *Reading Research Quarterly, 31*, 406–438.

Purcell-Gates, V., Degener, S., Jacobson, E., & Soler, M. (2002). Impact of adult literacy instruction on adult literacy practices. *Reading Research Quarterly, 37*, 70–92.

Purcell-Gates, V., & Duke, N. K. (2004). *Learning to read and write science genres: The roles of authentic experience and explicit teaching*. Washington, DC: National Science Foundation.

Purcell-Gates, V., Jacobson, E., & Degener, S. (2004). *Print literacy development: Uniting the cognitive and social practice theories*. Cambridge, MA: Harvard University Press.

Cultural Practices of Literacy Study: Semistructured Literacy Practices Interview[1]

(Each participant should have already read and discussed the Informed Consent letter with the interviewer and have signed the consent form.)

Start the interview with this narrative elicitation: "What does literacy mean to you?"

OUT-OF-SCHOOL LITERACY

Current Literacy Practices

I. What kinds of things do you **read** in your life (that are not part of any school work you might be doing at this time)?

For each text or practice mentioned, elicit information about why (purpose of reading); social context (as part of what type of activity, like work, church, committees, shopping for family, etc.), participant structure, that is, other people involved in the literacy events (like reading to a child, writing to a relative, etc.); and how important, enjoyable or fulfilling it is. (Don't belabor this; the goal is to remain conversational and informal.) Ask which language these activities happen in, if you are not sure.

PROMPTS (With each of the following, you can give example texts but don't ask about any one specifically.):

---

[1] A Spanish version of this interview protocol was used for Spanish-speaking informants.

- For daily tasks?
- For personal care/health?
- For political/civic participation/voting?
- With your children? With your spouse? With your friends? With your co-workers?
- For official purposes like getting a visa or work permit?
- For paying taxes?
- At your job?
- For entertainment?
- For relaxation?
- For information?
- For shopping?
- For worship (or religious purposes)?
- Internet?
- For group/community activities (e.g., Boy Scouts, Jaycees, book groups)

II. What kinds of texts do you **write** in your life (that are not part of any school work you might be doing at the present time)?

For each text or practice mentioned, elicit information about why (purpose of writing); social context (as part of what type of activity, like work, church, committees, shopping for family, etc.); participant structure, that is, other people involved in the literacy events (like reading to a child, writing to a relative, etc.); and how important or fulfilling it is. (Don't belabor this; the goal is to remain conversational and informal.) Ask which language these activities happen in, if you are not sure.

PROMPTS (With each of the following, you can give example texts but don't ask about any one specifically.):

- For daily tasks?
- For personal care/health?
- For political/civic participation/voting?
- With your children? With your spouse? With your friends? With your co-workers?
- For official purposes like getting a visa or work permit?
- For paying taxes?
- At your job?
- For entertainment?
- For relaxation?
- For information?
- For shopping?
- For worship (or religious purposes)?
- Internet?
- For group/community activities (e.g., Boy Scouts, Jaycees, book groups)

Historical Literacy Practices

I. When you were a child, what kinds of texts (or "things") did people in your family (or house) **read** regularly (except for those things that kids or adults read for school assignments)? *(Use questions from above to prompt.)*

For each text or practice mentioned, elicit information about why (purpose of writing); social context (as part of what type of activity, like work, church, committees, shopping for family, etc.); participant structure, language the reading/text was in; and how important and/or enjoyable/fulfilling it was to whomever was doing the reading. (Don't belabor this; the goal is to remain conversational and informal.)

PROMPTS (With each of the following, you can give example texts but don't ask about any one specifically.):

- For daily tasks?
- For personal care/health?
- For political/civic participation/voting?
- With your children? With your spouse? With your friends? With your co-workers?
- For official purposes like getting a visa or work permit?
- For paying taxes?
- At your job?
- For entertainment?
- For relaxation?
- For information?
- For shopping?
- For worship (or religious purposes)?
- Internet?
- For group/community activities (e.g., Boy Scouts, Jaycees, book groups)

II. When you were a child, what kinds of texts did your family **write** regularly (except for those things kids or adults wrote for a teacher in school as an assignment)?

For each text or practice mentioned, elicit information about why (purpose of writing); social context (as part of what type of activity, like work, church, committees, shopping for family, etc.); participant structure; and how important and/or enjoyable/fulfilling it was to whomever was doing the writing. (Don't belabor this; the goal is to remain conversational and informal.)

PROMPTS (With each of the following, you can give example texts but don't ask about any one specifically.):

- For daily tasks?
- For personal care/health?

- For political/civic participation/voting?
- With your children? With your spouse? With your friends? With your co-workers?
- For official purposes like getting a visa or work permit?
- For paying taxes?
- At your job?
- For entertainment?
- For relaxation?
- For information?
- For shopping?
- For worship (or religious purposes)?
- Internet?
- For group/community activities (e.g., Boy Scouts, Jaycees, book groups)

III. What kinds of texts did other people in your community read or write when you were a child? (These should be texts that the participant remembers seeing people use, not those that he "supposes" people used.)

For each text or practice mentioned, elicit information about why (purpose of writing); social context (as part of what type of activity, like work, church, committees, shopping for family, etc.); participant structure; and how important and/or enjoyable/fulfilling it was to whomever was doing the writing. (Don't belabor this; the goal is to remain conversational and informal.)

PROMPTS (With each of the following, you can give example texts but don't ask about any one specifically.):

- For daily tasks?
- With your children? With your spouse? With your friends? With your co-workers?
- For official purposes like getting a visa or work permit?
- For paying taxes?
- At your job?
- For entertainment?
- For relaxation?
- For information?
- For shopping?
- For worship (or religious purposes)?
- Internet?
- For group/community activities (e.g., Boy Scouts, Jaycees, book groups)

Do you think that the way you feel about reading and writing—like how useful they are or how enjoyable they are—is about the same or different in some way from how people in your community and in your family felt? (Probe for explanations and examples.)

SCHOOL LITERACY PRACTICES

Current School Literacy Practices (if applicable)

I. What kinds of texts do you read in your school as part of the school instruction/assignments (e.g., textbooks, novels, basal readers, encyclopedias, Internet, short stories, poetry, worksheets, picture books, information books, science books, math books, etc.)?

For each text or practice mentioned, elicit information about why (purpose of reading); social context (as part of what type of school activity); participant structure (e.g., read to or with whom and write to or with whom?); and how important and/or enjoyable/fulfilling it is. (Don't belabor this; the goal is to remain conversational and informal.)

II. Which of these literacy practices/texts did you particularly enjoy? Dislike? Find difficult? Boring? Why? Examples?

III. What kinds of texts do students **write** in your school as part of the school instruction/assignments (e.g., stories, poetry, spelling practice, reports, worksheets, essays/compositions, journals, class books, etc.)?

For each text or practice mentioned, elicit information about why (purpose of writing); social context (as part of what type of school activity); participant structure (e.g., read to or with whom and write to or with whom?); and how important and/or enjoyable/fulfilling it is. (Don't belabor this; the goal is to remain conversational and informal.)

IV. Which of these literacy practices/texts did you particularly enjoy? Dislike? Find difficult? Boring? Why? Examples?

V. Do you think the reading and writing you do at school prepares you for the kinds of things that you read and write outside of school? Why or why not, or in what ways?

VI. How do you think the reading/writing you do at school similar to or different than the reading/writing you do outside of school?

Historical School Literacy Practices

I. What kinds of texts did you read in your school as part of the school instruction/assignments (e.g., textbooks, novels, basal readers, encyclopedias, Internet, short stories, poetry, worksheets, picture books, information books, science books, math books, etc.)?

For each text or practice mentioned, elicit information about why (purpose of reading); social context (as part of what type of school activity); participant structure (e.g., read to or with whom and write to or with whom?); and how important and/or enjoyable/fulfilling it was. (Don't belabor this; the goal is to remain conversational and informal.)

PROMPTS (for each of these, it will help to conduct a brief conversation about the grade level, like where the participant lived then, do they remember the school, teacher, etc.):

- During kindergarten?
- During Grades 1–3?
- During Grades 4–6?
- During Grades 7–8
- During Grades 9–12
- During post-high school education (technical school; college; education classes in the military, etc.; for this, be sure to elicit what type of education/school they connect to specific literacy practices).

II. Which of these literacy practices/texts did you particularly enjoy? Dislike? Find difficult? Boring? Why? Examples?

III. What kinds of texts did students **write** in your school as part of the school instruction/assignments (e.g., stories, poetry, spelling practice, reports, worksheets, essays/compositions, journals, class books, etc.)?

For each text or practice mentioned, elicit information about why (purpose of writing); social context (as part of what type of school activity); participant structure (e.g., read to or with whom and write to or with whom?); and how important and/or enjoyable/fulfilling it is. (Don't belabor this; the goal is to remain conversational and informal.)

PROMPTS (For each of these, it will help to conduct a brief conversation about the grade level, like where the participant lived then, do they remember the school, teacher, etc.?):

- During kindergarten?
- During Grades 1–3?
- During Grades 4–6?
- During Grades 7–8
- During Grades 9–12
- During post-high school education (technical school; college; education classes in the military, etc.; for this, be sure to elicit what type of education/school they connect to specific literacy practices).

IV. Which of these literacy practices/texts did you particularly enjoy? Dislike? Find difficult? Boring? Why? Examples?

V. When you were in school, do you remember how you felt about what you thought about learning to read? About learning to write?

VI. Do you think the reading and writing you did at school prepared you for the kinds of things that you read and write now? Why or why not, or in what ways?

VII. How do you think the reading/writing you did at school similar to or different than the reading/writing you do now as an adult?

Demographic Information

(to follow the Literacy Practices interview)[1]

Date: _____ Researcher: _____

(1) Name: _____

(2) Age Range: 8–12 _____; 13–18 _____; 19–30 _____;
                31–55 _____; 55–70 _____; 70+ _____

(3) Gender: Male   Female

(4) Race: _____   (4) Ethnicity: _____

(5) Country of birth: _____   (6) Native language: _____

(7) Language spoken in the home: _____

(8) Are you a U.S. citizen?   Yes   No

(9) If no, what is your status? _____

(10) Are you currently a student?   Yes   No

      (10a) If yes, where do you attend school? _____

      (10b) What type of school is it? (e.g., high school, university,
              community college, etc.) _____

---

[1]A Spanish version of this survey was used for Spanish-speaking informants.

(11) Highest level of schooling you have **completed**:

☐ Some elementary/primary school   ☐ Some college

☐ Primary school (8th grade)   ☐ College degree (B.A./B.S.)

☐ Some high school   ☐ Master's degree

☐ High school/12th grade   ☐ Graduate degree (Ph.D., M.D., J.D., etc.)

☐ Vocational training   ☐ Other: _____

(12) Highest level of schooling your **mother** completed: (somewhere in here a question about WHERE this schooling occurred; i.e., What country? What location in the country—like rural village, capitol city, major city?)

☐ Don't know   ☐ Some college

☐ Some elementary/primary school

☐ Primary school (8th grade)   ☐ College degree (B.A./B.S.)

☐ Some high school   ☐ Master's degree

☐ High school/12th grade   ☐ Graduate degree (Ph.D., M.D., J.D., etc.)

☐ Vocational training   ☐ Other: _____

(13) Highest level of schooling your **father** completed: (See above for location of schooling.)

☐ Don't know   ☐ Some college

☐ Some elementary/primary school

☐ Primary school (8th grade)   ☐ College degree (B.A./B.S.)

☐ Some high school   ☐ Master's degree

☐ High school/12th grade   ☐ Graduate degree (Ph.D., M.D., J.D., etc.)

☐ Vocational training   ☐ Other: _____

(14) Your occupation: _____

(15) Your **mother's** occupation: _____

(16) Your **father's** occupation: _____

(17) Where you live now (choose one):

_____ Urban   _____ Suburban   _____ Rural   _____ Small town

(18) Number of people who live in your household: _____

Marital Status? Parental Status? (Maybe just parental status related to family/ child literacy issues.)

(19) Number of people **under age 18** who live in your household:

_____

(21) Do you have a computer in your home?   Yes   No

    (21a) If yes, is it connected to the Internet?   Yes   No

If no, do you have access to one? If yes, where? (e.g., office, library, friend, etc.) and do you use it for e-mail or for the Internet?

Author Index

Note: f indicates figure; *n* indicates footnote; *t* indicates table.

A

Althusser, L., 2, *21*
Alvermann, D., 156, 161, *167*

B

Bakhtin, M. M., 4, *21*
Barnes, J. S., 86, *96*
Barton, D., 4, 5, 19, *21*, 49, *54*, 58, *83*, 96,
   96, 101, *113*, 123*n*2, 127, 128*n*4,
   131, 152, *153*, 160, 161, *167*
Batibo, H. M., 43, 44, *54*
Bennett, C. E., 86, *96*
Berkenkotter, C., 200, *215*
Betancourt, J., 144, *153*
Bok, F., 57, 59, 60, 62, 63, 67, 68, 69, *83*
Bolter, J. D., 188, 192, *195*
Bourdieu, P., 2, 6, *21*, 134, 148, *153*
Brandt, D., 5, *21*
Brecht, B., 190, *195*
Burns, M. S., 151, *154*

C

Camitta, M., 162, *167*
Campbell, A., 53, *54*
Canagarajah, A. S., 2, *21*, 37, *39*, 210*n*10,
   216
Cazden, C., 96, *96*, 166, *167*

C

Chafe, W., 200*n*4, *216*
Christie, F., 200, *216*
Cole, M., 14, *21*
Comrie, B., 39, *39*
Coogan, M. D., 69, *83*
Cope, B., 131*n*6, *131*, 134, *153*, 180,
   180, *195*, 213, *216*
Crowder, M., 44, *54*
Cushman, F., 6, *21*

D

Dahl, R., 124, *131*
Dale, J., 144, *153*
Danielewicz, J., 200*n*4, *216*
Degener, S., 4, 14, 15, *22*, 76, 83, *84*,
   101, *113*, 178, *178*, 200, 200*n*6,
   201*n*7, 205, *216*
Deng, F. M., 59, 59*n*1, 63, 63*n*3, 68, 72,
   76, 78, 80, *83*
Denton, K., 94, *97*
Dewey, J., 134, 151, 153, *153*
Dorsey-Gaines, C., 152, *154*
Duke, N. K., 76, *83*, 199*n*2, 200*n*6,
   201*n*7, 202, *216*
Duncan-Andrade, J. M. R., 6, *22*
Dyson, A., 6, 9, *21*, 159, 165, 167, *168*

E

Eckert, P., 194, *195*

229

Erickson, F., 138, *153*

F

Foucalt, M., *21*
Freire, P., 9, *21*
Frensch, P. A., 96, *96*

G

Galper, K., 94, *97*
Gee, J., 48, 53, *54*, 96, *96*, 110, 111, *113*,
    127, 128, 129, *131*, 162, 167,
    168, 178, *178*, 193, 194, *195*
Gipson, F., 148, *153*
Gonzalez, N., 6, *22*
Goody, J., 3, *21*
Gregory, E., 6, 11, *21*
Griffin, P., 151, *154*
Grusin, R., 188, 192, *195*
Gutierrez, K., 165, *168*

H

Hagood, M., 161, *167*
Hall, L., 76, *83*
Halliday, M. A. K., 16, 20, *21*, *216*
Hamilton, M., 4, 5, 19, *21*, 49, *54*, 58,
    83, 96, *96*, 101, *113*, 123n2,
    127, 128n4, *131*, 152, *153*, 160,
    161, *167*
Hasan, R., 20, *21*, *216*
Haynes, C., 187, *195*
Heath, S., 96, *96*, 172, *178*
Herbert, P., 58, *83*
Hildyard, A., 3, *21*
Hinchman, K., 156, *167*
Holmevik, J. R., 187, *195*
hooks, b., 3, *21*
Huberman, M., 198, *216*
Huckin, T. N., 200, *215*
Hudders, M., 26, 27, *40*
Hull, G., 6, 9, *20*, 171, *178*
Hymes, D., 96, *96*

I

Ivani, R., 95, *97*
Ivaniĉ, R., 4, 19, *21*

J

Jacobson, E., 4, 14, 15, *22*, 76, 83, *84*,
    101, *113*, *178*, 200, 200n6,
    201n7, 205, *216*
John, V. P., 96, *96*

K

Kalantzis, M., 131n6, *131*, 134, *153*, 180,
    180, *195*, 213, *216*
Katz, K., 159, *168*
Knobel, M., 15, *22*
Kress, G., 183, 184, *195*, 213, 214, *216*
Krol-Sinclair, B., 96, *97*

L

Lankshear, C., 15, *22*, 192, *195*
Lareau, A., 149, *153*
Lave, J., 14, *22*
LeCompte, M. D., 18, *22*, 198, *216*
Lee, C. D., 6, 9, *22*
Luke, A., 11, *22*, 38, *39*, 47, *54*, 58, 82,
    83, 95, *96*, 101, 112, *113*, 120,
    131, 135, *153*, 156, *168*, 171,
    178, *178*, 194, 195, *195*, 199n3,
    208, *216*
Luke, C., *22*, 186, *195*, 213, *216*

M

Maddox, B., 58, *83*
Mahiri, J., 6, *22*
Martin, A. M., 173, *178*
Martin, J. R., 200, *216*
Matheson, I., 60, *83*
Matthews, S., 39, *39*
Mayer, M., 146, *153*
Mazrui, A. A., 39, *40*
Mazrui, A. M., 39, *40*
Melzi, G., 96, *97*
Metzger, B. M., 69, *83*
Miles, M., 198, *216*
Moje, E., 156, 159, 160, 161, 167, *168*
Moll, L. C., 6, *22*
Moore, D., 156, *167*
Morrell, E., 6, 9, *22*
Morris, N., 26, 27, *40*

N

Nyati-Ramahobo, L., 48, *54*

O

Oakes, J., 148, *153*
Okagaki, L., 96, *96*
Olson, D., 3, *21, 22*
Oren, A., 187, *195*
Ormerod, F., 95, *97*
Othman-Rahman, M., 58, *83*

P

Paratore, J., 96, *97*
Passeron, J.-P., 2, *21*
Pelzer, D., 164, *168*
Pennycook, A., 37, 38, 39, *40*
Perry, K., 9, *22*
Phelps, S., 156, *167*
Pitt, K., 95, *97*
Polinsky, M., 39, *39*
Purcell-Gates, V., 4, 9, 14, 15, *22*, 53, *54*, 76, 83, *83, 84*, 101, *113*, 153, *154, 178*, 199n2, 200, 200n6, 201n7, 202, 205, *216*

R

Ramírez-González, C. M., 27, *40*
Rey, H. A., 150, *154*
Robinson, C., 58, *83*
Rogers, A., 58, *84*
Ross, E., 60, *84*
Rothery, J., 200, *216*
Rowling, J. K., 90, *97*, 150, *154*, 165, *168*

S

Sanchez, R., 188, *195*
Schensul, J. J., 18, *22*, 198, *216*
Scheweers, C. W., Jr., 26, 27, *40*
Schultz, K., 6, 9, *20*, 171, *178*

Scribner, S., 14, *21*
Seefeldt, C., 94, *97*
Smieja, B., 43, 44, *54*
Snow, C., 151, *154*
Snyder, I., 186, 192, *195*
Soler, M., 4, *22*, 200n6, 201n7, 205, *216*
Stein, R. I.., 143, *154*
Stone, L. D., 165, *168*
Street, B., 3, 4, 10, *22*, 58, 59, *84*, 96, *97*, 110, 112, *113*, 167, *168*, 184, *195*
Sulzby, E., 49, 53, *54*

T

Taylor, D., 49, *54*, 152, *154*
Teale, W., 49, 53, *54*
Tlou, T., 53, *54*
Tolkein, J. R. R., 90, *97*
Torres-González, R., 27, *40*
Tower, C., 76, *83*

V

Vonnegut, K., 174, *178*

W

Waff, D., 156, *167*
Wenger, E., 14, *22*
Wilder, L. I., 173, *178*
Williams, A., 6, 11, *21*
Wright, M. W., 58, *84*

Y

Yang, D. C., 60, 61, 64, *84*
Yin, R., 16, *22*
Younoszai, T., 94, *97*

Z

Zentella, A. C., 26, *40*

Subject Index

Note: f indicates figure; *n* indicates footnote; *t* indicates table.

A

Academic literacy, 4, 7–10
  enhancing, 5–6
Academic underachievement, 6–7
Achievement, 130
Addis Ababa agreement, 63, 63n3
Adolescent initiation schools in
      Botswana, 44
Adult literacy practices, 115
African American youth (abilities of), 6
Age, 17
Agency, 175–177, *see also* Individual,
      agency
  frames, 12
  and power, 208–211
Agronomist, 37
American Anti-Slavery Group, 62
American Girls, 144
Apprenticing, 212
Arab
  language, 59, 62–63, 78–79
  people, 59, 61
Asian Americans, 86
@dig command, 192
"At risk" students, 116, 120, 131,
      204–205
  classroom of, 157–158
  literacy practices of, 155–167
Authentic reading, 200–201

Autonomy, 2–4, 7n3, 11, 15
Awareness to students' sociocultural
      background, 96

B

Babysitters Club, The, 173–174
Bangwato, 45n3
Batswana, 44n2
Beliefs, 14
Bible, 8, 20, 49, 69f, 69–70, 141
  in Setswana, 45
  translator, 62, 69
Bilingualism, 89, *see also* Chinese, Ameri-
      can bilingual families
  literacy practices and, 90–95
  in Puerto Rico, 27–28
Boat exodus from Cuba, 99
Bogwera, 44
Bojale, 44
Bonding, 176
Borderland literacy practices, 163–166
Botswana
  Christianity in, 45
  colonial education in, 45
  geography of, 43–44
  language of, 43–44, *see also* Setswana
  language and literacy contexts in,
      41–54
    informants for, 42–43

233

National Survey on Literacy, 50–52
   precolonial education in, 44–45
Breakfast of Champions, 174
Bureaucracy, 123

C

Castro, Fidel, 56
Cheat codes, 162
Child and the Curriculum, The, 134
Child Called It, A, 164
Child-centered curriculum, 133
Chinese
   American bilingual families, 85–96
   immigrants, 55
   literacy for school and social pur-
         poses, 90–91
   newspaper, 87, 88*f*
   paper-cut, 86, 86*n*2
   print literacy practices, 91–92
Chinese schools in the U.S., 85, 87–88,
         205–206
Chinese-language texts, 86
Christian
   missions, 76
   religious pamphlet, 70*f*
Christianity in Sudan, 69
Class, 7, 17
Classism, 10
Code-switching, 41
Cognitive development, 3
Colonial languages, 23
Communicative technology, 184
Communism, 100
   in Czechoslovakia, 100–101
   and education in Cuba, 100–102
Communities of practice, 183, 193–194
Community
   academic, 4
   change, 134
Chinese American, 86–87
   cultural processes of, 162
   defined, 138
   key aspects of, 58
   literacy, 20, 49–54
   organization, 72, 74
   power of, 4
   southern Sudanese, 71, 82–83
Community-based knowledge, 6
Community social networks, 159–161
Connection
   of home and school literacies, 53,
         148–152

between language and literacy, 81–82
   between published works and profes-
         sion, 177
   of work and political life, 32
Construction of deficiency, 157
Content, 130
Costa Rican literacy rate, 8
Credentialing, 74–75, 207–208
Crossword puzzles, 169, 175–177
Cuban
   literacy practices, 99–112
   lottery for immigration visas, 99, 102
   refugees, 55, 99
Cultural
   awareness, 105–106
   capital, 120
   contexts, 3
   dominant, 134
   reproduction, 6
   transmission, 96
Cultural Practices of Literacy Study
         (CPLS), 16–21, 115–116,
         119–120, 122, 127, 130, 197
   demographics, 225–227
   evolving data base, 198
   procedures of, 19–20
   researcher location, 18–19
   semi-structured literacy practices in-
         terview, 217–223
Culture-specific practices, 159
Curious George, 150
Czechoslavakia, 100–101

D

Daily oral language exercises, 128
Dear America, 144
Decontextualized thinking, 3
Democratic education, 58
Demographics of literacy, 11
Dialect in Botswana, 44
Digital literacy, 179, 182, 213–215
   defined, 184–187
   instruction, 194–195
   multimodal, 187–190
   teaching, 191–193
Dinka
   Bible, 78
   culture, 67
   literacy development, 77–78
   script, 70*f*, 81
   tribe, 61–62

Disconnect
  between child and curriculum,
       133–134, 151
  between students and teachers, 156
Discourse
  codes, 2–3
  digital, 193–194
  domination, 3
  Gee's notion of, 183
  technology, 193
Discourses
  acquired in schools, 120, 178
  available, 135
  dominant, 6, 12
  family, 178
  with implications for teaching, 6
  of literacy, 127
Discursive literacy practices, 4
Disney Adventures, 91
Diversity, 55, 134
  in classroom, 157
  local, 179
  of out-of-school literacy practices of
       struggling adolescents,
       158

E

Economic self-sufficiency, 129–130
Economics, 23
Economy, 2
  and literacy learning, 5
Education, 7, *see also* Formal education;
       Informal education; Traditional
       education
  and economic development, 45
  philosophy of, 134
  as a social venture, 13
Educatiʃn desde la cuna, 105
Emergent literacy, 53
  research, 211
Emeril Live, 159
Emotions, 162
Empowerment, 105–106
English
  complicated notions about the need
       to speak, 37–38
  hegemony of, 46–49, 55
  as the official language in Botswana,
       44
  as the official language of education
       in Puerto Rico, 26–27

and power, 48–49, 207
and social class in Puerto Rico, 28
texts in Chinese American home,
     89
English-speaking environment, 42
Enlightenment theories, 2–3
Epistemology, 2–3
Escape From Slavery, 62, 67, 68
ESL teaching, 29, 48
Ethical responsibility, 18
Ethnic divisions in the Sudan, 59
Ethnicity, 6, 17
Ethnographic researcher, 138

F

Face-to-face communication, 108
Family
  cohesion with, 212
  influences on literacy practices,
       110–111
  literacy, 31, 49–54, 101–102, 138,
       144–147, 152
  practice of storybook reading, 161
Farmers, *see* Puerto Rican, farmers and
       English literacy practices
Financial
  stability, 130
  text, 125
Formal education, 44
Forms, 200
Framing, 130
Free trade, 23
Full literacy, 7–8

G

Gender, 7, 17, 50*t*, 51*t*, 198
Genre theory, 199
  texts and, 199–200
Geopolitical positioning, 7
Gifted and talented programs, 116, 147
Globalization, 11, 23, 134, 179, 209
Goals, *see also* Life goals
  academic, 170
  achieving, 8
  of CLPS, 198–199
  professional, 170
  social, 58
  of "Writing and Technology" course,
       182
Goosebumps, 143

Government
  attitude towards, 26
  of Botswana, 44
  Ethiopian, 60
  paper, 47
  Puerto Rican, 26–28
  redefined function of, 120
  Sudanese, 59
Grand narrative, 2
Great China, 86, 87*f*
Group cohesion, 137–138

H

Harry Potter, 90, 150, 165
Heathen precolonial education, 45
Hegemony, *see also* Linguistic, hegemony
  of English, 23, 55, 210
Helping, 212–213
Hemingway, Ernest, 174
High-stakes testing, 134, 153
Home-based literacies, 8, 14, 20,
      115–117, 159–161, 171–172
  and conflict with school literacies,
      173–174
  and connection with school literacy
      practices, 148–153
Home computer, 94
Home–school connections, 198–215
Hybrid literacy practices, 165–166
Hypermediacy, 192

I

Ideological models, 2, 4
Ideology of privileging academic literacy,
      6
Identity
  key aspects of, 58
  marginalized, 120
  of Southern Sudanese, 82–83
Illiteracy, 1, 8
Immediacy model, 129, 192
Immigrants, 55
Immigration visas, 99
Imperialism, 30
Indeterminateness, 3
Individual
  agency, 2
  thought, 3
Industrialization, 5
Influence(s), *see also* Social, influences

  of home literacy practices on literacy
      learning, 211–212
  that impact literacy worlds of people,
      56
  of poststructuralist perspectives, 12
  of school-based literacy, 15
  of siblings of literacy practice,
      174–175
  of sociotextual domains on literacy
      development, 85
Informal education, 44
International Adult Literacy Survey
      (IALS), 8
Internet, 91, 94, 125, 161, 213
  life story, 145
Interpersonal communication
  in Chinese immigrant families, 95
  for literacy practices among the Suda-
      nese, 71
  text use in, 125
Islam, 59–60, 62
  converting to, 62

J

Jet, 161

K

Kakuma News Bulletin, 72
Kakuma Refugee Camp (Kenya), 57, 60,
      62, 69
  language and literacy in, 64–65
Kenyan educational system, 64
Knowledge, *see also* Community-based
      knowledge; Linguistic, knowl-
      edge
  background, 135
  developing one's, 8, 94

L

"Laffy Taffy," 119, 124
Language, 7, 17, *see also* Tribal language;
      Written, language
  acquistion of new, 55
  barriers for refugees, 100
  brokers, 38–39
  hybrids, 104–105
  and literacy (in Sudan), 81–82
  students marginalized by, 6
  theorists, 3

Library as resource for books, 174
Life goals, 130
LingaMOO, 189*f*
Lingua franca, 44, 79–80
Linguistic
  contexts, 10–12
  discourses, 120
  hegemony, 6, 12–13, 16–17, 55,
      209–211
  knowledge, 14
  markets, 120
  mediation, 2
Literacy, *see also* Emergent literacy;
      Home-based literacies; Literacy
      development; Literacy prac-
      tices; School-based literacies
  within adult roles, 146–147
  as credentialing, 206–208
  definition of, 7–8, 58, 184
  dominant view of, 3
  educational theory, 1
  events, 4, 7, 128, 128*n*4, 134–135
  freedom of, 33
  inappropriate model of, 131
  learning, 13–15
  as meaning making, 45–46
  as multiple, 2–4
  nature of, 1
  new perspective on, 2
  rate, 8
  school-only, 201
  with siblings, 145–146
as social, 3–6
Literacy of Adult Students study, 202,
      203*n*8, 205
Literacy in American Lives, 5
Literacy development, 174
  in school, 115
Literacy instruction
  authenticity in, 200–202
  definition of, 201
Literacy in the New Media Age, 184
Literacy practices, 4, 13
  of adolescents, 166–167
  by children, 212–213
  children's connections to family mem-
      bers', 144–147
  defined, 127
  in a foreign language, 99–110
  among the Sudanese, 68
Literacy Social Action Group, The,
      135–140, 153

Literacy in Theory and Practice, 3
Little Critters, 146
Little House on the Prairie, 173–174
Lived literacy spheres, 115
Livingstone, David, 45
Local literacies, 4–5
Localism, 3
London Missionary Society, 45
Lord of the Rings, 90
"Lost Boys" of Sudan, 55, 57,
  in America, 61–62
  journey of, 60–61
Low-income
  families, 152
  public housing, 121

M

Madi
  language, 79
  tribe, 62
Magic® cards, 91
Map Quest®, 147
Marginalization, 9–10, 134
Marxism, 2
Material
  dimension, 2
  well-being, 3
Meaning in written language, 4
Meaning-making process, 134
Media, 144–145
Metalanguages, 192
Military
  conflict, 11
  power, 23
Minority populations, 11
Minute Math, 128
Modernism, 2, 127
Moffett, Robert, 45
Mother Courage and Her Children, 190
Motivation
  lack of, 133
Motswana, 44*n*2
Multiliteracies, 186
Multiliteracies, 131*n*6, 179
Multimodal/multiliteracies pedagogy,
      183, 190
Multiple literacies, 2, 9–10
  research spawned by construct of, 4–5
Multiuser domain (MUD), 187
Multiuser virtual environment (MOO),
      182, 187–188

remediation within, 188–190
Muslim sharia law, 59

N

Namibia, 44
Narratives, 144
National Adult Literacy Survey (NALS), 8
New literacies, 2
New London Group (NLG), 179, 182
Newsweek, 65
Nintendo, 176
No Child Left Behind (NCLB), 120
Nondominant literacy practices, 123,
    123n
Nonmainstream students, 9, 131
Note passing, 165
Nucleus of production, 29, 37

O

Objective reality, 2
Old Yeller, 148
Oral
    education, 45
    exams, 108
    language, 4n2, 47–48
    literature (in Botswana), 52
Oral-culture practices, 127
Out-of-school literacies, 5–6, 115–116
    current literacy practices (interview),
        217–218
    of at risk students, 155–167
    eating out, 142–143
    historical literacy practices (interview),
        219–220
    journaling and creative writing,
        143–144
    religion, 141
    shopping for food and clothing, 142
Outside-of-literacy instruction, 201
Oxford Bible Companion, 69

P

Paintball, 165
Parenting, 20, 44
Parent's roles in children's literacy activi-
    ties, 94–95
Pedagogy, 1, 134
Pedogogy of Multiliteracies, A, 182, 187
Peter Pan, 60

Pink literature, 103, 103n5
Poetry, 93, 158, 173, 176
    as authentic genre, 204–205
    codes in, 162
Political, *see also* Geopolitical positioning
    borders, 11
    conditions for literacy learning, 5
    influence on literacy practices, 101
    power, 2–4, 10
Politics, 17
    and Spanish literacy practices, 31–32
Polyhedrons, 93, 205
Pony Pals, 144
Popular culture, 6, 9
Postmodernism, 2–3
Poststructuralism, 2–3, 12–13, 208
Potter, Beatrix, 147
Power, 3, *see also* Political, power
    used in academic underachievement,
        6
    and agency, 208–211
    of community, 4
    and English, 48–49
    impact of, 7
    literacies of, 10
    relations of, 23, 58
Preparation of students, 134
Print Shop®, The, 145
Print-based "high culture" literary tradi-
    tion, 127–128
Print literacy, 9, 45
    development, 14
    documenting, 138–140
    local language, 80–81
    practices for Sudanese refugees,
        76–81
Printed texts, 46–47
Puerto Rican
    farmers and English literacy practices,
        28–39
        resistance to, 33–39
    identity, 26
    language history, 26–28
Puerto Rico
    American signs in, 25–26
    Americanization of, 26
    anglification of, 26
    historical role of English in, 30
Punishment of children when speaking
    local languages, 48
Puppy Patrol, 144

R

Race, 7, 17
Racism, 10
Rap as a language form, 9
Rationality (development of), 3
"Read alouds," 128
Reading, *see also* Authentic reading;
  Storybook reading; Whole-class
  reading
  ability, 1
  "faking it," 130–131
  for fun, 124
  hour, 124
  learning, 150–151, 202–203
  as literacy practice, 4–5
  literacy rate determined by, 8
  personal interest in, 174–175
  as "uncool" 173–174
Reading Research Quarterly, 120
Reciprocity, 18
Recognition
  symbols of, 134
Refugee
  camps, 62–65
  resettlement program, 61
Religion(s), 2, 20, 141
  division of (in the Sudan), 59
  and local languages (Botswana), 49
  among the Sudanese, 68–70
Remediation: Understanding New Media,
  188, 192
Reproduction, *see* Cultural, reproduction;
  Social, reproduction
Research
  on literacy theory, 4–5
Resistance to learning English, 36–39
Resisting Linguistic Imperialism, 210n10
Robbins, Tom, 174
Roth, Philip L., 174

S

School
  curriculum, 134
  sense of validation in, 129
  success, 131
School-based literacies, 74–76, 115–117,
  126, 163
  bimodal education in one classroom,
  147–148

and conflict with home-based
  literacies, 173–174
current (interview), 221
historical (interview), 221–223
and influences on home/community
  practice, 203–205
transformed into home practices,
  92–93
Schooling
  activity of, 201
  discourse of, 9
  and gap between the child, 134
  as learning, 201
  for the "Lost Boys," 60
  in refugee camps, 62–65
Schools
  literacy privileged in, 6
  underachieving, 120
  urban, 145
School's Out!, 6
Selectiones del Reader's Digest, 30
Self
  positive sense of, 129
Self-maintenance, 124
Self-motivated learning, 93
Sensemaking, 58
Setswana, 41–42, 44
Signs
  in community, 138–139
  in English, 25
Slavery in southern Sudan, 59, 61–62
Social
  activity, 200
  changes, 133
  class in Puerto Rico, 28
  cohesion, 20, 126–127
  influences, 95
  institutions, 3, 58
  literacies, 2, 4–5
  networks, 117
  power, 134
  reproduction, 2, 6, 12, 148
  semiotics, 199–200
  symbol system, 2
Social–emotional development, 117
Sociocultural contexts, 4, 6–7, 10–12
Socioeconomic status, 120, 152
Sociolinguistic context, 4
Sociotextual practices, 20, 115–116,
  198–200
  of bureaucracy, 123

of clubs/organizations, 124
of community organization, 124
of daily routines/personal care, 124
of entertainment/pleasure, 124–125
of fashion, 125
of finances, 125
of interpersonal communication, 125
of personal writing, 125
of public writing, 125
of school, 126
of shopping, 126
of social cohesion, 126–127
of work, 127
South Africa, 44
Spanglish, 104–106
Spanish
    literacy practices in, 30–31, 103
        and politics, 31–32
        and work, 31
    as native language in Cuba, 99–100
    as official language of education in
        Puerto Rico, 26–27
Specificity, 3
Spoken literacy, 23
Storybook reading, 160
Storytelling, 67–68
Structuralism, 2–3
Subjecthood, 12
Sudan
    civil war in, 57, 59–60
    culture of, 68–76
Sudanese People's Liberation Movement
    and Army (SPLM/A), 59
Sudanese refugees, 55, 57–58, 207, *see
    also* "Lost Boys" of Sudan
    historical context of, 59–65
    and meaning of literacy, 66–67, 207
    print literacy practices of, 76–81
Symbolic resources, 6

T

Technological literacy, 182
Technology, 134, 144–145, 179,
    213–214, *see also* Multiuser vir-
        tual environment
    discourse, 193
    new, 182
Text
    as social interaction, 119
    use in nonschool activities, 124
    use for self-maintenance, 124

Texts
    associated with information and mul-
        timedia technologies, 134
    authentic, 201–202
    and genre theory, 199–200
    multimodal, 171
    public, 204
    school-only, 202
Textual
    practices, 23, 115
    resources, 120
Tracking system, 148
Traditional
    education, 44
    literacy, 6
Transculturation, 166
Transformed practice, 192
Tribal language, 209
Trust, 137–138
Twits, The, 124

U

Underclass groups, 6
United Nations High Commission for
        Refugees (UNHCR), 60–61, 64,
        74
Unofficial literacies, 165

V

Validating experiences, 129
Value
    of credentialing, 208
    of literacy for learners, 135
Values, 14, 67
    in Chinese American bilingual fami-
        lies, 85, 94–95
Vernacular literacies, 5, 7, 15, 123n2
    defined, 162
    documenting, 9
    and school, 5–6
Video games, 162
Virtual classrooms, 182
Vocabulary words, 157
Vocation education in Botswana, 45
Vonnegut, Kurt, 174

W

Wealth, 134
Whole-class reading, 130

Wisdom
  and relationships with the aged in
    Botswana, 44
Word-Up!, 161
Workplace
  changing, 134
  languages privileged in, 11–12
Writing
  ability, 1
  autobiographical, 176
  consultants, 170–171
  creative, 143–144
  learning, 150–151, 202–203
  as literacy practice, 4–5, 159
  literacy rate determined by, 8

  using MOOs for teaching, 187–188
  transforming through new technol-
    ogy, 182
"Writing and Technology" course,
    181–184
Written
  language, 4
  utilizing, 127
  texts, 58
  as documentation, 91
  in Chinese American home, 89

Y

Youth culture, 161–162